Multi-Party Britai

Other books by H. M. Drucker

The Political Uses of Ideology

Our Changing Scotland

The Yearbook of Scottish Government 1978

Breakaway: the Scottish Labour Party

Doctrine and Ethos in the Labour Party

Multi-Party Britain

Edited by

H. M. Drucker

University of Edinburgh

First published 1979 by
THE MACMILLAN PRESS LTD
London and Basingstoke
Associated companies in Delhi Dublin
Hong Kong Johannesburg Lagos Melbourne
New York Singapore and Tokyo

Filmset by Vantage Photosetting Co. Ltd.
Southampton and London
Printed in Great Britain by
Unwin Brothers Limited
Gresham Press, Old Woking, Surrey

British Library Cataloguing in Publication Data

Multi-party Britain
   1. Political parties – Great Britain
   I. Drucker, Henry Matthew
   329.9'41   JN1117

   ISBN 0-333-24055-3
   ISBN 0-333-24056-1 Pbk

Contents

Notes on Contributors

DENIS BALSOM is Senior Research Officer, Department of Political Science, University College of Wales, Aberystwyth, a Director of the Welsh Election Study and the author of the forthcoming *A Political and Electoral Handbook for Wales*.

R. L. BORTHWICK is Senior Lecturer in Politics at the University of Leicester. He is the author of several papers in *Parliamentary Affairs* and other journals.

H. M. DRUCKER is Senior Lecturer in Politics at the University of Edinburgh. He is the author of *The Political Uses of Ideology, The Scottish Government Yearbook, Breakaway: the Scottish Labour Party* and *Doctrine and Ethos in the Labour Party*.

ANDREW GAMBLE is a Lecturer in Politics at the University of Sheffield. He is the author of *The Conservative Nation*.

PETER MAIR is an Assistant in the Department of Political and Social Science in the European University Institute in Florence.

W. A. ROGER MULLIN is a Research Student in the Department of Sociology, University of Edinburgh.

SARAH NELSON has completed a thesis on loyalist groups in Northern Ireland at the Department of Politics, University of Strathclyde.

MICHAEL STEED is Senior Lecturer in Politics at the University of Manchester. He is the author of 'An Analysis of the Results' in *The British General Election of 1964* (edited by D. E. Butler and A. King) and for the succeeding volumes on the general elections of 1966, 1970 and 1974 (February and October).

MARTIN WALKER is a correspondent of the *Guardian*. He is the author of *The National Front*.

Foreword

This book is about the British political parties, about what they stand for, whom they represent, how they are organised, how they compete for power and how they use what power they may obtain. Despite the public interest in political parties, their central place in the country's politics, and the large number of books about the two major parties, there are few books about the British party system. Moreover, the available books have been outdated by recent important changes. They are about the competition between the Conservative and Labour Parties; they are about a two-party world. This book is an attempt to make good the gap opened up by the passing of that system. In it we have tried to do two different things. We have tried, first of all, to describe the currently significant parties. Each of the chapters about an individual party describes the organisation of the party, says something about its recent history, gives a sketch of the thinking of the party, and tries to put the party's problems into perspective. This is not to say that these chapters are written to a formula. They are not, and could not be, for the parties differ considerably from one another. This is not simply a matter of some being more popular at the polls than others; but rather that different kinds of politics matter more or less to the parties. We not only have more parties that matter, we also have more diversity of party. For some parties, the Conservatives and Labour especially, forming a government is the end of their activity. For others, such as the Liberals, electoral success is all. Still others concern themselves with elections hardly at all; they try to influence governments and the citizenry in other ways, some of which are illegal and even violent.

Despite the fact that the two-party system has lost its vigour, it remains the case that the greatest division between the parties in Britain today is between the Conservative and Labour Parties on the one hand and the other smaller parties on the other. Our book reflects this fact in that the chapters on the Conservative and Labour Parties are more interpretative essays than descriptions of their subjects. As there is already a considerable body of readily available reading on these great parties, the chapters on them concentrate on how they have adapted themselves to their newly reduced status.

But *Multi-Party Britain* is more than a textbook of contemporary British parties. It is also based on a theme: that the old system of two-party competition has been undermined and is being replaced by a different system of competition. This theme is explored in the introduction, in which the charms of the two-party model are described and the reasons for its demise examined; and in the Conclusion, in which the outlines of the new competition are summarised.

One of the bases of two-party politics, as long as it lasted, was the social homogeneity of Britain. It was possible to write books about British party politics – that is, about the Conservative and Labour Parties – and ignore the fact that the two parties competed not only in Westminster and the country, but also in England, Scotland and Wales. It was possible to speak of 'the country' as a homogeneous unit because the things which divided people in London also divided them (if not exactly in the same degree) in Glasgow and in Cardiff. Moreover, when people in one part of the country shifted their allegiance slightly from one party to another, it was a safe bet that people in the rest of the country were doing the same thing at about the same rate. This is no longer so.

For this reason it has been necessary for us to divide the book into parts. In the first part we deal with the two governing parties, Conservative and Labour, and the Liberal Party. These three parties compete all over Britain and each has behaved until very recently as if it expected and certainly hoped to form a government unaided by any other party after each successive general election. It may seem odd to include the Liberal Party with its much more successful rivals, but the inclusion is considered: so strong was the 'two-party' habit of mind that the Liberal Party leaders adopted it, and they led their party as if it were about to form a government, or at least to replace one or other of the major parties, at any moment. So strong, indeed, was the 'two-party' model that there was little else the Liberal leaders could do, for were they to admit that they were not one or other of the two major parties they would at the same time admit that they had no serious place in politics.

In the second part we deal with the Scottish National Party (SNP) and with Plaid Cymru (PC). These parties compete for votes only in Scotland and Wales. The fact that they have been able to compete successfully for votes and seats recently has made the party competition in Scotland and Wales distinct from that of England. At the same time the successes of the SNP and PC in winning parliamentary seats has made it more difficult for the Conservative and Labour Parties to form a government unaided. But the nationalist parties must not be considered simply as Celtic versions of the British parties. They do not aim to form British governments, nor do they wish to form a part of any British government. On the contrary, they wish to use their political muscle, at the ballot box and at Westminster, to break up the United Kingdom.

In the third part we deal with the extra-parliamentary parties – the Marxist parties and the National Front. Here we are dealing with organisations which are very considerably more removed from the old 'two-party' model than the SNP and PC. The extra-parliamentary parties engage in electoral competition only sporadically, and then usually for the purpose of gaining publicity for themselves or exposing the opportunism of the more conventional parties. These extra-parliamentary parties have been gaining prominence in recent years. The Marxists have learned to infiltrate the Labour Party, to the irritation of their host, and the National Front has shown the ability to organise sizeable cadres within the cities of England. These parties are attracting hard working activists at a time when the older parties have trouble retaining their membership. The success of the extra-parliamentary parties indicates the failure of the conventional parties, and conventional governments; and the ability of governments to deal with their extra-parliamentary opponents within the law is increasingly open to question.

Britain is not the United Kingdom. Northern Ireland is part of the Kingdom as well; it has twelve seats in the House of Commons. Until the recent troubles in Northern Ireland the Unionist MPs elected to these seats voted regularly with the Conservative Party, and governments of both parties let the Unionist majority in Northern Ireland rule the province as they wished, provided only that they did not bring themselves to the attention of the British public. The British parties do not, and did not, compete for votes in Northern Ireland. Indeed, the culture of the province differs so much from that on the mainland it is hard to believe that any political party could successfully compete in both arenas. Precisely because party competition within the province is so different from that in Britain, it has not been possible to include chapters here about the many Northern Irish parties. Any remotely adequate description of them would have taken up disproportionate space. One reason why so much space would have been needed is that the issues which divide the parties in Northern Ireland are so very distinctive. Instead we have included a fourth part, setting out schematically the differences between the politics of the province and that of Britain and indicating the main lines of recent changes within the province.

It was easy a decade ago to write about British parties and exclude not simply the Northern Ireland parties but also all of those discussed here in the second and third parts. Since then the existing dominant parties have been unable to prevent newcomers from taking the field and scoring some successes. We make only passing reference to the less successful and less important of the new parties, such as the Democratic Labour Party and the Scottish Labour Party. Neither have we been able to include a description of each of the small cadre parties which is operating on the Marxist Left. These omissions are regretted, but it seemed to us that the lessons which might be learnt by discussing these minute organisations did not justify the space necessary to accommodate them.

We have been aware in preparing this book that there is a serious argument for presenting the material in it in a quite different way. We could have presented it topic-by-topic rather than party-by-party. We might, that is to say, have had chapters on the breakdown of the two-party voting in England; the rise of the national parties in Scotland and Wales; the breakdown of intra-party discipline in the House of Commons; and so forth. We have decided not to proceed in that way for three reasons. Firstly, a book written on that principle would not meet the need for information about the minor parties. Secondly, since the changes we are describing in the book are still continuing, we thought it would be easier to grasp them if their effect on particular institutions such as the parties were made explicit. Thirdly, we have tried to make the material in the book as easily comprehensible as possible, and this can be better done by discussing the recognisable parties than the recondite themes.

The ideas advanced in this book were discussed by the contributors during a seminar in Edinburgh in December 1977. The costs of that seminar were borne by the Nuffield Foundation, to whom we are most grateful. We have had the benefit, both at the seminar and subsequently, of comments on our ideas from John Bochel, Andrew Bolger, Alan Cairns, James Cornford, Carol Craig, Ivor Crewe, Dennis Kavanagh, Ian McAllister, John P. Mackintosh, James Naughtie, Peter Pulzer and Fred Ridley. My wife, Nancy, helped with some of the editorial chores and Helen Ramm has typed the book more than once. I am indebted to them both.

The text was at proof stage when the Callaghan government fell. We are grateful for the forbearance of Rob Shreeve and Tim Fox of Macmillan, who allowed us to bring it up to date after the 1979 election.

May 1979   H. M. DRUCKER
Edinburgh

Introduction

Two-Party Politics in Britain

H. M. Drucker

Until recently it was a commonplace of political commentary that Britain had a two-party political system. Indeed, its two-party system was often extolled as one of the most stable and responsible systems in the world. Furthermore, the belief that Britain had a two-party political system was fundamental to many ideas about the Constitution. This belief can no longer be maintained. Britain no longer has a simple two-party political system. The old concept must be replaced.

The difficulties which we would now face if we were to try to describe Britain as two-party are so overwhelming that some readers may think I am tilting at a straw man. In order to make it clear that this is not the case, as well as to show how various were the features of the Constitution which were ascribed to 'two-partyness', I will begin with an examination of some major textbooks on British politics (roughly in order of publication).

An admirably lucid description can be found in Sir Ivor Jennings' now rather dated, but once popular, book *The British Constitution* (1941). Like many commentators, both before and since, Jennings began his account with a quotation from W. S. Gilbert:

> I often think it comical
> How nature always does contrive
> That every boy and every gal

> That's born into this world alive
> Is either a little Liberal
> Or else a little Conservative.[1]

In substance, Jennings asserted, Gilbert was right: there was a 'natural' tendency for the country to follow a two-party system. However, Jennings did not believe that voters in 1941 were either Conservatives or Liberal, for by then the Liberal Party had been replaced by the Labour Party as one of the major parties of state. Indeed, the speed and apparent ease with which this replacement occurred between 1918 and 1931 confirmed the two-party theorists in their notion that the modern constitution would accommodate only two major parties.

Jennings gave a classic statement of the two-party system in British politics:

> Above all, though there had been at intervals two-party conflict there was not until the Nineteenth Century, a two-party system of government. The foundation of that system is the recognition that, when a party wins a general election, a Cabinet will be formed out that party, that the Cabinet will accept the principle of collective responsibility to the House of Commons, and that opposing the Cabinet will be another party accepting the principle of majority rule, but expecting sooner or later to replace the party in office and form a Cabinet in turn ... the two-party system is less than 150 years old. Having once been established, however, it tends to be self-perpetuating.[2]

It is significant that he spoke of a two-party system of *government* (not politics), for like many writers of his period Jennings sought the evidence for what the Constitution was in the way it had developed. He was an historian. Many other writers of this older tradition were constitutional lawyers. As historians and constitutional lawyers, they tended to emphasise government when they discussed the party system: now it is more common to emphasise elections and the voting habits of the electorate.

This change of emphasis began to make itself felt shortly after the 1955 general election. At about that time British scholars began to learn new lessons from American and continental political scientists, who had been incorporating the techniques of sociology, psephology, and organisational analysis into their work. Henceforth, British political scientists could less happily concentrate on the behaviour of the parties in parliament and had to look more at their impact in the country. The success of this approach has been so overwhelming that it would be pointless to look back beyond the mid-1950s for further examples of two-party thinking.

Another reason for concentrating on works published since the 1955 general election is that it marked the point at which the two-party system began to unravel. At the previous general election, in 1951, the old system had been at its strongest. After that, each successive general election saw a small, often hardly perceived, weakening of the old system. So works published after 1955 were to an increasing extent – though not always noticed by their authors – patching up a model which was ceasing satisfactorily to explain how the constitution operated.

Professor R. T. McKenzie's *British Political Parties* (1955) is one of the standard works of the post-1955 genre. McKenzie adumbrated some of the central features of the slightly refurbished two-party system:

> Two parliamentary parties face each other in the House of Com-
> mons: Setting aside the party myths and the inter-party propagan-
> da, it is clear that the primary function of the mass organisation of
> the Conservative and Labour Parties is to sustain two competing
> teams of parliamentary leaders between whom the electorate as a
> whole may periodically choose . . . The democratic process ensures
> that there will be a periodic opportunity for the electorate to review
> the record of the decision makers who currently hold office; and, if
> the electorate wishes, it may replace them with an alternative
> team.[3]

Modern British Politics (1965) by Professor S. H. Beer offered a number of important challenges to McKenzie's thesis. But, so far from challenging McKenzie's assumptions about the two-party system, Beer's thesis assumed its operation:

> In post-war Britain, the new group politics – the group politics of
> the period of Collectivism – came to maturity through an intricate
> system of bidding and bargaining, consumer and producer groups
> came to exercise major influence on public policy. At the same

time, the ideological gap between the parties narrowed as Labour's retreat and the Conservatives' advance left the two parties occupying the common ground of the Welfare State and the Managed Economy.[4]

So powerful was the two-party model that, although McKenzie's book was called *British Political Parties*, he confined his discussion of the Liberal Party to an appendix ('. . . the party's domestic arrangements are only of very limited interest.').[5] Beer, acting on similar assumptions, gave the major parties' share of the poll as their share of the two-party poll. Both authors dismissed the Liberals – and other parties – as irrelevant.

Writing at about the same time, Professor Jean Blondel came to roughly similar conclusions from a different starting point. In *Voters, Parties and Leaders* (1963) he assumed that 'parties' meant only Conservative and Labour: 'British political parties are amongst the largest in the world. The Conservative Party has about 2.8 million members; Labour with its trade union members is 6.3 million strong and its individual members alone number 800,000.'[6]

When Professor A. H. Birch turned in his *Representative and Responsible Government* to consider the party system, he focused on still other features of the pattern:

Another and most important tradition of British political behaviour is the tradition that the government of the day should be given all the powers it needs to carry out its policy. The Parliamentary opposition does not normally make any attempt to obstruct legislation . . . The parties expect to take turns in governing the country, and each expects to pursue its course without undue hindrance when it has the reins of office . . . It is evident that the general public both expect and desire this tradition to be observed . . . decisive action by a government is nearly always approved of . . . This attitude is reflected in the reluctance of people who vote Liberal in municipal and by-elections to do the same in general elections, for fear that a Liberal revival might result in the election of a Parliament in which no single party had a majority . . . the British people still like being governed.[7]

Of course, the leaders of the two major parties have an interest in keeping out additional competitors. They are in a position to make life difficult for potential additional parties by controlling the electoral law. Thus, in *The Government of Great Britain* (1964), Professor Graeme Moodie emphasised:

> ... On top of all this, the ascendency of the two major parties is ensured by the electoral system and since the end of the war, by the electorate's manifest dislike of any diversion from what is apparently regarded as the main issue, namely the decision as to whether there should be a Conservative or Labour government in the succeeding Parliament.[8]

With the electoral law reinforcing popular demands and pressure-group interest, some think that the two-party system is the product of logic: that it is a rational system. R. M. Punnett pointed to this element of the two-party pattern, in his *British Government and Politics* (1968):

> Much more rationally, however, it can be argued that the two-party system results from a tendency for most political issues to resolve themselves (at least in Parliamentary terms) into a choice between two alternatives ... With the British system of responsible government, issues in Parliament become a question of supporting or opposing the government of the day ... This situation leads logically to a two-party system, with one party as the Government party and the other as the Opposition.[9]

While the notion that the two-party system is the product of logic is sublime, this did not stop opponents of the model from bolstering it with the ridiculous as well. Without apparent irony, some authors gave the shape of the House of Commons as one reason why Britain has a two-party system. This 'explanation' was attributed to André Maurois by the French political scientist, Maurice Duverger. Ian Gilmour noted it in *The Body Politic* (1969): 'Britain's enjoyment of a two-party instead of a group system has been held by some to be due to the shape of the House of Commons – rectangular, instead of semi-circular like most chambers on the continent.'[10]

The British two-party system was sometimes singled out even amongst the favoured two-party group because it was said to be a *strong* two-party system. It was strong in the sense that the two parties were thought to be – and to be known by their electorate to be –

answerable for their actions in the sense that they would stand on their records at successive elections. The parties also, and this feature particularly attracted Americans sympathetic to the Labour Party, put much emphasis on their role as policy-makers, and tried in government to carry out the policies they had decided upon when in opposition. American Social Democrats recognised that their Democratic Party made no such claims.

Another attraction of this system, some American political scientists argued, was the responsible nature of the parties.[11] Because each party came to power on its own from time to time, it came, as governor, to speak for the entire nation. Its role in government thus forced it to speak for the interests of the whole people and not just for those who paid the party bills or voted for the party. In this way both parties were pushed toward the centre of the political spectrum and away from each ideological extreme. This movement was encouraged by the fact that the leaders of the parties knew that the way to return to, or stay in office, was to win the votes of those who were not committed by interest or ideology to either party. Thus each tried to promote the belief that it spoke for the interests of the whole country and each tried to work within the existing constitution.

*   *   *

If there has been such agreement amongst observers of British politics, this raises a question. What do they mean when they say that Britain has a two-party system? And why do they want to tag it with this label? To simplify considerably, we may say that the phrase 'two-party system' was used as one of a set of three by some specialists in comparative government. They distinguished between one-party systems, of which the states of Eastern Europe and Africa were the most frequently mentioned examples; two-party systems, of which Britain was often thought to be the best illustration, although other countries such as the United States and New Zealand were also mentioned; and multi-party systems, as in France, Italy and most other West European states. It is not unfair to suggest that both the 'one-party' and the 'multi-party' tags carry a certain opprobrium. One-party systems are dictatorships. Countries become one-party systems by the expedient of suppressing all opposition. Multi-party systems are also frowned on. It is alleged that in countries with such systems the affairs of state often lack direction because the members of the governing majority are always squabbling with each other. By contrast, two-party systems are said to allow free opposition while retaining the advantages of decisive government.

This flattering argument has been reinforced by an additional administrative argument. The notion was that once either party had been returned after a general election with an absolute majority of seats – it being inevitable that one or the other party would have an absolute majority – the rigid party discipline of the House of Commons enabled the government to carry on for longish periods without having to look constantly over its shoulder to see if it was still leading an army. Those who upheld this argument, such as Professor Birch, often spoke of the need to 'carry on the Queen's business' as an important feature of government. A two-party system removed any possibility of coalition government, and made it easier for the government of the day to carry on governing.

The ability of Ministers to carry out their policies unhindered by the House of Commons might not have been so highly praised if it had been thought that the Ministers were likely to carry out extreme policies. This feature of the two-party system was admired because it was under-written by another, in some ways the central, praise-worthy feature of the system, that the two parties were moderate. They each pursued the support of the middle-ground in politics as each tried to add the centre to its own base (right or left, as the case might be). No defender of the two-party system, as it operated, went so far as to argue that it worked because most people agreed about most political issues. But it was often argued that there was a fair measure of agreement about the rules according to which the political battle should be fought; and it was believed that the two-party system reinforced this agreement. Each party tried to speak for the nation. In a multi-party system, it was claimed, the various parties, fearing that they might lose their own base, did not try to build a consensus of opinion around themselves. Moreover, in a two-party system, the parties were content to conduct their battle for office and power within the law, and, by international standards, with little bribery. It was just unthinkable, so long as the two-party model held, for either party to take to the streets or invoke the aid of the armed services or the police to improve the position. Two-party theorists thought that anyone who even talked in such language was obviously an extremist. The nice thing about the two-party system was that it ensured the parties were not extreme and that no extremists led the parties.

All these general arguments were easy enough for students of British politics to listen to. But the two-party model was not adopted just because it was flattering to Britain, or because its proponents thought two-party politics would be a good thing if it existed. The model was consistent with a good many of the observable features of politics in the period after 1945. Moreover, it was possible to believe that the system was accepted by the great majority of the electorate. Several features of post-war British politics which were either attributable to the two-party system or which bolstered it were the following.

Most citizens voted in general elections. In the first post-war election, in 1945, the turnout was 72.8 per cent of the electorate; in 1950 it was 83.9 per cent; and even at its lowest, in 1970, it was still 72.0 per cent. People, of course, vote for parties, not the Constitution. But it is difficult to believe that highly disaffected people would bring themselves to vote for any party. It has been tempting, therefore, to take the high polls as an indication that the existing political arrangements were not too unacceptable to most people. Moreover, the fact that such a high percentage of the people did vote has been taken to mean that there is no large reservoir of untapped political support waiting for a new party to discover it. High polls have thus been seen as a sign of the legitimacy of the regime and a factor making for its stability.

Of those who have voted, the overwhelming majority have voted for one or other of the two major parties. The two-party vote was at its highest in 1951. In that general election 96 per cent of those who voted voted for either the Conservative or the Labour Parties. Even at its lowest, in October 1974, 75 per cent of those who voted voted for one of the two major parties. It was this vote of confidence which made many commentators believe that the electorate was unwilling to support third parties.

It is possible for a country to have two major parties, high polls and a high two-party vote, and for one party still to remain in office after each election. In that case we cannot say that the country has a two-party political system. This is, indeed, what happened within Northern Ireland between 1922 and 1969, but it is difficult to accept that such a country really had a two-party system. Britain might have had such a political system after the rise of the Labour Party if all, or a very substantial majority, of working-class voters consistently voted for the Labour Party. Not a few people in the Labour Party expected something of the kind to happen when their party came, as they thought it inevitably would, into 'its inheritance'. Fortunately for the Conservative Party, and for the two-party system, such uniformity of class voting by the working class did not occur. Instead, the two parties have alternated in power with remarkable regularity until very recently. Indeed, at every general election between 1880 and 1955 the party in office lost seats to the other party, even if this did not always mean that it lost enough to lose power. There seemed to be a pendulum in public life which swung in favour of each party in turn and just as inevitably swung against it. This regular alternation gave both parties a chance to rule – and hence a stake in supporting the status quo – and kept both refreshed with periodic bouts of rest out of office.

One measure of the authority of the two-party system has been the strength of party discipline in parliament. Governments have been able to carry their programmes into law because MPs elected under their party labels have acted as the Whips bid. When the two-party system was at its peak, backbench MPs voted so regularly with their Whips that there seemed little point even in trying to measure their loyalty. Parties possessed a powerful sanction should an MP step out of line: if the Whip was withdrawn, the MP had little chance of re-election. The electors voted for a party, and once an MP had lost the party label, he was very likely to lose his seat. Any temptation an MP might feel to rebel was also curbed, by the extreme difficulty he would encounter if he tried to change sides. In a less tightly structured party system – particularly in a multi-party system – changing sides is, if not an everyday occurrence, not difficult.

Governments were willing, so long as the two-party system lasted, to rely entirely on their success at general elections as democratic sanction for their action. They did not indulge in referenda, neither did the party in opposition generally obstruct the actions of the party in government or encourage its supporters in the country to do so.

*   *   *

Thus bolstered, the two-party system was thought to be a secure, valuable and important feature of British politics. But, like all models, the two-party model never accounted for all the facts. There were always things about British politics which did not fit into the pattern. But, for a long time, few people thought that the facts that failed to fit were anything more than interesting exceptions or minor anomalies. Before we go on to look at the changes that have come over British politics, which now make it difficult to uphold the two-party model at all, we should record some of the features that did not match up to the two-party model perfectly, even when that model was most credible. If we look at the system first from the vantage point of the electorate, several anomalies can be detected.

Even if we count the National Liberal and Conservative Party candidates as Conservative Party candidates, and even if we look at the 1950 and 1951 general elections only (these being the elections at which the minor parties' votes were lowest), we cannot say that Britain has had only two electoral competitors. In 1950 the minor parties (mainly the Liberals) earned 10 per cent of the vote; in 1951 they had 2.4 per cent of the votes. These were not large percentages but they were real votes cast by real people. Moreover, there were several periods after the formation of the two-party system in the nineteenth century when there were in fact three major parties. The most recent was between 1918 and 1931, when the Liberal, Labour and Conservative Parties were all considerable electoral forces.

The two-party theorists were able to say that these awkward facts were anomalies and not disproof of their ideas, firstly, because it was not so much popular votes as parliamentary power that they were interested in, and, secondly, because periods of multi-party competition were seen by the leaders of the major parties as aberrations. They always expected one of the three main competitors to disappear. In other words, what was seen as central to the system was neither votes nor even parliamentary seats, but the long-term prospect for party survival. Britain could be said to have a two-party system because the leaders of all the major parties (including the Liberals) thought it had such a system.

The general model described a country divided into two more or less equal camps – Conservative and Labour – in which first one and then the other gained the upper hand. People who voted for Conservative candidates and people who voted for Labour candidates could both have governments made up of MPs of their party from time to time. The picture made sense in general, but it never made much sense to most voters. Two-thirds of all parliamentary seats were safe at each election (not always the same seats, but, as it happened, roughly the same number of seats). This meant that two-thirds of the voters had no part in the choice of the government. A Tory in Durham or a Socialist in Cheltenham was unlikely ever to have a candidate he voted for elected. Of course, no two-party theorist ever said that the two-party system worked in every seat. But the fact that it did not work in two-thirds of the seats and that the party workers and the electors knew in advance with some accuracy which these seats were throws a new light on the model. It worked through a series of geographical and electoral accidents which contrived to ensure that there were roughly as many safe Conservative as safe Labour seats.

In addition, large areas of the country have always been one-party dominated. For the purposes of local government places like County Durham or Kent are more like one-party systems. The defenders of the two-party system tended to concentrate on parliamentary elections, but we do have elected local government, and the decisions of local governments do affect our lives in important ways, so that it is reasonable to bear this lacuna in the two-party system in mind.

Northern Ireland was never fully part of the two-party system in so far as the overwhelming majority, occasionally all, of its MPs were members of the Unionist Party. Its local parliament, at Stormont, was permanently in the hands of the Unionist Party. It was also not part of the two-party system in so far as sect rather than class was the main politically relevant social division. Northern Ireland was also never, and is not now, part of Britain. But these differences could be overlooked because the members of the dominant Unionist Party made it their business to cleave as closely as possible to the Conservative Party in the House of Commons.

If we examine the two-party system from the vantage point of the government, there are other important ways in which the claims advanced for the system can be challenged. The proponents of the two-party model can be accused of confusing stability with strength. Few governments have fallen as the result of a change in policy or through a decision of the House of Commons. That is true enough and, what is more, governments once elected have been reasonably sure of their control over the House. But that is very far from the same thing as strong government. A government may be able to dominate the House without knowing how it wants to handle the country's problems. It may also know what it wants to do but be unable to act because it is beholden to international bankers, or powerful trade unions, or overweening allies.

In the two-party model there is also a peculiar ambivalence about the role of the House of Commons. On the one hand it is exalted.

Governments are meant to be held to account before the Commons for their actions. They are meant to ask its permission for various acts and to need its approval for any new powers they may want. We hear much too about the advantage of the adversarial system of Question Time and Opposition Days' debates. The ability of the government to survive these ordeals is said to be necessary to its morale and hence to its ability to survive. But on the other hand the whole notion of stable policy-making and secure Ministries is predicated on the irrelevance of parliament, in the sense at least that party loyalty on the government side renders the Commons impotent for most purposes.

Occasionally, when government spokesmen are pressed about this, they take refuge in the 'responsible party' argument. They say that if the electorate does not approve of what they are doing, it can throw them out at the next election. But this argument is suspect, for it assumes that most people know the difference between the major parties on the major issues; that there *is* a difference between the parties on the major issues; and that people vote according to the issues. All these propositions are difficult to sustain.

*   *   *

Until very recently these weaknesses in the two-party model were not thought to be serious. There were still many features of British politics which it described well, and these features were thought to be of greater import than those which did not fit. This position is increasingly difficult to sustain. Many of the central features of two-party politics have disappeared, while some that are still in evidence are subjected to considerable criticism. This change is noticeable in many ways.

The proportion of the electorate who turn out to vote at general elections is declining. The decline has, it is true, been slow, and it would be misleading to imply that it has been steady. But if the 83 per cent turnout of the 1950 election was a vote of confidence in the system, the 72.3 per cent turnout at the October 1974 election is noticeably less convincing. It is also the case that the turnout at local government elections is low, and has remained stubbornly low, despite a reform of local government designed, in part, to raise it.

More to the point, the proportion of the electorate who vote for one of other of the two major parties is much lower than it was in the immediate post-war elections, as Table 1 indicates. It is not an exaggeration to say that the largest party at the October 1974 election was Labour and the second party, only 1.4 per cent behind, was the non-voters. The Conservative Party came third. More spectacular has been the increased vote for the Liberal Party and the other parties.

TABLE 1   *Party votes as percentages of electorate, 1951–79*

	1951	*1955*	*1959*	*1964*	*1966*	*1970*	Feb *1974*	Oct *1974*	*1979*	
Con	39.6	38.2	38.9	33.5	31.7	33.4	29.9	26.1	33.3	
Lab	40.3	35.6	34.5	34.0	36.4	31.0	29.3	28.6	28.0	
Lib	2.1	2.1	4.6	8.6	6.5	5.4	15.2	13.3	10.5	
Other	0.6	0.9	0.7	1.0	1.2	2.2	4.4	4.8	4.4	
Abst	17.4	23.3	21.3	22.9	24.2	28.0	21.2	27.2	23.8	

1983 (handwritten, top right)

27·3 (handwritten, right of Abst row)

SOURCES: F. W. S. Craig, *British Electoral Facts* (London, 1976) p. 34; *Guardian*, 5 May 1979.

The number of parliamentary seats now held by parties other than the two major parties has also increased. In the parliament elected in 1950 there were only twelve MPs who were not members of either the Conservative Party (or its allies) or the Labour Party. In 1951 there were only nine MPs in this category. In the parliament elected in October 1974 there were thirty-nine such MPs – the peak so far. In 1979 twenty-eight minor party MPs were elected.

As Table 2 shows, the number of Liberal and 'other' MPs and votes has grown considerably since 1951. This increase in the number of

TABLE 2   *Votes cast and members elected at general elections, 1951–79*

	Conservative		Labour		Liberal		Other	
	Votes	*Seats*	*Votes*	*Seats*	*Votes*	*Seats*	*Votes*	*Seats*
1951	13,718,199	321	13,948,883	295	730,545	6	198,966	3
1955	13,310,891	345	12,405,254	277	722,402	6	321,182	2
1959	13,750,875	365	12,216,172	258	1,640,760	6	254,845	1
1964	12,002,642	304	12,205,808	317	3,099,283	9	349,415	0
1966	11,418,455	253	13,096,629	364	2,327,457	12	422,206	1
1970	13,145,123	330	12,208,758	288	2,117,035	6	873,882	6
1974 (Feb)	11,872,180	297	11,645,616	301	6,059,519	14	1,762,847	23
1974 (Oct)	10,462,565	277	11,457,079	319	5,346,704	13	1,922,756	26
1979	13,697,753	339	11,509,524	268	4,313,931	11	1,799,582	17

SOURCES: F. W. S. Craig, *British Electoral Facts* (London, 1976) pp. 32, 33; *Guardian*, 5 May 1979.

1983   *13 012 315*   *8,456 934*   *7,780 969* (handwritten)

MPs representing parties other than Labour and Conservative has acquired more importance than it might have from the fact that it has occurred at a time when the difference in strength of the two largest parties has been small. The smaller parties have come nearer and nearer to holding the parliamentary balance. Only three of the elections since 1964 have resulted in parliaments in which one party has had a sizeable majority. The Labour government elected after the 1964 general election had a bare majority of four over the combined votes of the Conservatives and Liberals. Sizeable majorities were obtained by the Labour government elected in 1966 and the Conservative governments in 1970 and 1979. But the result of the February 1974 election was inconclusive – no party had a majority. Labour succeeded in gaining a small overall majority after the October 1974 election, but here again the difference between the two major parties was so small that it was obvious that the then normal process of government defeats at by-elections would soon wipe it out altogether. The failure of the 1964 and the two elections of 1974 to produce a workable majority of seats for any party points to a trend which is likely to be sustained. There may be temporary reversals in the trend, as in 1970 and to a lesser extent in 1979, but the pattern is clear.

The number of votes captured by parties other than the largest two has increased more dramatically than their number of parliamentary seats. In October 1974 the Liberals gained votes from 13.3 per cent of those who voted. Yet the Liberal Party succeeded in getting a mere 2.0 per cent of parliamentary seats. Disproportions such as these have led a number of commentators to question the fairness of the electoral system. Perhaps the most distinguished contribution to this debate has come from *Adversary Politics and Electoral Reform* (1975), edited by Professor S. E. Finer. 'Adversary Politics' was Finer's characterisation of the two-party system. It was the first unflattering characterisation to which the system had been subject by an academic for a long time:

> Briefly, the adversary system is a stand-up fight between two adversaries for the favour of the lookers-on . . . Since 1945 especially, our public life has been [an adversarial system], with two rival teams of politicians in open contention . . . What sharpens this contention is that the stakes are extremely high. British two-party politics (and since 1945 it is two major parties who have made all the running until the elections of 1974) is what is known as a

'zero-sum game': what one side wins the other loses; and what is won or lost is nothing short of the plenitude of governmental power. In our system the winner takes all.[12]

This system was not without its point so long as a very high proportion of the electorate voted Labour or Conservative, but in the wake of the 1974 elections the two-party vote was no longer so impressive.

One reason why the two major parties fared so badly in 1974 was that a large number of people who lived in Northern Ireland, Scotland and Wales did not vote for either class-based party. Many chose instead to vote for one of the national or sectarian parties. The simple social system which had supported two-party politics for so long was breaking up. The position in each of these parts of the United Kingdom was different. In Northern Ireland the battle lines between the numerous parties were drawn most sharply on the sectarian front. This was not new, but what was new about the position in October was that none of the parties of the Protestant majority were committed unequivocally to the Conservatives. As Butler and Kavanagh put it in their analysis of the October election: '. . . it would seem that henceforth there could be no prospect of any London-centred party relying on Ulster support'.[13] In Scotland the Scottish National Party became (in terms of votes but not seats) the second largest party in October, having overtaken the Conservatives, and looked then like growing still further to become the first party in the country. Wales was different again. In a sense the two-party system had never really existed there. The Labour Party predominated from the end of the Second World War to the 1970 election. In that period it had a majority of votes on every occasion. Its predominance in parliamentary seats reached its peak in 1966, when it held 32 of the 36 seats. In the 1974 elections Welshmen were still a long way behind the Scots in their willingness to vote for a nationalist party. In both elections Plaid Cymru came fourth. The English also moved away from the class-based parties in 1974. In February 21 per cent of English voters voted for the difficult-to-characterise Liberal Party; in October 20 per cent did the same.

*   *   *

The unwillingness of so many citizens to vote for either of the two large parties is thought by some observers to diminish the standing of the governments elected in this way. Whether for this reason or not, both major parties changed their minds on referenda after the 1974 elections; both have promised to use them. The Labour government held a referendum on continued membership of the European Communities in June 1975 and pledged itself to act on the referendum result. It also proposed a referendum on its ideas for the devolution of legislative and executive powers to elected Assemblies in Scotland and Wales. Both these issues are constitutional in character, and the government has sought to distinguish between major constitutional issues of this kind on which it may hold referenda and other political issues. Whether a future Labour government would call a referendum on a proposal to abolish the House of Lords remains to be seen. The Conservative leader, Mrs Thatcher, confirmed the scope of referenda by suggesting in a television interview in 1977 that a future government under her leadership might hold a referendum if a major union struck against government policy, as the miners had done in the winter of 1973–4. This is not strong government.

The discipline of the parties in the House of Commons is also weaker than it once was. Governments can no longer be confident that backbenchers will vote as they are bid. In 1968, when Richard Crossman was Leader of the House and John Silkin Labour Chief Whip, the Parliamentary Labour Party introduced a new Code of Conduct which aimed at a less strict discipline of members. In that parliament the government was forced to withdraw its plans for a reform of the House of Lords and for reforming the law on trades unions. The Conservative government elected in 1970, despite its overall majority of fifteen over all parties, and of forty-two over Labour, was defeated six times in the House of Commons on whipped votes. During that parliament there was also considerable cross-over voting on the European Communities Bill. In October 1971 sixty-nine Labour MPs voted with the government for entry into the EEC and thirty-nine Conservatives voted against. During the short minority Labour Government of 1974 no fewer than nine government bills failed to reach the statute book. Some of these failures were trivial, but some others, such as the Trade Union and Labour Relations (Amendment) Bill, were very important, and involved a conflict with the House of Lords. In the 1976–7 session the government's plans for devolution were wrecked when a revolt by forty-three Labour MPs against the timetable motion on the Scotland and Wales Bill meant the loss of this very important piece of legislation. Two MPs, Enoch

Powell (then an Ulster Unionist) and Robin F. Cook (Labour), welcomed referenda on membership of the EEC and Scottish devolution respectively because they hoped the electorate would vote in the referenda against the wishes of their party leaders. Cook actually went so far as to say that he was voting for devolution in the House of Commons in order to be able to campaign against it in the referendum which would follow the passage of the Bill. This is not strong party discipline.

Further evidence of the collapse of the authority of the two parties can be found in their constituency organisations, individual membership and finances. Fewer people are now engaged in the activities of the political parties at local level. A parliamentary committee on Financial Aid to Political Parties under Lord Houghton, which reported in August 1976, provided much evidence of the decline at local level of the two major parties and of the Liberal Party.[14] The committee disclosed that fewer than a third of the constituency parties included in a survey they commissioned claimed membership of 1000 or more. The Labour constituency parties had fewer members than their Conservative opponents: only 16 per cent had more than 1000 members. Only 11 per cent of constituency parties or associations were satisfied with their membership. Houghton's survey also measured the decline of political activity at local level by the decline in paid agents. The ability of constituency parties and associations to pay agents is dropping much more rapidly in the Labour Party than the Conservative Party. But the trend is clear in both cases. Houghton's survey also discovered that only a small proportion of the population thought parties important for policy-making, the day-to-day running of the country, or for looking after ordinary people. Partly as a result of this attitude, the public were ceasing to give the parties adequate financial support. This drop in individual membership has not, however, prevented Labour constituency parties from joining in the general depreciation of Westminster. Frequent demands are heard from constituency parties for the right to reselect their MP before each general election. There are also increasing demands for the party in the country to be consulted over the choice of leader.

*   *   *

Clearly, many of the once salient features of the two-party adversarial system are no longer evident. Various suggestions have been made to

18   *H. M. Drucker*

explain why the two-party system is unravelling. They are of two types: those which seek to explain the change on the basis of some prior change in the minds of the electorate, and those which seek to explain the change on the basis of some change in the conditions of governing. The two kinds of explanation are not mutually exclusive.

An important contribution has been made by Ivor Crewe and his colleagues in their article 'Partisan Dealignment in Britain 1964–74'.[15] On the basis of electoral and survey data over this 10-year period, they have been able to trace a number of important changes. By the end of the period many Labour voters, especially those who had previously strongly identified themselves with the party, no longer accepted its major tenets and were particularly unhappy about its proximity to the trade unions. There was also some evidence (though it was not unambiguous) of a weakening in the willingness of workers to think of Labour as 'their' party. This latter weakening was particularly strong among the older generation, who had entered the electorate between the wars.

This article suggests that an examination of the voting behaviour of Americans indicates some possible implications of decreased partisanship. It may be that in Britain, as in America, a larger pool of unattached voters will develop, and swing between the major parties at elections. And although they did not find evidence of increased attachment to the minor parties, Crewe *et al.* do suggest that the newly disaffected voters may vote for these parties in the future. What they did detect was an increase in the proportion of the electorate who consistently voted for minor parties whether they identified with them or not (from 2 to 10 per cent) and a substantial growth of those who switched between voting and abstention (from 24 per cent in 1959–64 to 32 per cent in 1970–October 1974).

Almost in passing, the authors noticed another possible reason for the decline in the two-party system. They noticed an increased scepticism or even cynicism in the electorate about politicians. Though they are careful to note that there is insufficient data over a sufficiently long period to say that this will be a continuing trend, it is worth mentioning. If a number of voters are convinced that there is little difference between the parties, or that all politicians are the same, or that all are liars, and if the number of people who believe this increases, the danger to the major parties is clear. These voters are a pool of potential support which the newly popular 'third' parties might try to win over. There is already some evidence that the popularity of the SNP with Scottish voters owes something to disenchantment with the older parties.

This observation leads to another suggestion: that voters in increasing numbers no longer identify themselves closely with their class, and feel the importance of their nation or sect more than in the past. It is impressive in this respect that Crewe's evidence of the weakening of the class–party identification occurred during a period of economic trouble, for if class had any pull left, one would expect it to exert itself more strongly when economic tensions were high. It is not difficult to believe that a return of prosperous times (were that ever to occur) would further weaken the tie of class and the ties of class to party, and hence hurt the major class-based parties even more.

The evidence from Crewe's research is, of course, worrying for those who like class-based politics. The 'end-of-ideology' school of the mid-1960s thought that the two major parties would increasingly come to seek the middle ground in political arguments as their old class-based antagonisms weakened. Yet more recent political commentators have noticed, on the contrary, that the two major parties are each moving very much to their own ideological extreme. The Conservative Party under Mrs Thatcher, and supported by people like Lord Barber and Sir Keith Joseph, is to the right of its predecessors. For their side the Labour Party's leaders are still content to identify themselves with the centre, but their Annual Conference has taken to electing a left-wing National Executive Committee and passing left-wing resolutions. Is it not possible that the electorate – who, as Crewe has argued, are less class-conscious than once they were – are avoiding the major parties because those parties no longer seek the middle ground? Crewe's work contains some evidence that this is true of Labour's voters.

With this last possible reason for the breakdown of the adversarial system of party politics, we are beginning to move from reasons which focus on the electorate to reasons which focus on government. It has been suggested that the British people no longer want 'strong' government but, on the contrary, they object to being overgoverned. If people object to government, there is certainly enough of it around to object to. If we confine ourselves only to elected tiers, we can list four – EEC, national government, county and district. This is before we add additional tiers for Scotland and Wales. If people do object to so much government, then perhaps some of this objection rubs off on the parties who control these tiers.

In 1976 Professor Anthony King published a series of BBC broadcasts on this problem under the title: *Why is Britain becoming harder to
govern?* This book is a convenient summary of the arguments that the
two-party system has failed because of a failure of government. King
himself said that government was overloaded:

> Britain, then, has become harder to govern. The reason it has
> become harder to govern is that, at one and the same time, the
> range of problems that government is expected to deal with has
> vastly increased, and its capacity to deal with problems, even the
> ones it had before, has decreased. It is not the increase in the
> number of problems alone that matters, or the reduction in capa-
> city. It is the two coming together.[16]

King and his contributors list a number of reasons why this overload
has made itself felt in the 1970s. They think parties have fallen into the
habit of promising more than they can deliver. They think the
economic policies of expansion which were possible when Keynesian
theories were accepted in the 1950s and 1960s no longer stand up, and
hence governments can no longer buy off dissidence through ever
increasing public expenditure.

All these explanations of the weakening of the two-party system
share an assumption: that it is still party campaigns for votes and
party competition within parliament which determine how Britain is
governed. But the authority of parliament itself is now open to
question from two different quarters. There are those who think that
the old British Constitution, with its emphasis on parliamentary
conflict, is being superseded by a new Constitution in which the
important conflicts are adjudicated in private negotiations between
the representatives of large organisations. Professor S. H. Beer's
Modern British Politics is often cited as a forerunner of this theory, but,
while he thought that the demands of the major organised economic
groups were the main forces under which politicians had to operate,
he believed that the major parties had succeeded in containing these
pressures. More recent authors think otherwise. What matters now,
according to authors as diverse as Ghita Ionescu and Pahl and
Winkler, are the negotiations between the Trades Union Congress,
the Confederation of British Industry and the government of the
day.[17] The agreements reached in these private negotiations are
presented to parliament by the government for ratification only. In so

far as much government policy concerns control over prices and incomes, and all sides agree that statutory control over them has only a subsidiary role to play, this by-passing of parliamentary authority is inevitable. To these negotiations the government of the day brings considerable power, but it brings with it only the power of one pressure group bargaining with others. The other groups are equal to it in the sense that government is in no position to force compliance with its policy should its negotiations fail. The miners' strike against the Heath administration is often cited as an example of this independent power. If these theorists are right, then it cannot be long before individual citizens come to seek protection for their interests much more in pressure groups than in parties. Some would argue that this change is already occurring and that it helps to account for the decline of the major parties.

But some groups who would influence government policy are not content with quiet negotiations. They seek to exert influence by a variety of extra-legal, illegal and sometimes violent actions. A significant part of the British army has been tied down within the United Kingdom for nearly 10 years trying unsuccessfully to put down a rebellion. Political parties, such as the National Front and the Socialist Workers' Party, have brought violence to the streets of England in order to further their aims. Manifestly, parliament is no longer the only important arena of political discussion. The ability of the two parties to dominate that arena, therefore, counts for less than it once did.

*   *   *

It is, of course, easy to react too strongly to the lavish praise once heaped on the two-party system. We would be doing this if we were to take the events of recent years and make projections into the future in the blind belief that recent trends must continue. We could also underestimate the continued strength of the two governing parties. We are arguing that there is a long-term trend away from two-party politics. The two elections of 1974 were the low point, to date, for two-party politics. The minority administration which Mr Callaghan led for much of the 1974–9 parliament was striking confirmation of the weakness of two-party politics. In that minority government, we had a small glimpse of a situation we are likely to see much more of in the future.

The subsequent 1979 election saw a small retreat back into two-party politics. The number of seats held by the minor parties and the proportion of the vote won by them fell back from its October 1974 peak. Indeed, the two-party system scored one success in that election which had eluded it throughout its strongest period in the 1950s: rural Wales moved strongly into the Conservative camp. Thus the Conservative Party was, for the first time in this century, able to establish itself as a credible party in Wales. More important, the Conservative government elected in 1979 won a clear majority of seats over all other parties. Also, the smallest parties, the National Front and the Marxist parties performed very badly in 1979. But even the 1979 return to two-party voting did not disrupt the long-term trend to multi-party politics. The Liberal Party won 13.8 per cent of the vote – a figure which was only bettered in 1974; similarly, the SNP won 17.2 per cent of the Scottish vote, a figure which it only bettered in 1974 as well. Together the two great parties won 80.8 per cent of the vote; this is an improvement on their October 1974 performance of 74.8 per cent but it does not restore the 1970 total of 88 per cent.

Our argument is not that the great parties are finished as political forces, or that their power will necessarily continue to diminish. Less ambitiously, it is that electoral support for them, the dependable alternation of the two of them in office, and the usefulness of office to them, are no longer assured. The leaders of the two major parties can no longer reasonably assume that one side or the other will be able to form a government after each general election. Neither will they be able to assume that a government, once formed, will enjoy the plenitude of power and the obedience of its citizens. The world described in the numerous textbooks on British government, quoted at the start, has passed.

Part I

The British Parties

1

The Conservative Party

Andrew Gamble

All other attempts to find a third force which is neither Marxist nor
Tory have proved ... unrealistic because they are founded on a
fallacy. They assume that the choice between Socialism and Conservatism is one between 'extremes' of Left and Right. But there is
nothing 'extreme' about the philosophy of balance and moderation
which is the ethos of modern Conservatism ... the facts of life *do*
invariably turn out to be Tory.

Conservative Central Office, *The Right Approach*, 1976

The challenge to the two-party system

When Quintin Hogg was invited at a campaign conference in 1964 to
define the main issue at stake in the general election, he announced
that it was quite plainly a choice between madness on one side and
sanity on the other. Those who voted Labour, he declared, were stark,
staring bonkers. Conservative voters by contrast were sound, well
balanced and sensible. This disturbance of the tedium of the election
campaign reflected more than the eccentricity and pugnacity of the
party's former chairman. It expressed a long-established attitude
among Conservative politicians to the role of their party in the British
two-party system. When Conservatives have not regarded their
opponents as malicious, they have thought them foolish or ignorant;

possibly well meaning but certainly misguided. An electorate that votes such politicians into office when it could choose Conservatives reveals a sad lack of judgement and maturity. Hogg's outburst displayed the profound confidence of Conservative leaders in their right to be the leading party in the state, a confidence that has since weakened but has not yet vanished.

Above all else the Conservative Party is a party of government. Its history and organisation cannot be understood apart from the preoccupation of its leaders with the tasks of governing. In the 95 years since the introduction of manhood suffrage in 1885 the Conservatives have been in office either alone or in coalition for 60 years, or two-thirds of the time. They have won thirteen of the twenty-six elections. Between 1885 and 1945 they won eight of the fifteen elections and were in government for almost 75 per cent of the time. It is hardly surprising, then, that the practical problems of organising government have busied Conservative leaders more than the practical problems of organising electoral support, a fact which highlights the paradox of Conservatism in Britain. This party of property and privilege enjoyed its period of ascendancy after the widening of the political market had made the votes of the propertyless manual workers potentially decisive in any electoral contest.

To preserve their ability to form governments in this strange egalitarian world, Conservative leaders had to devise an electoral strategy that could secure a substantial number of working-class votes. Unlike some parties on the right elsewhere, the British Conservatives had no reservoir of peasants or small landed proprietors to organise so as to offset the numerical strength of the industrial workers. Their political problem has always been how to win sufficient support for their party from the mysterious and occasionally volatile mass electorate in order to remain the normal party of government. But it may be argued that the party has never considered itself to be the servant or instrument of any part of the electorate, and this distinguishes it from the Labour Party, which was formed to express the ideas and interests of the Labour movement. Labour still has enough of that character to make recent claims by some of its leaders that it has become the normal party of government somewhat insecure. The Conservatives have never had this difficulty. Although they learnt to become a movement of the nation, they were always primarily a party of the state, and they approached politics from that standpoint – the state's institutions, functions and requirements. Any party playing a considerable part in government will tend to evolve a leadership group with this kind of perspective, but the Conservative Party stands out in the British system because its leaders have always been either the government itself or the alternative government. It is an important part of the Tory interpretation of history[1] that other parties come and go, born of the occasional ferments produced by new ideas and interests, whilst the Conservative Party is a permanent feature of British politics, with a permanent expectation of forming governments.

The Conservatives have long regarded the British state and the encircling civil society as their own. They supply its leaders and rulers, and its institutional labyrinth is peopled by the party's natural supporters. Liberals and Socialists and other alien breeds of rationalist radicals, descendants of Puritans, Levellers, and Chartists, were always regarded as intruders into the ordered, calm world of the British state. This reflects in part the extraordinarily long history of this state and its institutions,[2] its constitutional legitimacy having been established long before universal suffrage was conceded.

Conservatives have generally been pragmatic as to how the Constitution should be interpreted, but they have never wavered over its main principle – the sovereignty of Crown-in-Parliament, the undivided authority of the unitary state, the organisation of government from above rather than below.[3] Although Conservatives have steadily become more populist in their appeals to voters, they have never believed in popular sovereignty or that elections gave mandates to governments to carry out declared policies. The Conservative instinct has always been to keep policy and the popular will apart. The people can be consulted, grievances ventilated, opinion presented, interests pressed, and this can be organised through universal suffrage, regular elections and an electoral system based on single member constituencies and simple majority voting. But out of this arena of support flow no consequences for policy in government that Conservatives consider binding, and the party in parliament and the country is organised to ensure that this remains so. The principles which should govern the organisation of civil society and the state are thought too important to be subject to electoral caprice. The problem of mobilising and winning support in the mass electorate is subordinated to the tasks of government, and despite occasional lapses, it has been this ever renewed perception of Conservative leaders that the political system is not one and indivisible, and that the tasks confronting them in government and in the political market are different and must be kept separate, that helps explain the political success of the Conservative Party; for it encourages the flexibility, the pragmatism, the readiness to make concessions, and the absence of an entrenched ideology that so many observers have noted.

Yet in 1974 the position was that, despite past successes, the Conservatives faced an uncertain future. The most visible sign of the party's wider political predicament was the two election defeats of 1974, which meant that the party had lost four of the previous five elections; its share of the poll in October 1974 was the lowest it had received in any election in this century. So the party faced a serious problem of rebuilding its electoral support. But the elections of 1974 also called into question the stability of the two-party system for the first time since the 1920s. The substantial loss of support by both major parties and evidence of the weakening of partisanship for them meant that the Conservatives could no longer automatically rely on a swing of the pendulum to restore them to government at some future election, as had happened after 1906, 1945, and 1966, the only previous big Conservative defeats this century. They had to reckon with the possibility that they were no longer competing in a stable two-party system in which electoral competition centred around defining and capturing the 'middle-ground', and in which stable parliamentary majorities and alternation in government were guaranteed.

Beyond these problems of competing in the political market, electoral defeats meant that the pressures to keep support from within the party compelled the leadership to become more ideologically committed in its policies and pronouncements, so making it harder for the leadership to retain its former electoral perspective of recapturing the centre by presenting the Conservatives as the party of the 'Middle Way' and 'One Nation'. But even this aspect of the Conservative predicament is overshadowed by developments in the arena of state power since 1960, with the result that periods in office have not strengthened but weakened the standing of the party and its leadership. This has had the effect of further undermining the electoral position of the party and of making internal party management more difficult. It is to the exploration of this long-term predicament beyond changing electoral fortunes that this chapter is devoted.

The electoral problem: party of class or party of nation?

In February 1974 the Conservative share of the vote dropped by 8.5 per cent to 37.9 per cent. Although they remained the largest single party in terms of votes, their seats in parliament were cut to 297, four fewer than Labour. In October 1974 their share of the vote fell a further 2.1 per cent to 35.8 per cent, and the party's parliamentary strength declined slightly to 277. This share of the poll represented just over 25 per cent of the electorate; only one in four British electors supported the Conservative Party in October 1974. The drop in support from 1970 was the largest suffered by any party since 1945, although the Conservatives had experienced comparable declines in the past and recovered. In 1906 the Conservative vote fell by 7.5 per cent, in 1929 by 10.1 per cent, in 1945 (after a 10-year gap between elections) by 13.9 per cent and in 1964 and 1966 (combined) by 7.5 per cent.[4]

In 1979 the Conservatives staged a considerable recovery, and won a comfortable parliamentary majority of 44 seats. But in terms of votes their performance was less impressive. They won 53 per cent of the seats on only 43.9 per cent of the vote (33.3 per cent of the electorate) – a lower percentage of the popular vote than that won by any winning party since the war except in 1974. Furthermore support for the Conservatives was still more heavily concentrated in the metropolitan heartland of the south. Their national mandate did not encompass Ulster or Scotland or even the north of England. In Scotland and the north, the Conservatives only won 77 seats, Labour 154; in the south the Conservatives took 195, Labour 55. The swing in the north in 1979 was lower than elsewhere but still considerable (4.5 per cent), but since the Conservative position was already much stronger in the south than in the north the party needed much *larger* relative swings in the north to correct the territorial imbalance in political allegiance.

The Conservative electoral strategy since the advent of democracy has been resolutely national. 'One Nation' is not an optional slogan for Conservatives but is dictated by the facts of the political market in which they have to compete. Their appeal cannot be based on class, since numbers are against them, and the scope for the exploitation of regional, religious, or racial divisions has remained limited. It is one of the ironies of political science that in one of the countries where the class alignment of voters has been shown to be the best predictor of the party an elector will vote for, the party that has had the greatest success in the political market has been the party which could not afford to emphasise class factors in its electoral appeals. The high correlations that have been found between 'middle-class' occupational status and Conservative voting, and the rather lower correlations between working-class status and Labour voting have tended to obscure the central reality of the British political market – the ability of the Conservatives to draw half their votes from manual workers, many of them trade unionists, across the occupational class divide. Organising a body of support sufficient to elect a Conservative government has necessitated an appeal that transcends class divisions and stresses common symbols and ideals.

Whilst for the Labour Party the main electoral problem has been getting out their vote and extending the relationship between class alignment and voting (since this would give them a permanent majority in the British political market), for the Conservatives it has been enlarging their existing vote by winning new support and detaching working-class voters from the normal political loyalties of their class. The party's electoral strategy has, it appears, been built around the intimate links the party has fostered between itself and the central symbols and institutions of the British state and civil society. Celebrating British national and imperial history from Crecy and Agincourt to Trafalgar and Waterloo, the Conservatives proclaimed themselves the patriotic party, the party of national institutions and the national economy.

But the party has appealed not simply as the party of nation but also as the party that knows how to govern.[5] It has done best electorally when it has found overriding national issues which have reinforced its image as the party of nation and have at the same time split the forces of the opposition, so allowing rival parties to be branded both as anti-national and as incompetent to handle the affairs of government. The bias in the electoral system punishes heavily any party that does not remain united and single-minded in its pursuit of government office. After 1886 the Liberals were divided over Home Rule for Ireland, and the Conservatives were able to make the unity of the state the central issue of domestic politics. After 1918 the Conservative leadership emphasised the need to contain the Labour movement,[6] both industrially and politically, making the defence of the constitution and British institutions the key issue. This strategy was to confirm the Labour Party as the second, though at first very subordinate, party in the two-party system, and in the short term proved staggeringly successful for the Conservatives. To the anti-national image of the Labour Party was added evidence of their incompetence in government in 1931, and as a result a large part of the remaining Liberal vote was stampeded into the Conservative camp – temporarily renamed the National Government. In 1931 and 1935 the Conservatives won over 50 per cent of the vote, the only occasion, apart from 1900, when the victorious party has managed this during this century. So remote seemed the chances of Labour ever forming another government that the British party system in the 1930s hardly qualifies as a two-party system at all.[7]

The years from 1918 to 1940 were the golden age of the British Conservatives. The Liberal Party was destroyed as a major competitor and Labour's challenge successfully contained. Although Britain was predominantly an urban and industrial nation, and the principle of democracy had been conceded in 1885, the presence of the Conservative Party delayed Social Democracy until 1945. The planning of Social Democracy and the welfare consensus by the war-time coalition, and the subsequent implementation of the reconstruction plans by the first majority Labour government, changed the electoral and political balance. Yet the arrival of Social Democracy did not relax the grasp of the Conservatives on government. In order to re-establish themselves as an equal contender with the Labour Party in the political market they shifted to the new central ground which Labour had marked out. They emphasised the might of the British abroad less and their ability to provide good government more, which, in the political circumstances of Social Democracy, meant the achievement of prosperity, security, and full employment. The Conservatives set out to prove themselves better managers of Social Democracy than the Labour Party, and, aided by the long boom in the Western economy, they succeeded beyond expectation, winning three elections in the 1950s in a row.

But electoral success concealed the new weakness of the Conservatives in British politics. For the first time since 1885 they lacked an overriding national issue on which to appeal to the electorate; in the 1950s they were forced to preside over the liquidation of the British Empire and Britain's decline as a world power; and they had become dangerously dependent on their capacity to govern better than Labour within a framework which ran counter to the electoral

ideologies of the party. This underlying insecurity of the Conservative
position within Social Democracy became evident once economic
conditions began to worsen, and was fully exposed for the first time in
electoral terms in 1974; for the new electoral strategy during the boom
was aimed at persuading large numbers of newly affluent manual
workers and white-collar groups to 'invest in success' and identify
their interests and aspirations with the Conservatives.[8] But although
30 years of Social Democracy and 20 years of accumulating economic
failures have undermined the stability of voting habits to a remarkable extent, in 1974 the Conservatives clearly suffered rather than
profited from the decline of partisanship and the weakening of the
class alignment, although these were the very things for which they
had been working and hoping.

If the Conservative Party was competing only with the Labour
Party, it might reasonably expect to perform increasingly well electorally, because the post-war two-party system was founded on the class
alignment and the Conservatives were able to pick up much support
from those manual workers who did not want or did not perceive their
class identity to be relevant to how they cast their vote, and who rated
as more important the Conservatives' image as the party of national
institutions and competent government. It is also true that, whilst
many policies and goals of the Labour Party are out of favour even
with their own supporters, Conservative positions on nationalisation,
taxation, and public spending are very much in line with current
'public opinion' perception of these issues and are strongly favoured
by Conservative supporters.[9] But in the present period the Conservatives are handicapped in their ability to profit from this by being
identified as the party of big business and finance. Although the party
has never been a class party in the electoral sense, and could not
afford to be, it has been widely perceived as a class party in government, the party of capital confronting the party of labour.

Those who identify with the two main parties believe that 'the trade
unions have too much power', but almost equal numbers believe that
'big business has too much power'.[10] The stalemate that has developed in economic policy as a result of defensive trade unions and
an internationally oriented business community has been reflected in
the rhetoric of two-party adversary politics, further reinforced by the
close political and financial links between trade unions and the
Labour Party and private capital and the Conservatives. The knowledge that in practice both parties pursue very similar policies whilst

flaunting 'the great divide' between them, and that economic decline has continued, uninterrupted by changes in government, was one reason for the support lost by both 'class' parties in 1974. The class stalemate in government has made an explicit class link in the political market an electoral liability. The Conservatives are now competing in a party system in which they may actually have less to fear from their major adversary, the Labour Party, than from some of the other parties. The extent of third-party voting in 1974, and the weakening of partisan support for the two main parties which underlies it, threatens the ability of the Conservatives to retain for long the electoral support they won back in 1979.

Where have all the Conservatives gone?

The Conservative vote fell in 1974 because in three crucial respects the Conservative image had weakened and the party was outbid on its own territory by other parties. The Conservatives lost some of their supporters who no longer wish to align themselves with them in class terms to the Liberals in England and to the SNP in Scotland, and may in the future lose some to the National Front. They lost credibility as the party of strong and competent government as a result of their record in government in 1960–4 and 1970–4, and this strengthened the image and the position of the Labour Party; and they lost some of those who voted for them as the defenders of national institutions to the SNP, the UUC, the National Front, and even, over the EEC, to the Labour Party.

As the national party, the Conservatives suffered in 1974 two important regional losses of support, in Ulster and Scotland. The historic links which bound the Ulster Unionists to the Conservatives were rudely severed when Stormont was suspended and Ulster placed under direct rule by the Conservative Government in 1972, and then by the Sunningdale agreement of 1973, which tried to solve Britain's political problem in Ulster by ending the Protestant supremacy and inaugurating 'power-sharing' between the two communities. The Orange card, which the Conservatives used to play with relish, had to be discarded. As a result, in February 1974, eight of the United Ulster Unionists elected for Ulster did not take the Conservative whip at Westminster. Their continued support would have left the Conservatives the largest single party in the House of Commons and permitted Edward Heath to carry on as Prime Minister. There seems little prospect that the rift can be healed, unless the Conservatives are prepared to break with the bi-partisan policy and re-establish a Protestant Stormont.

The second regional loss of support the Conservatives suffered in 1974 was in Scotland at the hands of the SNP. The Conservatives held thirty-six of the seventy-one Scottish seats in 1955, with more than 50 per cent of the vote. In October 1974 they won sixteen, and were pushed into third place in votes by the SNP, although they won more seats. Most of the SNP's ten gains in February and October were at the expense of the Conservatives. The success of the SNP lay in its ability to use the opportunity presented by economic failure and decline at the centre and the promise of North Sea oil on the periphery to redefine the national issue in Scotland. This has proved attractive for numerous Conservative voters who had previously supported the Conservatives as the British national party and lacked a strong class identification. The SNP has secured some of its strongest bases in the new towns – just the 'classless', 'meritocratic', family-centred communities where the Conservatives themselves once expected to succeed. Unionism remains a strong political force in Scotland and guarantees the Conservatives a continuing Scottish vote, as well as a continuing number of Scottish seats. In 1979 the party won back seven seats from the SNP but still trailed far behind Labour (only 22 seats to Labour's 44) and had no prospect of regaining the position it had occupied in the 1950s.

The loss of support in Scotland and Ulster is small in relation to the total electorate and parliamentary strength of the party, but failure to make good such losses could produce further hung parliaments at future elections and deny the Conservatives the chance to form governments without entering pacts and coalitions. The most serious losses, however, have occurred in England itself, and reflect not only the weakening of the Conservative image as the national party but also as the party of the non-aligned and the party of good government. In February 1974 the Liberals were the Conservatives' most dangerous challenger. Their national vote soared to 6 million, although they failed to make the breakthrough in seats that would have enabled them to maintain their momentum. Despite more candidates in October, the Liberal vote fell by 700,000; so did their share of the poll, and they lost one seat. The Liberals were thus already declining by October and that decline has continued. Although the Liberals in their periods of upsurge take votes from both main parties, they have so far only experienced periods of upsurge when Conservative governments have been in office. This is both bad and good news for the Conservatives. It means that they had an excellent opportunity to recapture a large chunk of their support that was lost in 1974. But, taking a longer view, the Conservatives have everything to fear from returning to office, since it might ignite a Liberal revival that went beyond even 1972–4, when four by-elections were lost in safe Conservative seats. If the Liberals were once to make a breakthrough in parliamentary representation, they would be unlikely to face a subsequent decline, since they could make the price of their support the introduction of proportional representation, and bust the two-party system wide open. They came close in 1974.

It is important to speculate, therefore, where the source of Liberal support lies and why the Conservatives are finding it increasingly hard to keep these voters loyal when they are in government. Apart from the core Liberal vote, the great bulk of Liberal voters identify themselves as supporters of the two main parties. As partisanship for the two main parties has declined, however, a larger and larger part of the electorate has no firm ties to any party, and votes accordingly. The experience of the Conservative Party in government, grappling with the political problems of managing Social Democracy, has in three previous parliaments (1955–9, 1959–64, 1970–4) precipitated an avalanche of less strongly aligned voters to the Liberals, each time on a larger scale. When Labour is in office, the Conservatives appear able to retain and win back such voters. With the decline in the importance of the class alignment in shaping the political perceptions and loyalties of the electorate over the last 20 years, the Conservative performance in government has not consolidated the position of the party as the natural representative of this 'middle-ground', but has thrice sparked a considerable movement away from it.

This is a strange reversal for the party, since formerly it looked to its performance in government to confirm and extend its electoral support. Since 1945 it is Labour that has more often derived electoral benefit from being in government, while in opposition it fails to increase its support.[11] Even more striking than the Conservative failure in February 1974 was the Labour failure. An unpopular government might be expected to lose votes, but for the main opposition party to do so as well was unprecedented.

Another rival that the Conservatives may have to face is the National Front, although as yet the threat remains potential rather than actual. Like the Liberals, the Front wins votes from those disillusioned with the two main parties and makes no secret of its ambition to destroy the two-party system. One of its founding organisations was the League of Empire Loyalists, a Conservative pressure group in the 1950s, and the Front has continued to pick up some members from the disaffected right-wing fringe in the Conservative Party. It infiltrated the party in a few areas in the early 1970s, working closely with such organisations as the Monday Club, assisted by the respectability which Enoch Powell's speeches on immigration gave the Front's own policies. The other side of the Front's nationalism, its strident defence of the national economy and advocacy of protectionism, has appealed much less to right-wing Conservatives, in part because it runs counter to the free-market ideology which still rules the lower reaches of the party, and also because these ideological and material interests are so forcefully represented by alternative combat organisations, such as the National Association for Freedom.

The greater danger to the Conservatives is electoral – the possibility that the Front might begin to attract part of the Conservative working-class vote. Such voters already do not generally align themselves in class terms, and the Conservatives have won them by appearing as the party of patriotism, of success, and good government. Tory working-class supporters tend to be those who do not belong to trade unions, who work in small companies, who do not live in urban working-class communities, and who have the opportunity of starting small businesses themselves, and therefore have a strong belief in self-help.[12] But as the Conservative Party has changed from the party of Empire into the party of Europe, so its national image and its Britishness have been diluted, whilst its share as a government party in creating the British economic morass makes its claims to be the party of affluence, prosperity, and competence harder to believe. The Conservatives also appear at present to lack leaders who can effortlessly communicate with their working-class supporters, as in different ways Joseph Chamberlain, Stanley Baldwin, Harold Macmillan, and Enoch Powell all managed to do.

Lacking at present a major national issue, the Conservatives' best hope of retaining their working-class support and attracting young workers is to remain an alternative party of government, and show themselves, now they are again in office, capable of governing well and effectively. The Conservative image as the national party as well as the party of the wealthy, the powerful, and the successful, was an important condition in preventing the class alignment becoming all pervasive in voting behaviour, and preserving a balance between the two main parties. The Conservatives fought Labour to a draw on electoral territory which Labour had made its own. But now that the electoral map is shifting, the Conservatives risk a significant long-term weakening of their position unless they can develop a new electoral strategy that adapts to the changing electoral and political circumstances as successfully as the party did in the 1920s. A major attempt to devise such a strategy was made by Enoch Powell between 1968 and 1974, and the extraordinary popular following he achieved indicates an electoral potential that only the National Front has begun to explore seriously. He showed immigration to be a national issue which could override in importance all others for a substantial portion of the electorate. The Front's community politics, its thorough organisation, and its threat to outbid the two main parties on race, law and order, permissiveness, as well as prices, unemployment, and real wages, have not yet increased its overall level of voting support; but its very presence is already changing the competitive dynamics of the two-party system, obliging the two main parties to move away from their exclusive preoccupation with the middle-ground.

The party unfaithful

In 1974 with their electoral base under siege and their partisan support in the electorate, particularly among younger voters, dwindling, the party needed to re-establish its reputation as a party of good government in order to stay a major contender in the political market. In 1979 the party advanced from its low point of 35 per cent, and was able to form a majority government once more, but complete electoral recovery is possible in the long run if the Conservatives can find, firstly, a major new national issue with which they can become identified, and, secondly, a way of reversing in government the record of economic failure and decline. The two are inseparable to the extent that a strong nation requires a strong economy; without economic recovery, for example, the Conservative position in Scotland is unlikely to be retrieved. Success in managing the economy would make the party once more the party of nation and the party of the non-aligned. The major obstacles to achieving it are twofold; pressures within the party itself have pushed the party away from the middle-ground marked out under the welfare consensus, and made it a more ideological party, so reinforcing its image as a party of class; and the party on its own appears less able in a period of recession to cope with the political problems of winning consent for policies that restructure employment and rebuild profitability.

Since the shock of the defeat in February 1974 the party has been gripped by a debate as to which policies and which strategy can regain the support that has been lost and, at the same time, provide solutions to the intractable problems of government.[13] The party leadership has been more seriously divided than at any time since the Second World War, and the gap between party ideological aspirations and Conservative performance in government has grown, fuelling a ferment among active Conservative supporters and a strong challenge to the perspectives of the post-war leadership. Margaret Thatcher skilfully exploited this gap when party morale was low after the events of 1973–4 to win the leadership in 1975. Identifying herself with the party's traditional ideological concerns, she promised a return to Conservative principles and objectives and a break with the policies and guiding ideas of the welfare consensus. She removed six prominent supporters of Edward Heath from the Shadow Cabinet, a move which reflected both her boldness and her insecurity. The breach with Heath has not been healed.

During its two recent periods of opposition, 1964–70 and 1974–9, the Conservatives have become rather more like a democratic mass party, in which there is continual tension between the party as a mass movement and the party as an instrument of government, and therefore between the policy perspectives of the leadership and the ideological perspectives of the rank and file. The oscillation between consensus policies in government and radical schemes in opposition, so long a characteristic of the Labour Party, has begun to make its appearance. It is a kind of politics Conservative leaders are unpractised in, and signifies a reduction in the intensity of the party's preoccupation with government, and the growing importance of the mass movement within the party.

The Conservative Party organisation is rather like the British constitution – antique and ramshackle. Two separate organisational principles contend. On the one hand the party is organised as a mass democratic party, built upwards from its large individual membership and the 542 constituency associations in England and Wales (the Scottish Party has its own separate organisation). The associations choose the 5000 delegates at the Annual Conference of the National Union, and select the parliamentary candidates (with a little help from Central Office). On the other hand all important powers in the party are still concentrated in the hands of the leader and are delegated by her as she sees fit. The National Union has no formal role in the formulation of policy and has not been encouraged to assume one. Even the modest proposals of the Chelmer committee in 1973 did not find favour.[14] The Central Council and Executive Committee of the National Union do not have the kind of policy role that is played by Labour's NEC. All the crucial committees in the party report direct to the leader, as does Central Office, and through it the Conservative Research Department, the Conservative Political Centre, and the twelve area offices in the regions. The Shadow Cabinet is appointed by the leader, not elected by the party, and the same is true of the chairman and other leading officials of the party organisation.

Since the constituency associations have overwhelming voting strength at all levels in the National Union (there are no affiliated bodies), the exclusion of the National Union so comprehensively from policy-making could be explosive, and occasional proponents of Tory democracy have hoped it would be. Officials of the National Union, however, have always been noted for their loyalty and self-restraint, and the danger is averted by the informal processes of diplomacy, which oblige the leadership to take account of the opinions of its followers and to anticipate opposition. The different ways in which the party is organised does in any case mean that there is considerable pluralism. The main point of conflict between the constituencies and Central Office has tended to come over the selection of candidates, and occasionally over the confirmation of incumbent MPs. The Maxwell-Fyfe reforms after the Second World War ended the buying of constituencies and gave Central Office the right to approve and suggest candidates, but any moves for complete central control over whom the constituencies may consider as candidates have always been strongly resisted. The independence of the constituencies is buttressed by the fact that they raise a great deal of party funds (over £4 million per annum) and contribute about £250,000 to the expenses of Central Office in a total budget of around £1¾ million – most of the rest being contributed by individuals and companies. The financial strength of the party allows it to employ three times as many full-time constituency agents (363 in 1974) as Labour, although they were once able to afford many more.

The tasks of the constituency associations are electioneering and fund-raising. Although the party does not release figures, the individual membership remains sizeable (2½ million in the 1950s, now thought to be only half that – the average constituency membership was estimated by the Houghton Committee to be 2400). It is largely a sleeping membership. The party is scrupulous in seeing that each organised section of the membership – the women, the Young Conservatives, and the trade unionists – are fully represented at every stage of the organisation and have their own National Advisory Committee and Annual Conference, but this only gives their representatives influence over administrative and not policy decisions.

Apart from the informal consultations at all levels that the party leaders must take in formulating policy, there are also many organised groups within the party which seek to influence the climate of opinion. They have no formal status in the party's deliberations and often draw members from all parts and all levels of the party. The most influential since the Second World War have been the Bow Group, founded in 1951, and the Monday Club, founded in 1960. More recent examples are the Tory Reform Group and the Centre for Policy Studies. In its heyday in the 1960s the Monday Club attempted to create an organised faction in the parliamentary party. There are also a number of pressure groups which, while not formally linked to the Conservative Party, are closely involved with the evolution of its thinking and policies: examples are the Institute of Economic Affairs, the National Association for Freedom, the Institute for the Study of Conflict, and Aims for Freedom and Enterprise.

Even though the National Union is formally powerless in the direction of the party, the leader could hardly survive a major revolt by her followers in the country. Both in relation to them and to her backbenchers in parliament, organised in the 1922 Committee, the leader exercises her monopoly over policy-formation on sufferance.

In its origins the party was an aristocratic party which reluctantly established a democratic mass organisation to assist the party leadership maintain its grip on government. It was not intended to provide a channel for demands and pressures from the party's supporters. Yet gradually it has become so. Whilst Conservative leaders may sometimes wish they could follow Balfour, who proclaimed that he would sooner consult his valet on policy than a Conservative Party Conference, that possibility has vanished along with valets. Party management has become a delicate process of negotiation and compromise, and though the Party Conference has not developed into a policy-making body, its importance as a forum for reconciling the demands of party supporters with the exigencies of government, and the rekindling of party faith and loyalty, has grown. The various tendencies of party opinion have become more vocal and better organised, and factions more common.[15] Since 1967 there has been provision for ballots to be held after debates, and since 1965 the leader has begun attending the whole of the Conference. Previously the leader arrived only when the Conference sessions had finished to deliver a message at a specially convened rally.

Heath and Thatcher have undoubtedly had more trouble in managing their party because both became leaders in opposition, the first Conservative leaders this misfortune had happened to since Austen Chamberlain. Central Office remains under the personal control of the leader but the National Union and the parliamentary party now assert their independence more than they used to. The informal processes of diplomacy for which the party used to be notorious, and whose summit was the magical method for choosing the leader before 1965, by which he 'emerged' rather than being vulgarly appointed or elected, have given way to greater formality and, therefore, more public conflict and dissension. In the 1970–4 parliament backbench revolts cost the party five defeats on whipped votes; two-thirds of Conservative MPs voted against their government in at least one division, twelve members more than fifty times; whilst Enoch Powell voted against the government on no less than 113 separate occasions.[16]

Like every good ideological party, what the Conservative Party now appears to cry out for in opposition is an independent Conservative policy – a policy that is independent both of .their electoral opponents and of the prevailing consensus that Conservative actions in government do not challenge. In the past Conservative leaders have generally been content to give support to the priorities of the prevailing consensus, on the pragmatic grounds that such a consensus reflects the balance of forces and interests within the state and so defines the limits of the politically practicable. These limits may sometimes be tested but the Conservative leadership has never seen its role in British politics as being to lead constant assaults on those limits in order to recast the state consensus. Yet this is what Enoch Powell and New Right opinion demanded in the late 1960s, and it is what Sir Keith Joseph and the National Association for Freedom demand today.

New Right opinion has grown from grass roots discontent almost to engulf the leadership itself. What Joseph and the New Right demand, following the path that Powell blazed, is that the Conservative Party break with the established consensus on policy, and in doing so repudiate their own record in government since the Second World War. Over 30 years of the mixed economy, over 30 years of Keynesian economic management, over 30 years of the welfare state, have signalled the steady advance of collectivism. The pendulum has been replaced by the ratchet because Labour governments extend collectivism, while Conservative governments only preside over what they inherit and never put the clock back or significantly reverse their opponents' measures, and compete electorally for the middle-ground. As a result, it is argued, the Conservative Party in government during 1951–64 and 1970–4 has been an accomplice in the drift towards socialism and corporatism – terms which are used (often interchangeably) to mean suspension of the market and increasing control exercised by government over the economy and society through non-elected agencies, particularly the TUC and the CBI.

The importance of such a position for a party seeking reorientation in opposition is obvious, but its weakness as a basis for prescribing policies for a future government is also clear. To release the ratchet that stops Conservative governments from turning back the great wheel of collectivism, more is required than merely changing the ideological outlook of the Conservative Party or the electorate, for the existence of the ratchet does not reflect the pressures in the arena of support so much as the institutional realities, class interests and organisational imperatives of the modern economy. There is little sign that the party has developed the political will or perspective that will enable it to confront these realities, but there are many signs that the hopes of the ideological militants in the party will again be disappointed.

Margaret Thatcher appears to appreciate in a way that her predecessor did not the differences between the politics of support and the politics of power. Whilst employing to the full the electoral ideologies of her party, she has been studiously careful to avoid detailed policy commitments. Whereas Heath had insisted on detailed blueprints for government and had scorned ideological simplification of issues he knew to be complex, Thatcher deliberately engages in 'populist' simplification of issues for party and national audiences whilst keeping all options for government open. It is for this reason that the new Thatcher government is likely to prove less radical than the Heath government was. Heath's policy committees may not have helped him in his struggle to retain party support against Powell's challenge to his leadership, but they certainly provided the new Ministers in 1970 with an essential means for imposing new policies and priorities on their departments. Failing either such preparation or the mobilisation of external support, Ministers must necessarily bow to the pressures arising from daily economic management and consent to become the brokers and spokesmen for the consensus policies that emerge from the interplay of interests and circumstances.

There is no doubt that Heath's programme for government – the competition policy – was more ideologically charged in 1970 than when it was first launched in 1965, owing to the liberal edge to Conservative thinking that had been injected by Powell and New Right opinion. It represented the first significant break with the understandings of the welfare consensus that any government had achieved.[17] Under Thatcher's leadership policy was kept much less detailed, and there is considerable doubt whether the earlier ideological expectations she raised will be matched by policies to realise them. The 1979 Conservative Manifesto promised only modest measures on trade union reform and was vague on plans for cuts in public expenditure and taxation, and the sale of nationalised industries. The cautious pragmatism of the Shadow Cabinet, even when purged of its more vociferous Social Democrats, ruled out a political assault on the priorities of the consensus.

Here is the dilemma of the Conservatives. Although they may flirt with immigration control and law and order, they lack a major national issue that can divide the opposition to them; and they apparently have yet to evolve a strategy for government that will enable them to escape the straitjacket of Social Democracy which has imprisoned them for the past thirty years – a strategy which enables them to combine policies that satisfy the ideological demands of the party with the policies necessary to govern effectively and so win votes. Thatcher is a traditional Conservative in that she clearly will bend to the realities of power, but she is also a new Conservative in that her style of leadership is to lead from behind, by clearly identifying herself with the perspectives of her party's ideological militants. Heath may prove to be the last Conservative leader who could still assume that his party was primarily concerned with government. Under Thatcher it has become significantly more preoccupied with the absorbing carnival of the politics of support and opposition. The party may well, as a result, suffer the costs imposed by greater ideological stridency – the image of a factional rather than a national party – without reaping the benefits of being able to reshape the consensus by redefining what is politically practicable.

Organising consensus

The spread of ideological politics within the party is one sign that the Conservatives have become less central to the process of devising coherent policies for the direction of the state. Another is that Conservatives have become estranged from some of the principal institutions of the state and civil society. In Conservative eyes the Crown, the Judiciary, and the Armed Forces remain above suspicion. It is almost unthinkable that any prominent Conservative should criticise a member of the royal family, a judge, the armed forces or the police. These are sacred institutions to which Conservatives accord the highest legitimacy. Yet many of the other prominent institutions of the state – parliament and the civil service – as well as some of the most important public institutions of civil society – the Church, the universities and the media – have become steadily more alien to Conservatives, and in several instances blistering and general attacks have been launched on them by sections of the party and by the Conservative press. Many of them are no longer viewed as sound Conservative institutions, the nurseries of Conservative sympathies and patriotic thinking, the professional havens for Conservatives either by birth or aspiration, but as bastions of opposition to the values Conservatives uphold.

The civil service, once the Rolls Royce machine that administered the Empire, has become an expanding bureaucracy administering the 'unproductive' welfare state and intervention in the economy. The universities, once the purveyors of English common sense and patriotism, have been expanded either into centres of left-wing agitation and disorder, or centres of technical expertise, and staffed by professional intellectuals instead of the more reassuring gentlemen intellectuals that used to return Conservative MPs for the university seats. Parliament has become an ineffective bulwark against the growth of 'corporate' government, an 'elective dictatorship', and no longer always protects the rule of law. The churches have grown increasingly meddlesome in race relations and other social questions, whilst the opinion formers in the media – the BBC is particularly singled out as the former voice of Tory Britain – have promoted social, moral, and political ideas that have helped subvert traditional values and social cohesion. The degree of disaffection ebbs and flows, but there is no doubt that cumulatively the Conservatives have been transformed from natural defenders of British institutions into frequent outsiders and critics. Conservatives now feel remote from many areas of state and public activity, and hostile towards some of them. The Establishment is no longer overwhelmingly Tory.

A further difficulty is that Conservatives find their ideologies of imperialism and the free market more and more distant from the policies they have been obliged to pursue in government. The displacement of Britain as an imperial power and the decline of the British economy has forced on the Conservative leadership practical choices that have undermined the former national appeal and identity of the party. This change was most clearly demonstrated in the passage of the party from party of Empire to party of Europe. Being a governing party within the imperial British state naturally gave a profound international orientation to the outlook of the party leadership, but whereas such an orientation was formerly compatible with nationalism and the defence of national institutions, it is so no longer. The commitment to Europe has not strengthened but diluted the Conservatives' national image, and the party has found it hard to turn the EEC into an electoral asset.

Abandonment of the nation–state and the symbols of national sovereignty as the apparently indispensable framework for Conservative thinking reflects the realities of a Britain which, shorn of imperial territory and industrial superiority, is yet dependent on its political and trading relationships with the world economy for food and raw materials to support its specialised industries and urban population. The loss of self-sufficiency in the free-trade era of the nineteenth century eventually destroyed the material basis for nationalist and protectionist policies on the right. The international organisation and perspectives of, first, British financial interests and the great export industries, now reinforced by British multinationals, have exerted enormous direct and indirect pressure on British governments to maintain and, where they can, increase the openness of the British economy to the free flow of goods and capital. The only significant attempt by the Conservatives to challenge this order of priorities was the Tariff Reform campaign organised by Joseph Chamberlain before the First World War. In the 1920s, when the party became the umbrella party for all sections of property, it naturally fell under the tutelage of the leading section of British capital, the financial interests of the City, a spell which has been occasionally modified but never broken.[18] Since that time British prosperity has been linked to the prosperity of the world economy, a stance powerfully reinforced by American influence after 1945; and in the bracing sink or swim atmosphere of the world market British governments have struggled to keep the national economy from capsizing.

It has presented the Conservatives with grave political dilemmas when they are in government. As the party of the free market since the 1920s, they have learnt to chant 'Let the market rule', and never more so than under Margaret Thatcher. But the market in question is no longer a national but an international market, which gives no certainty of prosperity or security to national economies, however large. This is of little concern to the advanced sections of British business, which have long since gone international and learnt to move their capital around the world in search of the highest return and the lowest tax burden. But it threatens the security of a large population dependent on industries which are being rendered obsolete by the progress of the world division of labour.

As a political organisation, the Conservative Party is rooted in the nation–state. It cannot disengage itself in the way that capital can disengage itself from the national economy. Yet the present leadership has no strategy for rebuilding or rescuing the national economy from the effects of long-term regional and industrial decline, save urging ever more complete adaptation to the severe disciplines of the world economy; and hoping in the meantime that sufficient rentier incomes can be earned from investments abroad, plus windfalls like North Sea oil, to cushion the social and political effects within Britain. On present form the Conservatives are unlikely to tackle politically the causes of economic failure, even to the extent that Heath was prepared to do; and, if not, it seems probable that they will not succeed in remedying the most important cause of the loss of public support for the two main parties. Pursuing a rentier strategy will only leave the Conservatives eventually with rentier supporters. Even the moderate nationalism of a British Gaullism appears ruled out by the extent of British dependence on the world economy and by the grip of liberal economics on Conservative thinking about problems of economic policy.

But that means that in the political conditions of Social Democracy the Conservatives risk surrendering their claim to be the party of the national economy. As the world recession deepens, so the issue of the national economy is likely to become the central national issue of British politics, because the low levels of productivity and profitability in Britain make so much of British industry vulnerable to overseas competition. Within the constraints of the existing consensus, the build-up of pressure for import controls, planning agreements, permanent incomes policies, and direct controls of investment will be remorseless. Thatcher's opponents in the party argue that only action from government can plug the gaping holes that seem likely to appear in the British economy over the next decade, with all their consequences for employment and living standards.

The hope of the Conservatives that support the perspective of the present leadership is that the party will avoid either a negative and defensive rentier strategy or an interventionist, protectionist strategy, because the next Conservative government will spark a British recovery by its thorough-going economic liberalism and will not be deflected from its goal as Heath was. Such a government would be hoping that major cuts in personal taxation and public expenditure would regenerate the British capitalist class by creating such a climate of profitability and enterprise that a host of new small businesses would be set up by new entrepreneurs that could compensate for the loss of jobs in heavy industry and the public sector, and widen the electoral base of the Conservative Party.

The main doubt about this policy does not concern the opposition of the trade unions, which would be outflanked instead of confronted; rather it arises from the time scale of the changes and the actual likelihood that there is a great reservoir of entrepreneurial talent waiting only for more incentives to thrust into the light. To get really free of the constraints of Social Democracy, and create the Social Market Economy of which Tory strategists dream, would require tough-minded adherence to a neutral policy stance – rigid monetary targets, no interference in wage negotiations, no help for lame ducks, the sale of the assets of nationalised industries at whatever price clears the market, and massive cuts in taxes and public expenditure. No interference in wage negotiations means free collective bargaining – the handing of responsibility for standing up to pay demands back to employers. The ability of many employers to cope is in doubt (the CBI has already voiced its misgivings about Conservative plans) and the likely effects in a depressed world economy would not be vigorous competition and growth, but high unemployment and stagnation, while attempts to raise productivity, reduce manning levels, and reorganise work processes would be successfully blunted by defensive trade unions. The reason for government intervention in the past has been to assist the efforts of employers in rationalising and modernising their businesses. The special contribution of Labour governments since the Second World War has been to divide the Labour movement in a way that Conservative governments can never hope to do. If the combination of ideological, political and economic pressures which governments have brought to bear on the work force have not succeeded in creating the right climate for profitable investment, it is hardly likely that a return to relying solely on economic pressures will succeed, particularly when the external environment is so unfavourable. In such a climate the boom in small-scale enterprise is extremely unlikely to take place on the required scale.

Without Ministers of Enoch Powell's vision and obstinacy, it is hard not to foresee the erosion of any hard-line monetarist strategy by the steady drip of day-to-day administrative decisions needed to keep economic performance and activity at tolerable levels. The proportion of the GNP passing through government hands has reached such a level that since 1940 all governments have been necessarily concerned with the management of demand, seeking to achieve desirable outcomes in the level of employment and prices, the balance of payments and the rate of economic growth. The course of policy under the Heath Government is a sharp warning. Heath's commitment to his overriding goal of rebuilding a strong national economy within the framework of the EEC was such that the meagre results, and the mounting opposition the liberal strategy had brought by 1972, precipitated a major change of direction and an intensified use of all the instruments for managing Britain's economic problems that previous governments had come to rely on. Heath and his lieutenants developed an appreciation for the special methods of Social Democracy which they have not since lost and which has for the present isolated them within the party.

Finding a future

Conservatism weakened in 1974 because of the undermining of the national strategy the party had pursued so successfully for the previous 100 years. The party now finds it harder to be identified as the party of the nation – state, the divide between its principles and its policies has grown, and it is blamed for its share in the two-party mismanagement of the British economy since 1951. Despite its success in 1979, therefore, the party finds itself in considerable long-term electoral danger, in part from its main competitor, but also from the smaller parties, who threaten to outbid it in traditional parts of its electoral territory. This danger is hardly temporary, because neither of the two main parties appears able to generate the conditions for overcoming economic decline and managing the recession that would restore electoral faith in parliamentary government and the two dominant parties. So long as the central economic problems are not dispelled, the loss of partisanship and fixed party loyalties, and the readiness of electors to switch their votes and party allegiances, will not decline and may grow.

The weakening of the two-party system and the feeling that government has become inept and ineffective have fanned the campaigns for constitutional reform on many fronts. Plans to devolve power to the regions, to introduce proportional representation for elections to Westminster, to draw up a bill of rights, to reform the House of Lords have all been canvassed. The Conservatives have so far proved very uncertain in their handling of them, particularly the most important – devolution and PR. That is primarily because the interests of the party and the interests of the state pull in different directions.

It was a constitutional question which once inspired the deep feelings in the party and gave the leadership little room for man-oeuvre. The unity of the UK remains a central symbol for the Conservatives, and although passions are nothing like as strong as during the political struggle over Irish Home Rule, the party has so far refused to agree to meaningful devolution proposals, and suffered the resignation of its Scottish Front Bench spokesmen in 1977 as a result. The stand taken by the Shadow Cabinet under Thatcher, with its renewed emphasis on the old Unionist principles, appears an attempt to safeguard what remains of the Conservative vote in Scotland. By rallying Unionist opinion once more behind it the Conservatives hope to survive as a substantial minority force in Scotland.

For the party of Europe, however, it makes little sense, since in a European perspective the Conservatives should be accepting the devolution of powers to different regions within the community. Such regions may well cut across or break up existing nation–states, the more historical whose boundaries, the more arbitrary and unwork-able they are likely to be. Convinced Europeans in the party like Edward Heath are strong supporters of devolution, since no clash of principle is involved for them. In opposing devolution the Conserva-tives are denying the logic of their acceptance of the EEC. A federal Europe appears to some of them as the best way of coping with the economic and political problems which British parties at the national level have failed to resolve. But at present electoral and party interests sway the leadership. For the party members, accepting Europe was always a matter of calculation and necessity rather than enthusiasm, so that the European commitment is easily overlaid by the traditional call to defend the unity of the kingdom.

Even more fundamental considerations apply to PR, which could destroy the Conservative Party in its present form. Those who support PR most vigorously do so in the hope that it would split the Labour Party, but the realignment of the centre which PR is expected to bring about might also detach part of the Conservatives from their party allegiance in the process of ending adversary politics, and altering the context of parliamentary economic management. The Conservatives have long been wary of electoral reform, from the days when their permanent majority in the House of Lords threw out the Lib–Lab plan to introduce the Alternative Vote in 1930 to the vote in 1977 on the modest proposal of PR in elections to the European

Parliament, which drew only sixty Conservative votes in its support.

Part of the opposition reflects deep seated Conservative attitudes on the Constitution. Arguments about the unfairness and the frequent absurdity of election results in the simple majority system excite little concern from most Conservatives, who have never believed that the primary function of the electoral system was to represent the views of electors accurately; its purpose is to ensure stability and authoritative government. Another reason for opposing PR is party advantage. The Conservatives could only rarely expect to form a government on their own under PR. In general elections since the Second World War only in 1955 and 1959 would the Conservatives have emerged with a straight majority of the seats. Naturally the party leaders prefer electoral rules that allow them to win a majority of the seats on a minority of the votes.

Yet if Conservatives are as afraid as many of them claim to be of the leftward movement of the Labour Party between 1970 and 1975, and of that movement being resumed at some point in the future, leading to the election of a government more committed to socialism than any of its predecessors, then the easiest way to reduce its likelihood is to back the introduction of PR. Otherwise the sheer pendulum mechanics of the two-party system are sure to bring Labour back into office eventually. Why sacrifice the national interest to the short-term party interest? The answer seems compelling to many in the party's ranks, particularly those whose experience of government has given them a special understanding of Social Democracy. Many of them have a strong feeling that the party is proceeding down an electoral cul-de-sac and putting at risk the interests it seeks to defend. Harold Macmillan's call in 1976 for the laying aside of party and the establishment of a national coalition at a moment when the Conservatives had an overwhelming lead in the opinion polls reflected the feeling that it might be unwise for the Conservatives to attempt to govern on their own again.

The reason why the bulk of the party and the present leadership so emphatically reject PR is that the party, as distinct from most of those who have led it since the war, has never fully accepted Social Democracy and the welfare consensus. Accepting PR means accepting that Tory England will never return; it means the consolidation of centre government and pragmatic policies to administer the 'mixed' economy and the welfare state, and safeguard the national economy, and the ending of the vision of a Conservative restoration, which those on the New Right still dream of so vividly. It would mean accepting that the Conservative Nation cannot again be as strong as it was in 1931 and 1935, establishing a commanding position over all other bodies of opinion.

If the two-party system weakens further over the next 10 years, then support for PR in the Conservative Party is likely to grow, just as support for the EEC grew in the 1960s, even though joining Europe meant the burial of much the party valued. The widespread sympathy in the party for the white settlers of Rhodesia since 1965 reveals the emotional dislike still felt for the withdrawal from Empire, which by skilful leadership in the 1950s and 1960s the party was brought to accept. It had already had to adjust at home to the uncongenial world of Social Democracy. As a result of these changes, the party has steadily lost the dominant position in British politics it once enjoyed. The logical conclusion, which the party is currently resisting, is to drop its claims to be the sole or even the principal organiser of consensus and to join with other political groups in building strong centre coalition governments to manage social democracy as it currently exists. That means accepting that Conservatism by itself is no longer a relevant response to the political problem of how to organise support for the institutions of the contemporary capitalist economy, a conclusion apparently reached by the financial markets in 1977, which fell sharply when there was a chance that the Conservatives might win their censure motion and rose again when the Lib–Lab pact was agreed, although after the winter of 1979 the City returned to its more normal allegiance.

As the 1975 Referendum demonstrated, a new centre party exists in embryo with abilities for mobilising national support superior to those of the Conservative Party on its own. Yet the Conservative response to the fragmentation of the party system and to its own loss of support in 1974 remains overwhelmingly defensive. The party has turned its back on proposals to change the constitutional rules and is instead chiefly concerned with regaining its lost position in the two-party system as quickly as possible. Between 1974 and 1979 it played the usual opposition adversary game in the two-party system, seeking to profit from government mistakes and misfortunes, exaggerating policy differences and hoping that the unpopularity of the government would bring election victory as it brought sweeping local election successes and important by-election gains in 1976–7. In such a mood the party is not prepared to discuss alliances with other parties; it always entered coalitions in the past from positions of strength, and its rejection of Liberal overtures in 1974 was because the party leadership would not trade continuance in office for a concession that might destroy for ever the Conservative chance of forming a majority government again. But if, during the next 10 years, electoral partisanship continues to weaken, the world economy remains depressed, and British industrial debility gobbles up the temporary benefits of North Sea oil, then the Conservative Party may be forced to change its conception of itself and its relationship to its rivals. Conservatives will not like forming coalitions or agreeing pacts with the Liberals or any other party, since it deprives them of their claim to be the moderate centre party, but they may eventually have no other choice.

In 1979 the Conservatives won the general election by a greater margin than had seemed likely in 1977 and 1978. The electoral collapse of 1974 could be forgotten. But the real test for the party was still to come. Since 1959 no government after serving a full term has managed to be re-elected. Margaret Thatcher is engaged on a bold but desperate attempt to preserve the Conservatives as an independent party capable of forming majority governments. If the Conservatives are judged to have failed in government again, the consequences for their own support in the country and for the future of the two-party system will be momentous. The alternative leadership within the party, both within and without the Cabinet, may then decide that the arguments for re-alignment have become overwhelming. In 1979 Margaret Thatcher still had to demonstrate that single-party government could find ways, within a single parliamentary term, of overhauling Britain's backward and stagnant economy, whilst maintaining social peace and electoral confidence, despite a deteriorating world economy. Whilst success would make the Conservatives dominant once again in British politics failure would almost certainly spell the end to the special role the Conservatives have played for so long and force a major re-organisation of the electoral system and the state. Proclaiming the facts of life Conservative is likely to prove easier than making the facts of government become so.

2

The Labour Party

R. L. Borthwick

Labour's place in the two-party system

For almost half a century one date has dominated the myths and actions of the Labour Party:1931. Since the traumatic events of that year, the party's guiding principle has been to avoid, in peace-time, co-operation in Parliament or at the hustings with other parties. The way in which in 1931 a Labour Prime Minister and some of his senior colleagues joined a coalition government, dominated by the Conservatives, and then used that coalition to inflict a crushing defeat on their former party, has served to keep all subsequent Labour leaders on the path of virtue.

The events of 1931 may be seen as confirming one view of Labour's position in the party system: that it is a party unlike all others in British politics. It seeks not merely to exercise power but ultimately to create socialism. In that respect Labour has always had a fundamental ambivalence about whether it is a movement or a party. It is, of course, both; but the sense of being a movement – a crusade, to use one of its own favourite descriptions – has had a profound effect both on the way the party has operated and on the scope it has had, and continues to have, to adapt to changing circumstances. In that respect Labour is quite unlike the Conservative Party, which, as Andrew Gamble points out in this volume, has tended to think of itself very much as the party of the state. Labour on the other hand has felt a deep sense of being a party of society (or ar least of part of it), which can hope to take over from time to time the reins of government and exercise the power of the state. Only in recent years has there been serious talk of Labour being the 'natural party of government', and even now there is an air of bravado about the use of such a phrase in connection with Labour, as though those who use it are not totally confident in what they assert.

However, the year 1931 has affected also the way in which Labour views the two-party system. Despite what has been portrayed as the 'betrayal' by its leaders, the party helped to confirm its place in the system in 1931 by its opposition to the 'National Government'. This confirmed deeply held suspicions that all other parties were fundamentally opposed to Labour and must in turn themselves be opposed, and that Labour must in future take office only when it had a parliamentary majority. More perhaps than any other party, Labour sees itself as having a special place in the two-party system. Since it represents, or claims to represent, one class (and the major class) of an inevitably divided society, its place in a two-party scheme of things has seemed assured. Yet for much of its life Labour has operated in a quite different world. After its foundation in 1900 it was perhaps more of a pressure group than a political party; its hopes of political success rested on its ability to persuade other parties to legislate on its behalf. There may have been those who believed it would one day grow into a major power in the state, but even they must have been surprised by the speed with which this happened. Less than a quarter of a century after it was founded, Labour found itself in office. However, both in 1924 and 1929 the party took office without having a majority in the House of Commons; as a result it found it had the responsibility of governing but without the power to govern in the way it wanted. Nevertheless, it could be said that on these occasions the Prime Minister, Ramsay MacDonald, took a decisive step towards ensuring that Labour in office would be a party of the whole nation and not merely of one section of it. This tension between representing the interests of a class and governing in the interests of the whole nation has been a permanent feature of Labour governments even when they have enjoyed parliamentary majorities.

Labour's current vision of its place in the two-party system rests rather heavily on its success in 1945. In a sense 1945 represents for the party the opposite pole to 1931. The landslide electoral victory of that year helped the party to exorcise the ghosts of the 1931 defeat. Ironically it is only since 1945 that Labour has operated in anything like two-party competition. It now appears that this period of 'two-partyness' lasted for little more than 25 years. If the two-party system is dead, Labour needs to re-evaluate its course.

The tension between the party of class and the party of the wider society reflects yet another ambivalence in Labour's attitudes. A movement it may be, but what exactly is it a movement for or towards? At least two different answers can be given to this question. For some it is, and always has been, a socialist movement with a vision of a society in which the means of production, distribution and exchange are publicly owned. Whether the party was in office or not, it has been important for these socialists to keep untarnished the purity of their ideals. On the whole this is more easily done in opposition than in government; consequently, there have always been those in this camp who have not seen the occupation of office as being especially significant. While retaining a faith that full-blooded socialism of this sort can be achieved by democratic means, they have tended to reject the compromises which holding office has brought with it. In this respect Labour has been quite different from the Conservative Party, which, though it may have disagreements about policy, never doubts the value of holding office.

The other wing of the Labour Party has tended to have a less clear view of where the party is going. The Social Democratic wing of the party expects it to become a semi-permanent party of government rather in the manner of its Scandinavian counterparts. This strain of thought emphasises the special qualifications of a Social Democratic party to govern a modern industrialised society, thereby avoiding the ideological extremes of Marxist Socialism on the one hand and laissez-faire Conservatism on the other. Social Democrats avoid taking a doctrinaire position on the question of the ownership of the means of production. They expect that some mixture of public and private control will prevail, but are reluctant to set out in advance just which parts of the country's productive capacity ought to be publicly owned and which bits privately owned. Indeed, Social Democrats are rather impatient with the argument between Marxists and Conservatives on this question, for they believe that the question of ownership is much less important than that of control and accountability. In that respect the Social Democrats believe that the state now possesses adequate statutory and fiscal power to direct the owners of capital, both public and private, to behave in accordance with the national interest. Social Democrats are unhappy about the obsession with the ownership of the means of production; for them the more important issue is the pursuit of social equality. To this end they place their faith in such things as comprehensive education, progressive taxation, a National Health Service with care free to the patient, full employment, a comprehensive system of social services and welfare payments provided by the state. All these, it is asserted, are within the capacity of the contemporary state to deliver, given the political will and administrative intelligence required.

This wing of the Labour Party has embraced office more willingly than its more fundamentalist brethren. Moreover, when the party has been in office, it has been this wing which has prospered, often to the dismay of other sections. Out of office it is sometimes a different story: then the fundamentalists may be more successful. Here we encounter yet one more paradox about the operation of the party: it is prepared to place much reliance, when in office, on plans drawn up while in opposition. Because of its instinct as, or yearning to be, a democratic party, it has always laid great stress on the right of the party at large to lay down policy. Inevitably, it has been easier to do this when Labour has been out of office. In office the countervailing pressure of a Cabinet, advised by a civil service and, through them, in contact with a range of interest groups, has given a wider, or at least a different, perspective. Yet the policy commitments drawn up in opposition, whether sensible or not, tend to acquire the status of holy writ if the party wins power. There is a clear understanding that what is in the manifesto is what the party is in office to implement, and this may well include the small print, which played no part in the election campaign and which can hardly be said to have been, in any meaningful sense, approved of by the electorate. How else, it may be asked, can the party of social change be kept on the path of rectitude in the face of what are seen as the corrupting influence of office and hostility of institutions like the civil service? Evidence for the truth of these propositions is not required; the sense that Labour is engaged on a righteous struggle is sufficient. In that context co-operation with other parties is bound to be almost impossible. Those who are not with Labour are against it, and, even if not obviously the main opponent, they must be merely in disguise; thus the Scottish National Party, for example, must inevitably be 'Tartan Tories'.

What perhaps lies behind the faith in the manifesto is that Labour has retained the constitution of a party of opposition rather than of government. This is reflected too in the party's attitude to leadership.

Like the constitutions of the trade unions who helped to build it, the constitution of the Labour Party is formal and elaborate. It allows little scope for the imaginative ideas of the leader of the party. On the contrary, it is based on the assumption that the leader is in office to carry out the properly constituted will of the party. In theory the supreme body is the Party Conference, which meets annually. In practice policy is decided by the National Executive Committee (NEC), which the Conference elects, and, when Labour is in office, by the Cabinet. The conflict between the representative theory and the practice is just one of the tensions within the party, which result from the fact that on the one hand the party was formed to represent, and on the other it has increasingly been ruling.

Until fairly recently the Conservative Party was happy to let its leader emerge and then give him or her enough freedom to get on with the job of acquiring and using the power of the state. Labour has never formally trusted its leaders in this way. Indeed, Labour's rules are largely an attempt to control its own elected rulers and make them as directly responsible to the mass of the party as possible.

To the two groups we have been discussing so far should be added a third, of much less numerical significance. Since the mid-1960s the party has been subjected to 'entryism' (or 'entrism', the spelling varying with the ideological perspective from which it is viewed) from Trotskyists. As Peter Mair explains in this volume, a number of small but highly active and well educated groups of Trotskyist revolutionaries have entered the Labour Party with the intention of turning it to their own uses. Sometimes these groups hope to break off a significant section – the more revolutionary section – and carry it back to the Trotskyist camp; and sometimes they hope to convert Labour to some of their own policies. The tension within the party between the Social Democrats and the fundamentalists has provided these Trotskyist groups with the opening they need to operate. The generally enervated state of local Labour Parties, particularly in working-class areas where there are often Labour MPs and Labour councillors, has made it relatively easy for the entering groups to gain a voice. Small run-down constituency parties in the inner cities are in a poor position often to resist such groups. So far their impact has been confined to a few constituencies and has served merely to make MPs nervously wary about what is going on in their own Constituency parties.

Crucial to any discussion of the strands that make up the Labour

Party are of course the trade unions. In the much quoted view of Ernest Bevin, the party grew out of the bowels of the trade-union movement. It is not clear whether the trade unions incline more to one wing of the party than another. Like the party itself, they are ambivalent about their role; is it to maximise the rewards to be had by their members in the existing capitalist economic system or to act as an agent in bringing about socialism?

Their importance in the party is clear: in 1977, 5,800,069 of the party's 6,459,127 members were affiliated to the party as members of trade unions. These trade-union members came from fifty-nine unions, or, to put it another way, fifty-nine union leaders controlled nearly 6 million of the $6\frac{1}{2}$ million votes at the 1977 Annual Party Conference. Under the terms of the party's constitution, the trade unions elect twelve of the twenty-nine members of the NEC, and in addition their votes are decisive in the choice of the five women representatives and of the Party Treasurer. In effect, then, the unions control a majority of the NEC; their own twelve slots are filled on the basis of a complex set of bargains among union leaders involving also membership of the General Council of the TUC. At Party Conferences the individual unions normally cast their votes as a block in favour of whatever position has been accepted by their union, no matter how small the majority for that position may have been. This habit of block voting increases the weight of their numbers even more. Collectively the unions also pay the bulk of the Labour Party's bills. Even though the party is invariably hard up, it knows that it can turn to its friends in the unions to pay for general elections and most of the running costs of the party.

However, occasions when the unions vote as a block against the rest of the party are rare. The unions do not usually need to use their power in any heavy-handed way: their position in the party is so strong that their weight does not have to be flaunted to be felt. For much of the party's history the weight of trade-union opinion has been in the centre of the party, or, perhaps more accurately, the centre of the party has been defined by the position of the majority of the larger unions. Be that as it may, the unions have not usually become closely involved in the ideological battles within the party. However, this is not always the case. When the party was led in the late 1950s and early 1960s by Hugh Gaitskell, the larger unions frequently backed him when he fought the fundamentalist left led by Aneurin Bevan. But the unions would not follow Gaitskell when he tried to water down the party's commitment to fundamentalist change as embodied in 'Clause 4' of the party constitution; nor did they back him automatically when he clashed with the left over unilateral disarmament. It is at this time we begin to see a shift in the position of leaders of some of the major unions. By the late 1960s a number of larger unions, including the Transport Union, the Engineers and the Miners' Union had elected left-wing leaders. The result was that the unions took up much more ideological positions within the party. Against this background in 1969 the Labour government announced plans to legislate on the vexed question of industrial relations. These plans produced such opposition from the unions that the government was obliged to abandon its proposals. By the time of the June 1970 election, outwardly at least, the breach was healed.

In order to make such breaches less likely in future an informal but very powerful liaison committee was set up in 1972. This consists of nine members of the Parliamentary Labour Party (PLP), ten representatives of the NEC and seven representatives of the TUC. This liaison committee was the form in which the party and the unions first agreed to the 'Social Contract' and to a number of the more important pieces of legislation passed by the Labour government elected in 1974.[1] In general the support and interchange between party and TUC is so close and so powerful that, when united, they can ignore the other elements within the party. This may be one reason for the somewhat benign view that the party has taken of such things as entryism.

It is perhaps unavailing to discuss whether the Labour Party would have been stronger had its links with the trade-union movement been less close. Clearly in some ways it gains enormously from the union connection. As Andrew Gamble points out in this volume, the Conservative Party's links with its natural allies among groups are both more distant and increasingly uncertain. Compared to that, Labour's relations with the unions are firmly based. Not, of course, that the unions cannot adjust to governments of other parties (indeed, given the strains imposed in the 1970s by policies of wage restraint, it has sometimes seemed that some union leaders were speaking a language of free collective bargaining that was closer to that normally used by the Conservative Party); it is simply that the connection with Labour suits them best and gives the party a secure place in the political market-place. In the light of the difficulties experienced by the Conservatives in the early 1970s and of the more general concern over the governability of Britain, it has become abundantly clear that the trade unions are a central instrument in the functioning of the society, and a group whose co-operation is of some importance to the success of any government's policies. In that respect a party with such close links to the trade-union movement must be a potential partner in any coalition governments that are to be formed if two-party politics is no longer the rule.

Electoral position

A further consequence of the special relationship between the Labour Party and the TUC, outlined above, is to place a premium on the winning of office; this in turn has weakened the position of the fundamentalists, for the TUC is not interested in having its party sulking in opposition. Outwardly over the past 15 years the party has been remarkably successful: power has been acquired at four out of six elections. When the two-party system was losing its force, the party was enjoying an unparalleled run of success. The irony here is that Labour became the natural party of rule in a two-party system just when that system was losing credibility.

In fact Labour's popularity is slightly illusory. The party's highest ever vote came in a year it lost – 1951 – when it had 13,948,385 votes, 48.8 per cent of the poll. In 1964 the party won office with 12,205,808 votes, 44.1 per cent of the total. Its vote then rose to 13,096,629, 48.1 per cent, in 1966 and has been falling ever since. Labour actually won half a million fewer votes in February 1974 when it won office than in June 1970 when it lost. In October 1974 Labour suffered a further drop to 11,457,079, which represented 39.2 per cent of those who voted (and just 28.6 per cent of the electorate). In 1979 Labour's share of the poll dropped to 36.9 per cent. This is its smallest poll since 1931.

Labour's success has owed a good deal, too, to the benefits conferred by the simple plurality electoral system. It is not surprising therefore that the party has not shown much enthusiasm for proposals to reform that system. Under pressure from the Liberals, the Labour government gave lukewarm support (to the extent of allowing a free vote) to the idea of a regional-list system (a form of proportional representation) for elections to the European Parliament when this matter was considered in the House of Commons in December 1977;

but the House, in its wisdom, decided against the idea by 319–222, with 146 Labour MPs voting in favour of the idea.

General elections are only one indication of the level of public support for the party; another is by-elections. Whereas the Labour government of 1945–51 had the proud record of never losing in a by-election a seat it was defending, more recent Labour governments have not been so favoured. Between 1966 and 1970 Labour lost fifteen out of the twenty-six seats it defended, including a spectacular run from September 1967 to June 1969 when it lost eleven out of the fifteen seats. The party's record in by-elections after the general election of October 1974 was equally unhappy.

The picture presented by local-government elections scarcely provides more encouragement for the party. While the Labour Party performed tolerably well in such elections in the early 1970s (with a Conservative government at Westminster), more recently it has seen its representation severely diminished. In the District Council elections of 1976 Labour lost many seats, including control of Birmingham, Leeds, Leicester and Nottingham. In the 1977 County elections the picture for Labour was perhaps even more depressing: the party was left in clear control of only five counties in England and Wales (Durham, Tyne and Wear, Mid Glamorgan, West Glamorgan and South Yorkshire). Rarely can the party's heartland have been so narrowly defined. This situation might have been expected to make Labour groups on councils more willing to consider co-operation with other parties, but, with very limited exceptions, this does not seem to have happened. Their assumption – that the usual swing of popularity will restore Labour's position – was to some extent realised in the 1979 district council elections.

This drop in Labour's popularity at the polls has been paralleled by a drop in the number of its individual members. We noted that the overwhelming majority of members are affiliated to the party through the trade unions; but the day-to-day life of the party depends on its individual members. They pay an annual subscription of a mere £1.20 and have a large part to play in choosing the party's candidates for local and parliamentary elections, and it is they who organise the party's election campaigns. More important, it is on their number that Labour bases its claim to be a mass party. It is little consolation that Labour is not the only party to have difficulty in maintaining its local support at anything like a healthy level.

Officially individual membership of the party is about 675,000 (this figure includes some who are also members of affiliated unions). Recent studies,[2] however, have shown these figures to be a considerable overestimate; 250,000–300,000 is probably nearer the mark. Even the party's own figures admit that only thirty-four constituencies have more than 1500 members and only five have more than 3000. The decline in members appears to be worst in inner-city constituencies. This is particularly worrying, as these seats are usually safe for Labour. The party does not appear to be faring anything like so badly in marginal or Conservative seats. This pattern of decline leaves it with very little presence in the areas which have suffered the most from industrial decline and which have the highest proportions of poor and elderly citizens. Martin Walker points out that the National Front has been particularly successful in recruiting in these areas of England. Roger Mullin points out also that the Scottish National Party (SNP) also recruited well, if not in the inner-city areas of Scotland, certainly in a number of previously Labour areas where the party had become enervated. Entryism of the kind described by Peter Mair is likely to be most effective where the Labour Party is small. Thus it is worrying for the party that it is weak in precisely those seats where its parliamentary and local government representatives are chosen.

The decline in the mass membership has been accompanied by a narrowing of the activities undertaken by local parties. In the not too distant past, where Labour was strong, the ward and constituency parties used to enter fully into the lives of ordinary people. The social functions once provided by Labour parties, and which were so important in binding people to the party, have now all but disappeared from these areas. The tradition lives on only in a few coal-mining areas. It is perhaps no accident that some of the most vigorous of the younger parties described in this book, the Welsh and Scottish National Parties as well as the National Front, resemble the old Labour Party more than the contemporary machine does.

Threats and responses

The main threat to Labour continues to be the Conservatives: Labour's most damaging electoral losses have been to them and, in so far as elections continue to be thought of (not least in the Labour Party) in terms of forming governments, the Conservatives remain the main alternative. Yet this overall picture obscures important regional variations. In Scotland the SNP, though it won most of its Westminster seats from the Conservatives, was poised to challenge Labour in many of its seats. Given the importance of Labour's Scottish seats for its prospects of winning a majority at Westminster, this was a threat to its chances of forming a government by itself and conditioned, as we shall presently see, a number of important policy responses in the 1970s. The challenge of the Scottish Labour Party did no serious damage to Labour.

In Wales Plaid Cymru (PC) has not been a serious threat to Labour's dominance: its area of success, at least in parliamentary elections, has tended to be away from the main areas of Labour strength. In England Labour is challenged not only and most obviously by the Conservatives, but also by the Liberals, who, after their pact with Labour in 1977–8, hoped to pick up votes from Labour sympathisers. In a different way the party also feared inroads from the National Front in a limited number of constituencies, mostly in London and the Midlands. This threat was less real after the Front's failure in 1979.

One can examine the response of the Labour Party to the changed party situation in a number of ways, but it may be as well to bear in mind that what is being observed is not necessarily a new phenomenon so much as old remedies applied to new situations. When in office, the main responses have been to use the powers of government to undercut support for its opponents or strengthen support from its own voters. Secondly, there is the use of legislation to achieve the same ends. Thirdly, there is the search for parliamentary allies to enable a Labour government either to survive or to act. Then there is the use of the weapon of publicity to attack opponents.

It is sometimes argued in the 1970s that it is no longer a clear advantage for a party to be in office, because of the electorate's tendency to blame government and react against what it is trying to do. Office, however, still has some advantages. The powers exercised by Ministers, even in the straightened economic circumstances of the past few years, are still very considerable and are a major asset when trying to secure political support. So, over the past few years one can point to a number of decisions which seem, in part at least, to have been motivated by the desire to weaken political opponents. Most noteworthy are those decisions which were designed to weaken the

SNP and help Labour in Scotland. The decision to use public money to help Chrysler (UK) Ltd, which had an important Scottish dimension; government support for a shipbuilding order for Poland; and the reversal of a decision to close a number of Scottish teacher-training colleges all fall into this category.

Legislation can be used in much the same way. The efforts to legislate for devolution to Scotland and Wales clearly owed a great deal to the threat posed to Labour by the nationalist parties, and the particular form of the proposals represented a desire to weaken support for the nationalists by making concessions while at the same time maintaining representation of Scotland and Wales at Westminster at present levels, so as to maximise Labour's prospects of forming a government (and a single-party government) in the future. In this connection it is worth noting that the Scotland Bill was guillotined successfully, whereas the earlier Scotland and Wales Bill could not be, partly because the government was able to promise extra support and status for development funds in England, which enabled them to win back the support of Labour MPs from Northern England. But all this is not in itself a new tactic, it merely illustrates anew how pursuit of the common good can, happily, be made to coincide with the self-interest of the government of the day.

The least ambiguous response on the part of the Labour Party has been within Parliament itself. The fact that Labour found itself in a condition of minority, or very small majority, government for virtually the whole period from March 1974 to the 1979 election placed a premium on finding parliamentary support outside its own ranks. The most obvious manifestation of this was the pact with the Liberals from March 1977 to the Summer of 1978. This represented not only a very public form of such parliamentary arrangements but also a major innovation in the post-1945 history of party politics in Britain. For many Liberals it probably represented a breakthrough into what they hoped would become a more permanent style of government, but for Labour it was always regarded as no more than a temporary expedient to be dispensed with as soon as circumstances allowed. The assumption was that after a future election 'normalcy' would be restored.

Other parliamentary allies have varied in their reliability. The Social Democratic and Labour Party (SDLP) member from N. Ireland has provided regular support, while a Republican MP can sometimes be prevailed upon to vote for Labour, but his attendance has been infrequent. More surprisingly, Labour has been able to obtain support from among the ranks of the United Ulster Unionist Coalition MPs. In addition the SNP and PC representatives have given a good deal of support to Labour, which, in view of the concessions they have gained, is much less surprising.

The party itself has responded in a variety of ways to this new situation. At one level the party has used the weapon of publicity to attack its rivals: perhaps the clearest instance of this was a celebrated Party Political Broadcast in December 1977 attacking the National Front. While this was perhaps more extreme in tone than usual in such broadcasts, it can be seen as merely the extension to a new area of one of the well established uses of such broadcasts.

It is significant that the Labour Party has remained essentially united in its responses to the various threats facing it. Despite its historical and ideological disposition to be a party of centralisation, it has managed the somersault to being a party of devolution with considerable smoothness. Sometimes the cracks have shown through, as when, in 1974, the Party's Scottish Conference had to be reconvened to enable it to come up with the 'correct' response on devolution. The impact of regional nationalism has been less than might have been expected. The only serious crack in the structure of the party over this issue has been caused by the breakaway Scottish Labour Party (SLP). Formed mainly by the Labour MP Mr Jim Sillars, and subsequently joined by Mr John Robertson, MP, it failed to grow as its founders hoped. Its early promise was much diminished by internal disputes and by its failure to capture any solid body of support either within the Labour Party or the trade unions; as a result it seems destined to join that group of fringe elements on the left of the Labour Party. It was somewhat unlucky in that for the first two years or so of its life there was no by-election in Scotland, and it was thereby denied the chance to demonstrate any popular appeal at a crucial stage of its life. Its successes in local government were very few, and confined to district level.[3] There have of course been differences of opinion elsewhere in the Labour Party over devolution, but these have not involved a threat to the structure of the party.

Managing the party

The struggle between fundamentalists and Social Democrats is very evident within the parliamentary party; each has developed its distinct organisation. The left in the PLP is organised around the Tribune Group, and though bearing that name since 1965 they are the successors to the earlier 'Keep Left' and Bevanite groupings. On the right of the PLP the idea of a separate identity is less well established, but since 1974 the Manifesto Group has operated as a kind of counter to the Tribune Group, and has spent much of the time supporting a Labour government against the Labour Party. Straddling the party inside and outside parliament, one finds the Campaign for Labour Party Democracy appealing more to fundamentalists and countered by the Campaign for Labour Victory. This line-up is parallel to the early 1960s, when the Victory for Socialism Group gave rise to the opposed Campaign for Democratic Socialism. The labels change but the tendencies are abiding.

The general decline in membership has not prevented a number of constituency parties from demanding a greater say in the reselection of their MPs. In theory every constituency party's General Committee (GC) has the right to select its candidate before each general election. In practice, this right is effective only where it is unimportant – in seats held by parties other than Labour, where a new candidate is selected before each election. In principle, even where there is a Labour MP, the GC has the right not to reselect him or her; but the convention that such reselection is virtually automatic has grown up. In recent years, however, a number of MPs have experienced difficulties with their constituency parties, notably Mr Prentice in Newham North-East, Mr Sandelson in Hillingdon, Hayes and Harlington, Mr Tomney in Hammersmith North, Sir Arthur Irvine in Liverpool Edge Hill, and Mrs Colquhoun in Northampton North. The individual issues raised by these conflicts are perhaps less important than the growth of a movement for the general right to compel all Labour MPs to face reselection once in every parliament. This movement, organised by the Campaign for Labour Party Democracy, has not so far achieved its aim.[4] There were dire warnings from Mr Wilson, while he was still Prime Minister, that such a campaign risked dividing the party completely. Were it to be successful, one consequence would be to place more power in the hands of GCs, which are untypical of Labour voters. It is of course fair to say that MPs rarely complain that they were selected by such unrepresentative bodies in the first place. Nevertheless, were the constituency parties to increase their hold over MPs, this would be very likely to lead to efforts to control the MPs' views. Already Labour MPs have been heard to complain that they may be in trouble with their constituency parties for loyally supporting a Labour government in parliament.

Clearly, if reselection were to become automatic in the party, it would be desirable to widen the selectorate. At present GCs are relatively small bodies, and ones on which representatives of the individual members of the party may be in a minority. At the very least, some would argue, the whole of the membership should take part, and perhaps even all Labour voters should be given a voice, though the practical problems raised by the latter proposition are considerable.

More extreme problems have arisen where MPs have completely lost the support of their constituency parties. Four notable cases in the 1970s have been Mr S. O. Davies at Merthyr Tydfil, Mr Taverne at Lincoln, Mr Milne at Blyth and Mr Griffiths at Sheffield Brightside.[5] Each shows rather different features. Mr Davies was not readopted in 1970 on grounds of age, but he stood nevertheless and won the seat decisively, holding it until his death in 1972. Mr Taverne's local party were so opposed to his stance on the Common Market that they indicated their intention of adopting another candidate at the next election. Mr Taverne resigned his seat to provoke a by-election in 1973, in which he defeated the official Labour candidate, a feat which he repeated in the general election of February 1974, only to lose in October of that year. Mr Milne had had a number of disagreements with his constituency party, and additionally had stirred up opposition by his allegations that the Labour Party were not investigating sufficiently allegations of corruption in North East England. He was not readopted for the February 1974 election, but nevertheless beat the official candidate of the party, only to lose in October by 78 votes. In 1979 his defeat was much heavier, however. Mr Griffiths was thought to be too right-wing by his constituency party; as a result he was not readopted for the October 1974 election. In his case, defeat was swift: he lost to the official Labour candidate by almost 8000 votes. Together these examples go some way to suggesting that some MPs can hope to fight successfully against their former party.

In the case of both Mr Taverne and Mr Milne their protests produced local political parties that have enjoyed some success. In Lincoln Mr Taverne's Democratic Labour Party controlled the district council for a time. However, when the party has tried to fight elsewhere, it has done badly, as it did in Lincoln itself in 1979. Mr

Milne's Independent Labour Party has been a substantial force in the Blyth Valley Council, having gained nine seats there in the 1976 elections to make them the second largest party on the council. It is instructive to compare these two cases with the SLP. Neither Mr Sillars nor Mr Robertson showed evidence of the ability to develop a strong base from within their own constituency parties. Especially in the case of Mr Sillars, this may have been a major error. Moreover, as noted earlier, the SLP made little headway in local elections, and lacked the opportunity to demonstrate popularity in parliamentary elections.

To those who have been driven out, one should add the names of those who have left voluntarily. (Exactly which category Mr Sillars and Mr Robertson belong to is an open question.) The departures of Mr Jenkins and Mr Marquand to the European Commission, and Mr Walden to television, may be compared to similar departures that affected the party in the early 1960s. In part no doubt they reflect individual frustration, but perhaps in part also some dissatisfaction with aspects of adversary politics.

The position of the PLP within the party has never been quite so secure as the position of the parliamentary groups within other major parties. This is partly a matter of origins. The Labour Party was formed by extra-parliamentary organisations such as trade unions and socialist societies, and these organisations have never been willing totally to relinquish their hold over the PLP. In the Conservative and Liberal Parties, however, mass country-wide organisations were created by parliamentary groups to win votes for the already existing parliamentary groups. Nomenclature is a useful guide here: the Conservative Party is the Conservative Party in parliament, and the mass organisation is called the National Union of Conservative and Unionist Associations. The Labour Party does things the other way round. Labour's ideologists have continued to argue that the PLP is still, in important respects, responsible to the decisions of the Annual Conference and the NEC. This contention has been disputed by Professor R. T. McKenzie in his book *British Political Parties*.[6] McKenzie maintained that Labour governments, and hence Labour parliamentary parties when the party was in office, have been forced to adapt themselves to the demands of office, and that these demands have meant the *de facto* domination of the entire Labour Party by its Cabinet.

Labour's theoretical insistence that it is still controlled by and responsible to the party in the country – in other words, it is still a democratically controlled organisation – fits in well with the 'opposition-mindedness' of some of these ideologists. The difference which used to exist between Labour and Conservative Parties on this issue neatly underlines the difference between Labour as a natural opposition party and the Conservatives as a natural party of rule. Andrew Gamble has shown in this volume that the Conservative Party has recently been changing its internal practices so that it now looks more opposition-minded than it previously did. Labour has made next to no changes in its formal practices in this regard in recent years.

Labour's method of choosing its leader is a case in point. For a long time Labour had the most formal and elaborately democratic rules for the selection of its parliamentary leader of any of the major parties. It chooses him from amongst the PLP by an exhaustive ballot of the PLP. In theory the leader must be re-elected every year when the party is in opposition; in fact he is rarely challenged (there have been only two such challenges in the past 40 years: in 1960 by Harold Wilson and in 1961 by Anthony Greenwood, both against Hugh Gaitskell). In the system of exhaustive balloting the candidate with the fewest votes drops out and this process is repeated until one candidate emerges with a majority of the votes. This is a cumbersome system, but it does ensure that candidates who can win support from all areas of the party have an advantage over candidates who have a small but devoted following. The more generally popular candidates can win the second and third preference votes of those who have voted for candidates who have dropped, or been dropped, off the ballot.[7] Since 1935 there have been only four leaders of the PLP: Attlee (1935–55), Gaitskell (1955–63), Wilson (1963–76) and Callaghan (1976–). In part the slow turnover of leaders is due to the loyalty which Labour people attach to their leaders, and in part to the success of the electoral system in securing the election of leaders who are sufficiently popular with the PLP to last.

Strictly speaking, the person chosen by the PLP to head it is only the leader of the PLP. In practice he is all but universally described as the leader of the party. Recently there have been demands to change the system of election so that the electoral college is more representative of the party as a whole. Such demands reflect partly the diminished respect in which parliament is held: as an institution, it and those who are members of it, no longer have the authority they once enjoyed. However, the demand for change springs also from the political fact that those sections of the party who are stronger in Conference and in the NEC would like to have more voice in the choice of the leader; in that sense the choice of the PLP is likely to lie too firmly in the Social Democratic wing of the party. This ideological preference can be advanced behind some respectable democratic arguments, made more so by virtue of the fact that in the past few years both the Conservative and Liberal Parties have altered their procedures for selecting leaders.

Another sign of the changing nature of the party system and the reduced status of the parliamentary party is the increase in acts of indiscipline in recent years. Votes by MPs of either party against the Whips used to be relatively rare; this is clearly no longer the case. The Conservative government of 1970–4 was the first in recent times to suffer in this way, but the record of the subsequent Labour government has made those earlier rebellions seem almost insignificant. Obviously much is due to the composition of the House of Commons since the elections of 1974, but more perhaps to the realisation pioneered by the Conservatives that no very drastic consequences need follow from individual MPs voting against their parties. The constitutional rules about when governments resign have been re-drawn over the past few years, and it now appears that resignation is necessary only if a government is defeated on a specific vote of confidence; with this increase in the security of governments has necessarily come an enormous weakening of the power of the Whips over backbenchers. Traditionally the Labour Party has taken a tough attitude to the question of discipline, but increasingly it has been forced to adapt to a more tolerant era. Of course MPs may still have difficulties with their constituency parties, but even there, as we have seen, the traditional assumption that a disowned MP could not hope to stand successfully against his former party has had to be modified.

Freedom of this kind has extended in recent years much further than the backbenches. The doctrine of the collective responsibility of Ministers, another key element in the two-party constitution, has been breached. In the 1960s two Ministers, Mr Cousins and Mr Callaghan, publicised their differences with their Cabinet colleagues over, respectively, wages policy and industrial relations legislation. Concerted support for policies opposed to those of the Cabinet has been shown from time to time by Ministers. In October 1974 three Ministers (Mr Benn, Mrs Hart and Miss Lestor), who were also members of the NEC, implicitly supported the NEC's motion criticising the government for allowing a visit by a Royal Navy ship to South Africa. They escaped with a rebuke from the Prime Minister.

On occasion Ministers have ignored the doctrine of collective responsibility by leaking Cabinet discussions to the press before the Cabinet has made up its mind on a particular matter. The purpose of leaking the discussion was, of course, to stir up support for their own position when that position was not powerfully backed in the Cabinet. Government proposals to aid the American-owned Chrysler Corporation in 1975 led to such leaks. It became clear that the Minister most closely involved, Mr Varley, was being overruled in the Cabinet. On this occasion the leaks were so extensive that it was possible for an apparently accurate reconstruction of the debate to be presented on television. By far the most dramatic indiscipline suffered by the Labour government came over the issue of Britain's continued membership of the EEC. The Labour Party had promised in its 1974 election manifestos to put the matter to a test of public opinion – either a new general election or a referendum. When the government decided on a referendum, the depth of the split in the party became clear. Most of the Cabinet and some of the NEC were in favour of a 'Yes' vote for remaining in the EEC. On the other side were some Cabinet Ministers, many other members of the government, most of the NEC and a large majority of the party outside parliament. The government held itself together in this instance simply by suspending the doctrine of collective responsibility. Members of the government were licensed to campaign for the side of their choice, subject only to the restriction that they were not to speak against each other in the House of Commons. These divisions, which were paralleled in less dramatic fashion among Conservatives, led to remarkable scenes of leading figures in both the Labour and Conservative Parties sharing both the 'Yes' and 'No' platforms. Clearly party ties are not what they were. Confirmation of this came with the debates over devolution, where once again Conservative and Labour politicians were to be found on both sides of the issue, and where once again the device of the referendum had to be resorted to in an effort to find the legitimacy that parliament no longer seems to provide, which in turn of course accentuates the divisions within the parties.

The changes in Labour which can be traced to a weakening of party loyalty and discipline are not confined to the PLP, however. The

NEC, acting as the board of management of the party between Conferences, has operated rather differently since the mid-1960s. Meeting monthly, it oversees the activities of the party through a series of sub-committees. The first change has been that the NEC is much more willing than it used to be to stand up to Labour Cabinets. It has proposed reductions in defence expenditure and extensions of nationalisation against the wishes of the Cabinet. Such indisciplines would have been unthinkable during the Attlee government.

At the same time the NEC has tolerated a vastly greater degree of indiscipline from constituency parties than it would previously have done. In the 1950s General Management Committees could be, and were, suspended on the basis of the suspicion of being taken over by Communists. In the 1970s the NEC chooses to ignore the political motivations of GCs; it will listen sympathetically to appeals against their actions – for example, in refusing to reselect an MP – only if the appeal is based on some alleged procedural impropriety. Appeals from Mr Wilson in 1975 and Mr Callaghan in 1976 to take a tougher line against Trotskyist infiltration have met with as little positive response as has greeted a report by the National Agent on the same subject. Here, as over the matter of the NEC's greater willingness to oppose a Labour Cabinet, the explanation would seem primarily ideological. The domination of the NEC by the left wing of the party in recent years has led it both to be at greater odds with its own government and at the same time to be ideologically closer to the entrists.

Readjustment

For all the reasons outlined above, Labour has not found its unaccustomed experience of frequently winning elections either particularly comfortable or satisfactory. Moreover, Social Democracy has had its most extended opportunities at precisely the time when the relevance of its doctrines has been open to question. The traditional attitude of Social Democrats, that the expensive character of their programmes could be afforded, no longer seems as true as it once did. Neither increased taxation, which has lost whatever limited appeal it once had, when it could be presented as a levy on other (i.e. wealthy) people, nor the more favoured prescription of paying for the programmes from the newly created wealth in a growing economy, have much plausibility. The latter has lost its appeal as a painless way of having the best of all worlds by the obstinate failure of the British economy to grow in the 1970s at anything like the rates that were confidently relied upon in the 1950s and early 1960s.

Even in those boom years Britain achieved less than some of her major competitors, and since then she has allowed herself to be more adversely affected than them by the changes in the world economy. The failure of industrial production in the past few years to match up even to the levels achieved during the famous '3-day week' of 1973–4 is evidence both of the state of the British economy and the depressed world situation. The acceptance of a level of unemployment in the 1970s that would have been thought outrageous in the 1950s is another indication that we are operating in a very different world. Inflation has cut the ground from beneath the feet of the Social Democrats, a fact recognised by them in mid-1975, once the EEC Referendum had been disposed of, and accepted subsequently, though reluctantly, by the trade unions.

However, it is not just in terms of accepting unpleasant economic realities that the ghosts of the 1930s have been exorcised. The willingness of the Callaghan government to continue in office after 1977 with the open help of the Liberals is further evidence that the lessons of 1931 are thought no longer relevant. Nor is it only the Liberals who have provided support in the hour of need. Theirs is merely the most explicit arrangement; there have been more or less public understandings with other parties, as we have seen. These understandings need to be borne in mind, for they throw the 'agreement' with the Liberals into context and because they indicate the extent to which Labour was prepared to play the multi-party game in order to stay in office. To this extent Labour has shown itself more willing to adapt to the new game than have the Conservatives; the latter may have rejected too quickly their chance to play this new game after the February 1974 election.

It is not, however, a game that Labour plays with much enthusiasm: it is reluctant to believe that it is more than a temporary necessity, and it has a clear preference (shared apparently by the Conservatives) to play for regular outright victories rather than the possibility of more frequent, if less exclusive, occupation of office. Like the Conservatives, Labour has not yet embraced the idea of proportional representation, seeing it still as having within it the potential to divide the party and making explicit that division between socialist and Social Democrat that much of the party's effort is devoted to patching over. This patching over was achieved yet again in the 1979 general election, when the party's manifesto and conduct of the campaign were dominated by Mr Callaghan. Its defeat in that election suggested that in opposition the Labour Party will continue to offer from within its ranks, its own version of 'multi-party politics'.

3

The Liberal Party

Michael Steed

The Liberal Party provides at once the confirmation and the denial of the view that Britain naturally has a two-party system. In its period of growth and greatness from the mid-nineteenth century to the out-break of the First World War, the Liberal Party functioned as the left wing of a two-party system. Breakaway parties, such as the Peelites or the Liberal Unionists, were duly absorbed into one wing or the other. Then, when the Labour Party emerged on the scene, the demise of the Liberal Party seemed to confirm the essentially dualistic character of British politics. During the 1930s, 1940s or early 1950s the persistence of the Liberal Party at a minor level was seen as the obstinate refusal of a dying party to accept that fate. The only outcome other than death allowed by the inexorable system was absorption into one of its two wings.

Yet a two-big-plus-one-small party system lasted longer than any other party system in Britain's history – from 1924 (when, with the slump in the Liberal vote from 30 to 18 per cent, it ceased to be one of three similarly sized parties) to 1974 (when Liberals were joined in parliament by other small parties). Throughout this half-century the Liberal Party did not just survive; it recruited new supporters and provided a source of new political thinking. It never showed the characteristics one would expect to find in a dying party – an ageing electorate and core of active supporters, steady retreat to declining areas or groups, or obstinate defence of outdated policies. During the late 1950s there was a tendency, both among Liberal leaders and among commentators who had previously written the party off, to see the Liberal revival as a new phenomenon, appropriate to present and coming times. For both, the party's past was something of an irrelevance; the mood was caught by the titles of a book (*The Liberal Future*, 1959) and pamphlet (*The New Liberalism*, 1957) by Jo Grimond.

But the continuity was more significant than the novelty. Jo Grimond himself had fought his first election in 1945 (at the age of 32), as had the two Liberals who were managing the party with him around 1960 – Frank (now Lord) Byers (30) and Mark Bonham Carter (28). And whilst at the 1945 election the Liberal vote had been falling in rural areas (and Liberal seats were lost), the party made signal advances in its voting support in the suburban constituencies which had seen the most rapid inter-war population expansion, such as Bromley, Hendon, Ilford or Manchester Withington. The simple electoral record shows the mid-1930s to the mid-1950s as the party's bleakest period; yet during these two decades the party was readily finding new electoral support and new activists.

Two notable Liberal recruits were the two social scientists who probably exercised most influence on public policy during this period – William Beveridge (who served briefly as a Liberal MP in 1945) and John Maynard Keynes. Liberal publications in the inter-war period had looked forward to mid or late twentieth-century ideas of management of the economy, of partnership between capital and labour and indeed to some form of industrial democracy. The striking changes in Britain's world role during the latter part of the twentieth century were also foreseen by the party. The Liberal Party shared the vanguard with Labour in promoting decolonisation – and was indeed ahead of it by several years in realising that this meant withdrawing from the United Kingdom's East of Suez military role. It was well ahead of both larger parties in advocating membership of the Common Market, and dealt with resistance to the European idea among its own traditional free-trading wing more easily than the two bigger parties did with their imperialists or Little Englanders. Whatever the explanation for the relative irrelevance of the Liberal Party in parliamentary or public policy terms, it is clearly not the failure to keep abreast of the times.

The perspective of this volume is one of a two-party system which, having once been dominant, is now seriously undermined. The Liberal Party occupies a very special position in this perspective. It is unique among the parties covered herein: neither a part of the system under threat, nor yet a new challenge to it. Apart from the war-time experience, it had no part in government between September 1932 (when Liberal Ministers left the National Government over tariffs) and March 1977 (the parliamentary agreement with the Labour government). Yet it has been continuously present in both Houses of Parliament,[1] and has always been accepted as one of the three parties entitled to such perks as coronation honours, more recently life peerages, and party political broadcasts – the subtle ways in which the British system confers recognition on political parties without any formal mechanism. It has been uniquely and peculiarly part of, and yet not part of, the system of party government in the United Kingdom.

Its own attitude has reflected this ambivalence. Its position as the leading minor party, and the obvious beneficiary of any breakdown of the existing party system, together with its advocacy of a proportional voting system, would seem to make it a whole-hearted challenger to the system. Yet the Liberal Party has tended to reflect, and perhaps even to purvey, attitudes which uphold that system. It retained the sense of being a majoritarian party which had temporarily lost its natural place in the system, and when its electoral fortunes were on the mend in the 1950s, it found it easiest to think in terms of a realignment of the left which would restore its position as the radical party in an essential two-party world. Though the troubles inside the Labour Party seemed to fit such an objective, since this was a period when the Liberal vote was, temporarily, more anti-Socialist than anti-Tory, such an objective made little immediate sense. But then, despite demanding proportional representation, it always thought in terms of single-party government. Its manifestos and conference resolutions were couched in terms of what a Liberal government would do, and it disliked talk of more limited objectives, such as gaining the balance of power or entering a coalition Cabinet, as undermining its ultimate hope.

When the United Kingdom found itself suddenly without an overall majority for one party in the House of Commons on 1 March 1974, the Liberal Party was as much taken by surprise as anyone – and more inhibited from grasping the opportunity than the two larger parties. The official briefing to candidates during the February 1974 election campaign had suggested that the possibility of holding the balance of power should be handled as follows:

What happens in this situation is surely a matter for the other two parties, the Liberal MPs will have to decide whether to support one particular party in government or, if such an agreement is unsatisfactory from the Liberal point of view, whether to vote for every piece of legislation according to its merits.[2]

From 1931 to 1974 overall parliamentary majorities had been invariable; in the Commons the largest parliamentary party functioned as a government party, the second largest as the opposition and alternative government party, while the third largest had, in the way the two larger parties viewed it and the media reported it, no real business there. Hence the handful of Liberal MPs never found a natural role. Most of them have represented remote, rural constituencies, and have made much of their role as constituency representatives; several would not have won, or held, their seats without a great deal of mundane hard work on behalf of their constituents – the personal, electoral reward for this role has always been far greater for Liberal MPs than for Conservative or Labour ones. This role, and the consequent sense that they have depended for re-election more on their own efforts than on their party's fortunes (a half-truth in fact), means that for many purposes the Liberal MPs have looked more like a league of independents in the House of Commons. Certainly, lacking any overriding goal to be pursued at the cost of relations with the larger parties and of Commons' conventional behaviour, and lacking (until recently) any leverage in terms of parliamentary arithmetic, they rarely made much impact as a group.

For the Liberal Party this has accentuated the unique importance that elections play for it. The two larger parties' predominance has always been more parliamentary than electoral; the still smaller parties have placed a greater emphasis on other spheres of activity, from the industrial field to direct action on the streets. The Liberal Party has been the most concerned with simply contesting elections and winning votes, and has naturally placed a greater emphasis on its achievement in votes than its victories in seats. Its survival, its revival and its periodic ups and downs in morale have been closely connected to its vote-getting record.

Vote-getting is made more important by the way in which the Liberal Party is reported in the political media. Unlike the territorially based SNP and Plaid Cymru, it has no media serving the section of the electorate at which it aims, and, consequently, through which it can debate its objectives. It eschews publicity-seeking direct action, though the Young Liberals have shown that there are rewards (in publicity) in that direction. Its parliamentary presence having merited little coverage, it is ignored by the national media, which tend to define the political as what happens in Westminster in normal times. (Wherever Liberal associations are locally active, they tend to receive a far higher share of local media attention.) However, in periods when it does well at elections, the national media switch national attention to the Liberal Party and give an impression that the party's significance depends rather simply on its electoral fortunes. Another consequence is that the extra-parliamentary part of the Liberal Party (which is of course a rather greater proportion of its whole than in the Conservative and Labour Parties) is one of the most under-reported areas of political life in Britain.

With the change in the Liberal Party's perception of its role, which started with the parliamentary agreement with the Labour government in March 1977, its impact has become very different. This chapter focuses on the need to explain the Liberal presence in the half-century before 1977. The change of strategy since 1977, and the question of how lasting that change will prove, is discussed at the end after we have looked at the party's political base. We start by examining the electoral record, which is so central to its survival and revival.

The electoral record

Since the Second World War, Liberal representation in the House of Commons has varied only a little: over ten general elections there have never been fewer than six Liberal MPs returned and never more than fourteen. The same is not true of the Liberal vote. The electoral system has not only grossly under-represented the Liberal vote in the Commons; it has also tended to insulate it from changes in its size.

The actual Liberal share of the total votes cast in Great Britain has been as low as 2.6 per cent (1951) and as high as 19.8 per cent (February 1974). But at only one election has the party fought almost all the seats at stake – in October 1974. On other occasions it has fought as few as a sixth (1951 and 1955), a third (1959), or around a half (1945, 1964, 1966 and 1970), extending to a broader front of 475 in 1950 and 517 in February 1974. The changes in these proportions are a good measure of grass-roots Liberal strength. Only occasionally has there been much centrally directed effort to place candidates (notably there was in 1950); normally seats have been fought or left unfought by local decision, reflecting organisational preparedness and political confidence in the constituencies concerned.

Other indicators of organisational strength are limited. Reliable figures of Liberal Party membership have simply not been collected (or are not collectable), although the party is now trying to establish a more regularised system of recording such membership. We can take the Liberal candidatures in by-elections and in local elections in conjunction with those in general election; the only other available index of organisational strength is the number of constituency associations that pay their annual affiliation fee.[3]

Taking these measures together, it is safe to state that the party suffered a sharp drop in organisational strength and morale following the 1950 general election, and had probably lost more ground following the 1945 Labour victory than it realised at the time. After a 5-year period of greatest weakness, it started a slow, steady revival, climaxing in 1963. Thereafter some ground was lost, particularly in the late 1960s, but it is more striking that, despite losses of votes at the 1966 and 1970 general elections, most of the organisational advance of the previous decade was held. Then came another surge forward in 1973-4, most of which has been subsequently held despite loss of votes in the late 1970s. Thus the party was able to fight every seat in England at the 1979 general election. Comparison with the record of votes cast shows that these changes follow, not precede, turns in the electoral tide. Liberal organisation and morale has improved as a response to increases in the numbers of people voting Liberal.

But the big changes in the numbers of candidates complicates the measurement of the numbers who are voting Liberal. Thus, between February and October 1974, the total Liberal vote dropped modestly from 6.1 million (19.8 per cent) to 5.3 million (18.8 per cent). However, half a million of the latter total were cast in seats which the party did not fight in February; had it fought on the full front then, it would have polled something like 6.7 million ($22\frac{1}{2}$ per cent), showing a much bigger loss of support in October.

It is quite possible, though, to project a level of Liberal support for each general election (and also for groups of by-elections); that would be the level of votes the party would have received if it had fought all seats in Britain, though assuming of course that this did not bring any

additional credibility and extra votes. This shows that the level of
Liberal support in 1945 was 14½ per cent, declining steadily to 11 per
cent in 1950 and 7½ per cent in 1951. Thereafter it climbed steadily to
a peak of 16½ per cent in 1964, dropping then at the 1966 and 1970
elections to 11 per cent. By-election and local election evidence puts
the turning point more precisely between 1953 and 1954; the rise in
support as more irregular in the late 1950s, with a big jump in the
Spring of 1956 and a falling away from a Spring 1958 peak to the 1959
general election; then a sharp rise to a high and isolated peak in the
Spring of 1962 (probably, on local election voting, a little under 30 per
cent); and a nadir of support in 1971 (the local election results in May
that year were the party's worst since 1955), followed by a massive
upsurge back to the 30 per cent level in the Spring and Summer of
1973.

By then, however, local elections were showing an additional
feature of striking variation in Liberal performance. Whereas up to
the mid-1960s the movement of Liberal support is fairly even, during
the last fifteen years there have been increasingly varied results,
especially during the years when the party was faring generally worse.
The most striking case is that of Liverpool, where the major electoral
advance was under way in 1971–2, when the party was at its weakest
nationally; and where a dramatic recovery was staged in by-elections
during autumn 1977. But the feature has been general, and has led to
the building up of a number of enduring local Liberal bastions, which
have ensured the presence of small Liberal groups on almost all major
British city councils in recent years.

This local government representation has come to play an important part in the Liberal Party. Its local councillors have often become
leading figures in the party, and their municipal elected position has
contributed to their status. Put against the party's weak Westminster
representation, and especially the great paucity of representation
from more urban areas of Britain, Liberal councillors have counted
for more than in other parties. Local government success has also
been a comfort to the party in its nationally weaker periods, and
encouraged the party to think in localist terms. Much of the strategy
of 'Community Politics' (see below, p. 101) was based on the apparent success of local campaigning. It has also contributed to tensions,
whenever the natural interest and thinking of the parliamentary and
municipal wings of the party have diverged. Much of the opposition
to continuing the Lib–Lab agreement at the party's special assembly

in Blackpool in January 1978 came from Liberal councillors in predominantly Labour areas, who thought in terms of fighting rather than co-operating with that party.

But the ability of the Liberal Party to win enough municipal votes to win seats is also highly significant for understanding the nature of the Liberal vote. However low the general readiness of people to vote Liberal has been, in years such as 1967, 1971, and 1977–8, there have been places and circumstances where more people have been willing to vote Liberal than in previous nationally 'good years'. This suggests that we may be misreading the significant variation in the level of Liberal voting by simply putting it into a time sequence, clear as the changes in time are.

The character of the Liberal vote

Research into political behaviour in Great Britain, being mainly concerned with questions and methodology appropriate to a two-party system, has left the Liberal vote largely unexplored. The bulk of the Conservative and Labour vote at any given time consists of regular identifiers; these can be, and have been, examined each as a group for their social characteristics, political views, strength of attachment to their party or whatever. General elections have been determined by small shifts between the two groups, summed up as swing. Most electoral research revolves around points raised in this manner, and their foundation – the class base of Conservative and Labour voting. Liberal voting is not like that.

The electoral record shows the level of Liberal voting since the Second World War ranging threefold, from $7\frac{1}{2}$ to $22\frac{1}{2}$ per cent, at general elections, and fourfold with the 1962 and 1973 by-election peaks. The jumps up and down can be very short-term; thus the 1973 by-election peak was preceded in 1970–2 and followed a short while later in 1977–8 by levels little above the nadir of the early 1950s. Survey research shows that the circulation of Liberal voters is even greater. Despite the relative stability of the 1964, 1966 and 1970 total Liberal votes (over elections where Liberal candidatures were fairly steady), it has been found that at the two elections where the party lost ground in votes (1966 and 1970) something like half the Liberal vote consisted of people who had not voted Liberal the time before.[4]

This should not surprise us when we consider the very large

number of people who show some leaning towards voting Liberal whenever appropriately worded questions are put to them. Thus, over the years, the Gallup Poll has repeated a question, *'Would you be likely to vote for the Liberals if you thought they . . . would obtain a majority?'*, and regularly found something of the order of a third replying 'yes' at times, as in February 1950, when the party had low actual support. Opinion Research Centre asked a vaguer question in September 1968, *'If you thought that Liberals stood a chance of forming a government, would you ever consider voting for them?'*, and got a 52 per cent 'yes', although the party won only 10.5 per cent of the vote in three by-elections the following month.

In the two 1974 elections a large proportion of this potential Liberal vote did turn out for the party. The total Liberal vote that year exceeded 8 million, a figure which would have made a more dramatic impact if it had all voted at once; nearly half of those who voted Liberal in the first 1974 election failed to do so in the second.[5] We are thus dealing with a small core Liberal vote and a very much larger penumbra of Liberal sympathisers. The actual Liberal vote at any given time consists of a mixture between the former and a varying proportion of the latter; and there appears to be a constant movement of sympathisers in and out of the act of voting Liberal, whether the current level of party support is high or low.

This distinction between the core Liberal vote and the wider sympathy support, together with the constant circulation of Liberal voters, pose problems both for party strategists and for electoral analysts alike. Without the loyalty of its core support, the party could not have survived. But without its wider appeal, it would not have achieved those 'revivals' which have helped to re-establish a role for it in contemporary British politics. Yet those revivals pose their problems; they have turned out to be ephemeral, and have increased Liberal core support little, if at all.

One reason for this, as we shall see, is the difference between the attraction of the party to its core and to its sympathisers. The distinction has been so little recognised by political scientists that the evidence for this difference is limited and scattered. The normal treatment has been to analyse as the Liberal vote those who turned up in a sample as Liberal voters in a similar way to Conservative and Labour voters or partisans. A more useful approach would have been to recognise five categories of voters – Conservative partisans, Labour partisans, the partisans of each who display Liberal sympathies, and the small number of steady Liberal partisans. This might answer questions about the character of the Liberal vote, as well as to the presence and potential of the Liberal Party. It would also avoid some of the sillier statements about the Liberal vote which have been made. Thus it has been claimed that Powellite sympathies gained major ground among Liberal supporters in 1973, although in 1968 Liberal voters were less in agreement with Powell's immigration views than those of either of the two larger parties.[6] In 1968 the Liberal vote was low; in 1973 it was at a by-election peak. The evidence does not demonstrate a swing to Enoch Powell or Powellite views on immigration among the sort of people (largely the core Liberal vote) who gave a Liberal response in 1968; it indicates that on this issue there is a striking difference of attitudes between the core vote and those Liberal sympathisers who were added to the Liberal total in 1973 – at the latter period the party was receiving the votes both of those most opposed to Powell and of those who responded most to him. There is evidence of a similar situation with attitudes towards the European Community, with core Liberals giving British membership strong support and sympathisers among the more opposed to it.

The only serious study to date which comes close to identifying the core Liberal vote is from the British General Elections Study.[7] Alt *et al.* define as stalwart Liberals those who voted Liberal at least three times in the 1966, 1970, February 1974 and October 1974 general elections. Unfortunately this definition gives their stalwarts a distinct bias towards the middle class, since in 1966 and 1970, and to a lesser extent in February 1974, Liberal candidatures were concentrated in more rural and suburban constituencies and were much fewer in industrial areas. Hence middle-class core supporters had more opportunities to vote Liberal. The definition also deprives the youngest voters of the chance to be included as stalwarts.

Nonetheless, the Study does offer some insight into the attitudes of the Liberal core. Alt *et al.*'s stalwarts regard most economic and social issues as not very important – matters such as prices, unemployment, taxation or the social services, which conventional wisdom believes to be the central issues of elections, matter less to them. They are more concerned than major party supporters or less stalwart Liberals about industrial democracy and equal treatment for coloured people and women. Such priorities are similar to those found by Wilson, who argued in 1973 that Liberal voters should be seen as extremist rather than middle-of-the-road, and that their attitudes differ from those of voters of either of the two major parties on issues such as opposition to censorship or capital punishment or support for co-education or coloured immigration.[8] Alt *et al.* also found stalwart Liberals more critical towards the operation of the political system, and mentioning electoral reform, local government and the Common Market as specific good points of their party.

These issues do not cover foreign policy or environmental questions. But there is evidence of more distinctive Liberal voter attitudes there too. Thus, at the time of the Vietnam War, Liberal voters were more opposed to British government support for the United States than those of the two major parties. A 1977 *New Society* survey on attitudes towards nuclear energy found that whilst Conservative and Labour supporters had very similar views, Liberal supporters were markedly more opposed to nuclear power stations.[9]

Thus there is abundant evidence that the core Liberal vote is essentially distinguished by its attitudes, and that these attitudes differentiate it from major party supporters as a group rather than placing it between Conservative and Labour partisans. The evidence is culled from an unsatisfactory definition of Liberal stalwarts (at 4 per cent of voters) and from scattered poll data. If we had a measure of those who have (or would have if given the chance) regularly voted Liberal, we would probably have a Liberal core of around 7 per cent, or some 2 million voters, whose attitudes would probably be even more distinctive than this evidence indicates.

The Liberal core vote appears to be radical, humanitarian, libertarian, internationalist, environmentalist and particularly interested in constitutional questions, although by no means all of it shares all these attitudes; the other side of the coin is its relative indifference to the major economic questions of the day. In many respects it is a clear inheritor of Victorian radicalism, and argues that the survival of the Liberal Party owes a great deal to the maintenance of certain radical and liberal values in face of a party system which otherwise ignores them or pushes them to the sidelines of a free vote in the Commons. It is no coincidence that Liberal MPs have found it easier to vote unitedly on certain issues, such as opposition to the 1968 Commonwealth Immigration Act or in the May 1978 vote on Windscale where MPs from both other parties have been deeply divided.

The evidence of survey data is that the core Liberal vote is drawn evenly from all social strata. A Gallup compilation of over 8000 interviews in the winter of 1977−8 showed Liberal support of 8.7 per cent.[10] Across standard objective measures of social status, there was little variation – support was lowest within the market researcher's top social category of ABs (8.1 per cent) and highest where the head of the household was a semi-skilled manual worker (9.5 per cent). But when social self-rating was used, the Liberal vote was clearly distinctive – see Table 3.

TABLE 3   *Liberal vote by social self-rating (percentages)*

Social self-rating	Proportion of sample	Liberal vote
Upper, upper-middle or middle class	33.7	8.3
Lower-middle class	12.6	11.8
Working class	49.4	7.8
Don't know	4.3	12.0

SOURCE: Social Surveys (Gallup Poll) Ltd.

Whatever his actual social grouping, the Liberal voter is more likely to assign himself to the most intermediate social category available or to refuse any social categorisation. The core Liberal vote reflects, therefore, some personal rejection of social class. It does not include a disproportionate number of those who assign themselves to a class which differs from objective criteria; with Conservative and Labour voters such status inconsistency is strongly associated with voting deviant from class norms. This indicates that the 'lower middle class' Liberal vote does not reflect an attempt to identify with a Liberal class so much as indifference to the whole question. However, it is clear that where objective social factors support or undermine each other, Liberal support is affected. Within this Gallup sample, trade unionists were as Liberal as the rest (8.6 per cent), but support fell particularly where trade-union membership and council tenancy together reinforce Labour voting (5.4 per cent), and rose where trade-union membership among the ABs was in conflict with their Conservatism (11.9 per cent). The latter may also indicate that if there is a distinctly Liberal social grouping, it is the professional as opposed to the managerial middle classes. The one other social grouping which some evidence has shown as disproportionately Liberal is small farmers.

However, when we turn to religion, a slight embellishment to the basic class alignment of major party voters, we find that the core Liberal vote still reflects the strong impact of religious dissent. Among the samples collected for the 1969–70 Butler and Stokes surveys who were asked their religious allegiance, Liberal identifiers were close to a core level at 8.5 per cent. Among those who gave one of the established churches (England or Scotland), only 4 per cent were Liberal; among the Roman Catholic minority, the proportion rose to 8 per cent, among those without a religious preference to 17 per cent, and among the various nonconformists as much as 22 per cent.[11]

Butler and Stokes head this section of their study 'The Political Legacy of Religion', and to an extent this striking variation probably does simply reflect inherited behaviour.[12] But the party which has inherited the nonconformist conscience is now apparently also attractive to the atheist minority. Both nonconformists and rationalists may currently hold broader personal values, which may fit better with Liberalism than Conservatism or Socialism. Furthermore, membership of a minority group or the holding of unconventional views in any sphere of life both probably incline a person towards toleration and individualism in politics and help to weaken the pull of class norms. Not for nothing does the opening sentence of the preamble to the Liberal Party's constitution pledge the party to a society in which 'none shall be enslaved by poverty, ignorance or conformity'.

But the majority of people who vote for the Liberal Party when it is doing well are not committed to the distinctive values of the core voter, except in a loose, diffused way. That Liberal priorities are, in a weak and imprecise way, widely shared throughout British society as worthwhile liberal values is probably a precondition of the party's attracting such massive additional support. With most British people, the Liberal Party has a vague, nice image which leads so many of them to sympathise with it. The 1968 ORC poll, which found a potential Liberal vote of 52 per cent, also showed that 59 per cent thought the Liberal Party produced a lot of good ideas, and only 30 per cent thought it would be a good thing if the Liberal Party disappeared and voters had to choose between Labour and Conservative.[13] The British public has probably always rather liked having such a third choice, for all the textbook virtues of a two-party system.

But we must explain why that sympathy for the Liberal Party has been increasingly turned into a willingness to vote Liberal during the last quarter of a century. Probably the most important reason is a simple and negative one – the decline in attachment to one of the two main class-based parties. This is pursued as the thesis of a dealignment by the British General Election Study authors.

Linked to this is the strong dislike of both class-based parties that Butler and Stokes found in the (largish) 1963 sample of Liberals and Alt *et al.* found again in the 1974 Liberal voter.[14] It has also been shown that the 1974 Liberal vote was not irrational in policy terms, in so far as it was particularly prone to have specific policy disagreements with the major party to which social class would naturally lead it: for instance, the middle-class Liberal voters were more anti-Common Market (and therefore at odds with the Conservative Party) and working-class voters were more pro-European (and so at odds with Labour).[15]

Thus the Liberal Party's increasing level of voting support can be seen as the product of the class basis, policies and performance of the two major parties. Its own contribution has been its survival and attractive campaigning at elections, rather than any specific policy appeal or image. Yet there is evidence of a more precise orientation towards the Liberal Party on the part of Liberal sympathisers, to be found in the research into evaluations of parties. This leads one to suggest that there are two distinct types of disposition towards the Liberal Party, apart from those who identify with its own values.

The first we might call the centre voter, who is disposed to see the Liberal Party as a moderate or in-between party or the 'happy medium' (the theme which Butler and Stokes found most frequent when their respondents were asked what they liked about the Liberal Party). Such voters share with core voters a tendency towards a central stance on many economic and social issues, but lack that sense of distance from both larger parties which characterises the more loyal Liberal, and since they are very conscious of the difference between them, most retain some sense of belonging to one side or the other. In 1974 the emphasis on moderation by the Liberal Party, coupled with the general fear of extremism, seems to have played on this centre voter's Liberal sympathies, and there was a distinct preference for the Liberal Party as being less divisive than the other two parties.[16]

A very special form of this centrist vote for the Liberals is the tactical vote, which has contributed critically to the election of Liberal MPs. Apart from the Scottish Highlands and Islands and from Montgomery, every Liberal seat won in the last 25 years has owed much to the preference of a majority of Labour partisans for the Liberal Party over the Conservatives, or to the similar anti-Labour preference of Conservatives.[17]

The second type we could call the anti-system voter. There is evidence, stronger for the 1972–4 peak of Liberal voting than for the 1961–3 peak, that many people vote Liberal as a generalised protest against the operation of the political system. The rising propensity to vote Liberal can be linked to other indicators of dissatisfaction with democracy and of powerlessness.[18]

An extreme form of this anti-system vote must be the explanation of the preference of a certain number of Liberal voters for the National Front over the two major parties. The evidence of a number of occasions where one can compare NF votes with or without a Liberal candidate leaves no doubt that certain Liberal voters may choose the Front if no Liberal is available.[19] There is also an evident willingness for such Liberals to opt for parties of the extreme left. The only thing that the National Front, the Liberal Party, the Communist Party and the Workers' Revolutionary Party have in common is being anti-system, making radical though utterly different criticisms of the way the country is governed.

The striking differences between the core voter, the centre voter and the anti-system voter can be seen if we express in diagrammatic form how they appear to judge the distance between the various parties (leaving aside the nationalists in Scotland and Wales) – see Figure 1.

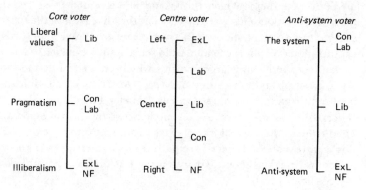

ExL indicates parties of the extreme left

FIGURE 1   *Voter perception of ideological differences between parties*

It is not being argued here that each Liberal voter can be neatly slotted into one of these three categories – many have overlapping or very vague motivations, and some personal or local ones. But recognising the existence of these three very different orientations towards the Liberal Party and towards the other components of the party system does illustrate the diverse character of the 1974 Liberal vote, and pinpoint the problem for the Liberal Party in holding on to or regaining that level of support.

There is one other feature of the increasing tendency to vote Liberal that has both affected thinking about its causes and influenced the Liberal Party's own strategy. The electoral record shows a series of peaks, in 1958, in 1962 and in 1973. Only the last of these continued into a general election; the dissolutions of 1959 and 1964 came after a peak was well over. This point sounds trivial now; but until February 1974 it was widely believed that the Liberal Party could only get a substantial by-election vote, which could therefore be disregarded. Tables showing only the succession of general election Liberal votes give an impression of a sudden change in the level of Liberal support in 1974, which belies the reality of the more irregular electoral record. Consciously or unconsciously holding the 'by-election only' theory, the two major parties and most political scientists paid far too little attention to the significance of the growing willingness to vote Liberal, and were all caught on the hop in 1974.

But there is a feature of the Liberal by-election peaks which is surely significant. Every period of Conservative government since the Second World War has seen a net Liberal advance, and every period of Labour government in history a net loss of Liberal support. It is not clear why this should be so, or how far it may be the character or behaviour of the main opposition party (Labour) as well as the government's performance which is responsible – certainly, while conventional wisdom has described Liberal by-election advances as being based on protesting Conservative voters, the evidence of the 1959, 1964 and February 1974 general elections is that the increment in Liberal support has been drawn remarkably evenly at the expense of the larger parties.[20] For the Liberal Party itself this phenomenon has reinforced its historic sense of being the natural opponent of the Conservative Party, and conditioned its tendency to think in terms of a realignment of the left as the way by which its breakthrough could occur.

The Liberal Party structure

The Liberal Party was never founded,[21] and its rather complex structure bears the marks of a long and varied history. Within what is claimed to be a federal party, the three national parties (Scotland,

Wales and Ulster) are defined as autonomous, and each chooses how far it wishes to be part of the structure contained in what is defined as the 'constitution of the Liberal Party of the United Kingdom of Great Britain and Northern Ireland'. The Scottish Liberal Party takes its independence furthest, having unilaterally declared it in 1946, and whilst participating at certain levels, such as the Annual Assembly or the election of the leader, regards this structure as being English rather than British. This accentuates the extent to which the constitutional organs of the party (often referred expressly as being LPO, see below) are viewed by some Liberals as being only a part of the full party. Whilst this view has no constitutional basis, it acccords with the way the party grew up around a number of distinct organisations.

The National Liberal Federation (NLF) was formed in 1877 simply as a federation of local (constituency and city) Liberal associations. The Liberal Party in the late nineteenth century was made up of at least four distinct bodies – the NLF, the Liberal Central Association (LCA), the Liberal Peers and, most important, the Liberal Members of the House of Commons. In the period 1916–36 successive splits meant considerable confusion, and at the same time a decline in the numbers and significance of both parliamentary parties, and also the atrophying, though not disappearance, of the LCA. In 1936 the NLF set up a convention, which agreed for the first time a constitution for the party, using the title 'Liberal Party Organisation'. But, over the years, the term LPO came to be synonymous with the headquarters itself, and this usage was made official in 1969. However, the term LPO is also used among Liberals to mean the Liberal Party outside parliament or (in Scotland) the Liberal Party in England only.

The Liberal Central Association is descended from the Liberal Registration Association, formed in 1860 by the parliamentary leadership of the party. It was a central party organisation created from above, in the classic manner of a caucus party expanding outside parliament. For many years, up to the First World War, it performed major tasks – preparing elections, dealing with all policy questions and placing candidates, as well as servicing the Chief Whip of the party, who was responsible for it to the leader. By the 1950s and 1960s the LCA had come to be a fund controlled by the Chief Whip, through which limited servicing of the Liberal MPs was performed; but it still had financial and organisational responsibilities for two departments in the party headquarters – candidates and research. Neither of these responsibilities remain now, though the vestiges can be seen in the constitutional arrangement for the appointment of chairman of the candidates and standing committees. But the one area where an ambiguous autonomous relationship remains, the Liberal Publications Department (LPD),[22] relates directly back to this history. The LCA only survives now to channel the state financial support for servicing opposition parties to Liberal MPs, and since Cyril Smith, MP, was briefly Chief Whip, it has come within the Party Treasurer's ambit.

At its base, the party membership is arranged into constituency associations, which in turn form twelve English regional parties and the three national parties; in addition members of the party may join ten appropriate 'recognised bodies'. Each of these is represented at various levels of the party; the more important are:

The Association of Liberal Councillors (ALC)
The National League of Young Liberals[23]
The Union of Liberal Students[23]
The Women's Liberal Federation
The Liberal Candidates' Association

These, in turn, are represented, directly or indirectly, in the constitutional organs of the party, which are elected as follows:

The (annual) Assembly: Constituency Associations, National and Regional Parties, recognised bodies;
The (quarterly) Council: The Assembly, National and Regional Parties, recognised bodies;
The National Executive Committee (NEC): The Council, National and Regional Parties, recognised bodies;
The Finance and Administration Board (F & AB): the NEC (4), the LPO staff (2), the Assembly (1 or 2);
The Standing Committee (policy): The Council, candidates, National Parties, plus a chairman appointed by the Liberal MPs;
The Candidates' Committee: the NEC, candidates, plus a chairman appointed by the Chief Whip;
The Assembly Committee: The Council.

The first three constitute a hierarchy, with additional Regional/National Party and recognised-body representation built in; the last four are independent functional bodies, each specially constituted and none clearly responsible to one level of the hierarchy. The Assembly Committee comes closest to a simple responsibility, to the Council: but, in practice, it may also report to the Standing Committee (on the policy content of the Assembly), to the NEC (on general organisation) and to the F & AB (on the budget).

The Finance and Administration Board is the key body for the headquarters. It was originally conceived, in the first draft of the 1969 constitution, as a body wholly elected by (but only vaguely responsible to) the NEC. The Assembly insisted on including a Treasurer directly elected by the Assembly, whose ambiguous independence from the other four members of the Board on matters of finance is a potential source of conflict. This was resolved during 1969–76 by electing the same person as chairman of the whole Board. In 1972 the 'worker control' current within the party secured the addition of two employee representatives to the Board. The Board appoints the Head of the Liberal Party Organisation, who has been styled the 'Secretary-General' since 1977; and he, in turn, then becomes the eighth full member of the Board. The precise extent of the responsibility of the F & AB to the NEC has been a matter of some dispute; in 1973 the phrase 'subject to the general policy and priorities decided by the National Executive Committee' was added to the constitutional definition of the F & AB's functions. The matter was further complicated in February 1976 by the creation by the NEC of an ad hoc officers' or steering committee, consisting of the holders of some constitutional offices (such as the Treasurer and the chairmen of the main committees) together with several members of the NEC, who have been designated as officers by that committee. Intended to co-ordinate the hydra-headed party structure, it has inevitably become a further head. The 1979 general election generated another such body; the general election committee was set up in 1977 to consist of four members elected by the NEC, four appointed by the leader and one each from the Scottish and Welsh parties – and therefore responsible to no one. But it is the Standing Committee that shares the leader's constitutional responsibility for the manifesto.

The Standing Committee represents an attempt to mesh together the parliamentary and non-parliamentary wings of the party. Its chairman is a Liberal MP elected by the Liberal MPs. The bulk of its members are elected by an electorate consisting of all members of the council, all adopted candidates and the MPs. This gives the parliamentary-inclined (candidates) a majority, and if the party had substantial parliamentary representation, MPs would acquire a substantial weight in the election. It could play a key role if the party were in government; other British parties have no similar body. It is responsible for 'the planning of the long-term evolution of Liberal policy; for expressing between meetings of the Council the views of the Liberal Party on urgent political issues and for setting up and co-ordinating the work of policy committees and panels'.[24] This leaves a fuzzy overlap with the powers of the NEC in the general area of political campaigning and strategy. The Standing Committee has tried to direct the party's political priorities, but the NEC and/or the F & AB clearly command the party's material resources.

These are limited. In the headquarters (LPO and LPD) there were, early in 1978, six executive and twelve non-executive (mainly clerical or secretarial) staff, plus three others working independently – for instance, the ALC employs a party local government officer, located in Hebden Bridge, West Yorks. There were only eleven full-time professional constituency agents, plus three full-time association secretaries, though several more have part-time help. About half the national and regional parties also employ staff. The party's paid staff has declined in numbers in the 1970s as shortage of income has hit all political parties.

The party's main resources, particularly when it comes to vote-getting, has been its active members, or activists. These are the basis upon which it has been able to fight elections (or failed to), and the expansion of organisational strength discussed above (see pp. 80–1) is largely in numbers and commitment of activists. Given the tiny number of Liberal MPs, it is from the activists that party leadership comes at national and regional level, and it is activists who man the committees of the party with little participation from Liberal MPs. Most of the committees tend, therefore, to meet at weekends in order to facilitate the attendance of activists and, under pressure from members arguing that the party should practise as well as preach its decentralism, many of the major meetings rotate around the country. Liberal MPs generally hold their constituencies by small majorities, so that they feel the need to defend reputations as good constituency members and spend Saturdays particularly on constituency work.

The tension between parliamentary and non-parliamentary sections of parties is a general theme of writing on political parties. The British Liberal Party reflects this tension in a special form, because its MPs are few in number and electorally vulnerable. The geographical distortion of the electoral system adds a further problem. Whilst the bulk of the British population, of Liberal voters and of activists (and also of Liberal councillors) comes from the more urban areas or nearby countryside, most Liberal MPs sit for remote constituencies. Those in Scotland and Wales often look first to their national parties (though the extent of this differs in the two countries, for in Scotland the party is run more by those who live in the urban central areas, where there are no MPs), so that the loose and unclear structures of the party accentuates the problem.

The tension has been behind, or the direct precipitant of, several crises in the party's recent history – the sudden selection of Jeremy Thorpe as leader in 1967, the 18-month civil war which ensued,[25] the difficulties that the party faced in reacting to the hung parliament situation over the first weekend of March 1974, and the row which simmered over the future of the Lib–Lab agreement in the autumn and winter of 1977–8. The growing Liberal Party of the late 1950s and of the 1960s had inherited a mixture of an apparently open and democratic party structure (which fitted the participatory mood of the times and the emphasis of the party's newer activists) and a club-like party elite through which a very Westminster-oriented MP, Jo Grimond, had had unrivalled sway. As Grimond departed and the newer recruits moved up the party hierarchy, some conflict was inevitable, thought not necessarily the depths of distrust and malcommunication which characterised periods of Thorpe's 10 years of leadership.

One of the main themes of the Radical Bulletin Group within the party (see below, p. 101) during its period of most activity, 1971–6, was the need for more internal party democracy. As a result of organising for internal party elections, several of its members had attained leading positions within the party in the late 1970s. However, that did not alter the underlying situation. One such officer, Gordon Lishman, resigned his position as director of policy promotion in 1977 on grounds of the National Executive Committee's incapacity to take decisions, and later set out his view of the situation inside the party under the title *The Inarticulate and the Deaf*. He emphasised how the process of selection of Liberal MPs accentuates the problem:

In order to be a Liberal MP, it is necessary to be born and to find a job in the appropriate Celtic constituency, or to have the leisure and money to travel to one, or to have a bye-election in the right place at the right time . . . the pre-requisites rule out most urban English Liberals with jobs and families almost immediately, apart from a major stroke of luck as a parliamentary bye-election at the right time or a major scandal involving your opponent.[26]

Not surprisingly, there has been a succession of attempts to review the party's structure to improve communication and to produce a leadership of the party which is more co-ordinated, effective and (from the point of view of some) democratic. In 1944 the party created the 'Liberal Party Committee', with a system of mixing election by the party and nomination by the leader, in a body which could give political direction to the whole party. By the 1960s the leader had simply ceased to convene its meetings. A comprehensive review was set under way in the 1960s, under the chairmanship of Nancy (now Lady) Seear. After much debate, this review's recommendations were half implemented and half rejected by the 1969 Assembly, which consequently left the structure more complex either than it was before or than it would have been if the Seear proposals had been fully adopted. A further review was set in motion in 1975, but it was disbanded by the National Executive Committee in 1977 because it suggested that drastic alteration of the NEC was the key to reform. The 1977 Assembly then decided to set up yet another constitutional review, which was still under way in mid-1979.

The one success of the 1975 review was the change that the party made in 1976 to the method of election of its leader. This gives a direct vote to every party member, weighted according to Liberal strength in each constituency. But the leader may only be chosen from among Liberal MPs, and the nomination system is designed to ensure that the leader has significant support among other Liberal MPs. David Steel's election by this method in July 1976 undoubtedly contributed to his strength within the party.

Liberal Party strategy

It is tempting to write about the strategy of a party in terms of logical pursuit of goals, or an intelligent choice of alternative courses. Liberal strategy is better understood as a response to the pressures and enticements engendered by the size and character of the Liberal vote, filtered through the preferences and interests of the various parts of the party's structure. The party lacks any sense of a simple, overriding route to the exercise of political power; arguments about its strategy periodically absorb it into an introspective debate, and not infrequently get entangled with internal constitutional questions.

There are certain strategies which the party has eschewed, although they are logically available to it, and parallel parties in similar political systems pursue them. One would be an attempt through political propaganda, and the mobilisation of its supporters into educational activities, to build up its core of committed supporters slowly through conversion. The ready availability of Liberal voters who are not too interested in the party's policies, let alone in its deepest principles, has discouraged thought of this. The majoritarian impulse within the party and the majoritarian element within the voting system have tempted the party to go for rapid expansion of its votes rather than the intensification of its voting base. The party's electoral and inter-election campaigning has focused on building up the credibility and standing of Liberal candidates, not on spreading awareness of Liberal policies or turning voters' minds towards Liberalism.

Another would be the position of a (semi-)permanent minor ally of another party. This was not a possibility with the Labour Party; but it was the course that a number of Liberals opted for with the Conservatives through the National Liberals. The latter were so completely absorbed into the Conservative Party that their name became an embarrassing memory within 20 years of the 1947 Woolton–Teviot agreement. In 1951 Winston Churchill offered the then Liberal leader, Clement Davies, a place in his cabinet; Davies, backed up to the hilt by his party, refused, and so turned down the option of a close alliance as the route to power at a period when every other prospect seemed bleak.

However, there were several electoral alliances with the Conservative Party at the 1951 election and three Liberal MPs in 1955 and two in 1959 were elected owing to the lack of Conservative candidates. At earlier elections there had also been Liberal MPs elected with Labour support, and during the 1950s a large proportion of the surviving Liberal municipal representation in the North of England was in alliance with another party. The Liberal Party, with growing self-confidence, broke the parliamentary electoral pact at the East Bolton by-election in 1960 and since then has firmly turned its back on any question of electoral pacts. Overtures from within the Scottish National Party for some form of electoral pact during the early and mid-1960s were rebuffed by successive chairmen of the Scottish Liberal Party. After the 1970 election David Steel suggested some withdrawal of Liberal candidates where the party was weak and a major party candidate was liberally inclined; the storm that met his remarks ensured that he has avoided repeating the idea.

At other periods in Britain (notably the Lib-Labbery of the 1906 and the 1910 elections) or in other countries, a single-member seat system has induced electoral pacts whereby smaller parties can not only survive but prosper. They should have an obvious attraction to sitting Liberal MPs, whose chances of re-election could thereby be enhanced. That the idea has become such an anathema to modern Liberals is a reflection of the powerful will to survive on its own that the party developed during its years in the wilderness, and the importance to it of its independence. But in turn these attitudes fit ill with the tactic of forming an alliance with another party in parliament.

During his years as leader Jo Grimond pursued the chimera of a realignment of the left – a strategy which fitted the growth of the Liberal vote esentially in opposition to the Conservatives, the succession of Labour general election defeats (1951, 1955, 1959) and the periodic disputes within the Labour Party during Gaitskell's leadership. With the Labour victory of 1964, the prospect of returning to its historic role as the major radical party faded for most Liberals, and so Grimond received little support and much misunderstanding among Liberals for his overtures to the Labour government in 1965. Grimond's leadership brought many activists into the party, and the idea that there could be an essentially radical role for a Grimond-type of Liberal Party has continued to influence the thinking of many of them. Though it does not correspond closely with any of the three types of Liberal voter suggested above (see p. 90), the radical self-image of the party that the realignment of the left presupposed fits broadly to the position of core voters as being at the radical end of their own dimension of politics.

During Jeremy Thorpe's years a series of strategies were pursued, in succession or at the same time. Thorpe himself never developed a political strategy; he put the emphasis much more on the attainment of credibility, and on the hope that winning more seats would constitute a bridgehead from which expansion would become easier as the bridgehead grew. There is much evidence that credibility has a direct effect on willingness to vote Liberal, but the bridgehead approach takes no account of the problems inevitably resulting from the increasing diversity of the Liberal vote as it expands.

In many ways Thorpe was a major asset to his party, especially his television personality, and most Liberals were conscious of his contribution to the party's vote-getting record. But there was an awkward disjunction between his somewhat dilettante, upper-class image and several of the strategies which the party, or sections of it, set out to pursue whilst he was leader.

During the 1966–70 Labour parliament the party made a concerted effort to build up support in industrial areas; LPO expanded and reorganised on the basis that the party's expansion would continue as dissatisfaction with the government boosted Liberal support once again, but in Labour rather than Conservative areas. Many in the party also hoped to improve the prospects of longer-term realignment of the left by giving the party a better electoral base in industrial areas.

The strategy was mainly, though not wholly, a failure. It was in 1966–8 that Liberal councillors started to build up electoral bases in inner city Birmingham and Leeds. But in general the electoral record was poor; the expansion of LPO left the party heavily in debt; and the 1970 election saw no change in the relative weakness of the party in more industrial areas.

At the same time the party tried to portray itself as opposed to the consensus between the two major parties. One Liberal poster of the late 1960s showed pictures of Harold Wilson and Edward Heath under the question 'WHICH TWIN IS THE TORY?'. This fitted the anti-system element in Liberal voting, and also the impatient youthful radicalism of the period. The Young Liberals became more militant after 1966 and increasingly made an impact on both public and the party – which some senior Liberals welcomed but others did not. On certain issues the Young Liberals succeeded in getting the party to campaign with them (notably in opposition to British government support for the United States in Vietnam), but the party did not find militant campaigning congenial. In 1970 a protest movement led by Young Liberals, the 'Stop-the-Seventies-Tour', achieved perhaps the most direct success of the youthful protests of the period – prevention of cricket matches between the MCC and a (white) South African team.

But the Liberal Party leadership was always unsure how far it wanted to take this radical protest stance. After the 1970 election there was a widespread belief that the party had lost votes and seats because of its association with students trying to stop sporting engagements, and some senior Liberals tried, unsuccessfully, to start a witchhunt of the Young Liberals. Once again the party found it could not pursue any strategy wholeheartedly without some loss.

At the 1970 Assembly two strategies were offered by pressure groups within the party. One, from John Pardoe's constituency, proposing that the party should find a *deus ex machina* in declaring that it would contest every single constituency, was turned down. The other, a resolution on what was styled Community Politics,[27] was adopted and became the strategy of the NEC and most of the party, though noticeably it never attracted significant support among Liberal MPs.

Community Politics brought together Young Liberals and Liberal councillors; the Radical Bulletin group, led mainly by former Young Liberals, maintained the lobby for the next few years. The strategy laid emphasis on both operating inside established political institutions and working directly with people to enable them to achieve changes in society directly. It was seen by many of its enthusiasts as meaning that the Liberal Party would provide a bridge between conventional electoral politics and movements such as women's liberation, gay liberation and environmental action groups. Its practitioners laid most emphasis on electioneering tactics which concentrated on local issues, intensive leaflet distribution and the involvement of Liberal candidates and councillors in day-to-day popular grievances. Derided as 'broken-pavement politics', these tactics were already paying off in Liverpool in 1970, and led directly to the party's becoming the largest party on the city council there in May 1973 and to the remarkable by-election victory at Sutton and Cheam in December 1972.

There was always an uneasy link between the ideals of creating ways in which people could participate in politics, and improve their living conditions themselves, and the winning of votes. In 1973 the other link, that between the electoral successes of the Community Politics strategy and the other images the party was pursuing, became more problematical. The Isle of Ely (July 1973) and Berwick-on-Tweed (November 1973) were won by more conventional electioneering methods – and both were to be held at the 1974 elections, in contrast to Sutton and Cheam. Developments in the Labour Party, in particular the resignation of Roy Jenkins as deputy leader in April 1972 and Dick Taverne's victory at Lincoln in February 1973, were encouraging thoughts – particularly among Liberal MPs – of a different form of realignment of the left. But this time it was envisaged as a centre-left, Thorpe–Jenkins party, with the 'extremist' Labour left pushed to one side of British politics. There was, of course, an essential contradiction between this view of the way forward for the Liberal Party and the Community Politics strategy, corresponding to the dichotomy between the centre-voter and the anti-system voter. But whereas Jo Grimond's vaguer concepts of the realignment of the left had enlisted the support of radically minded activists, these found the idea of a link with the moderate wing of the Labour Party much less congenial.

If the 1972–3 local government and by-election build-up had seemed to confirm that the party could gain ground through the Community Politics strategy and as a party of radical protest, the February 1974 general election seemed to confirm the appeal of moderation. A tremendous moral victory, and a pivotal role in the House of Commons, came to the party as a result, but it spent the middle months of 1974 muddling about how to respond. Rival perceptions of how the party had got to where it was, and the lack of co-ordination between different sections of the party, played their full role in this. For instance, the suggestion of a national or all-party government approach, which came from Liberal MPs, was a logical extension of the role of the party in bolstering the moderate centre against extremism; but it was regarded by many activists as a betrayal of the basis on which they had been appealing for votes. In the event the fact the party held so many votes in October 1974 and gained others was more surprising than that it suffered a net loss; the October 1974 campaign was studiously silent as to what would happen if the Liberal Party gained more seats and there was another hung Parliament – which nearly happened.

In the $2\frac{1}{2}$ years between October 1974 and the March 1977 parliamentary agreement to support the Labour government the party drifted uncertainly. The feeling that electoral progress could only be made when a Conservative government was in power had a strong influence. The uncertain future of the leader, Jeremy Thorpe (who was under threat before the Scott/Bessel/Holmes affair broke in January 1976), held back any constructive review of the party's

strategy. The 1975 referendum on European Community membership united the party, with its strong European ideals, as it did no
other; but it did not galvanise it, since the tenor of the 'Yes' campaign
did fit with the party's view. The success of the 'Yes' campaign,
however, encouraged the inclination of some Liberals towards co-
operation with others, and towards the idea of a central common
ground in British politics.

This was also encouraged by the growing belief in many circles that
British government was suffering from the system of adversary
politics, and by the increasing support for electoral reform, marked by
the formation of the National Committee for Electoral Reform. The
case for proportional representation on grounds of democratic principle and justice, which the Liberal Party had always propounded,
was being overtaken by a very different sort of argument about the
desirability of electoral reform in the interests of stable and effective
party government. Liberals had always tended to avoid the implications of proportional representation for party government.

At the same time many proponents of the Community Politics
approach remained convinced that the association of Liberalism with
the electoral reformers' idea of a centre force could only damage the
party's longer-term prospects. They were able to point to electoral
evidence: the only advances that the party made after 1974 were some
scattered but striking ones in local government and the Newcastle
Central by-election in November 1976, where the Liberal candidate
was the NEC's Community Politics officer.

The contest for the party leadership between John Pardoe and
David Steel in the summer of 1976 offered a choice of strategies.
Pardoe argued that the party should attack the political system
aggressively with a programme of radical constitutional reform,
which he believed would both galvanise the party's activists and
attract voters. Steel's campaign played upon his effectiveness at
Westminster, and David Steel made plain his belief that the party's
way forward lay in co-operating with other like-minded elements in
politics. The majority of leading NEC members and regional party
officers supported Pardoe, but Steel had impressive support from
some more radical activists (the Radical Bulletin group was deeply
split, with a pro-Pardoe majority) who distrusted what they saw as
Pardoe's populism and felt that Steel was a truer Liberal. Thus David
Steel's record (his parliamentary standing had been made over such
issues as the Abortion Law Reform and the 1968 Commonwealth

Immigration Act) and approach brought support from both those whose view of strategy was conditioned by allegiance to the values of the Liberal core vote and those who thought more in centre-party terms; Pardoe's stance and aggressive style appealed to the anti-system view but offended others.

The Labour government's loss of an overall majority in March 1977 gave David Steel his chance, which he grasped eagerly – too eagerly perhaps, for his credibility as leader of an independent party and his negotiating position. The initial decision to make the agreement to support the Labour government followed widespread consultation throughout the party, and was generally supported. The agreement was renewed in July 1977, without further similar consultation and without any improvement in the terms. This renewal, taking account of the position of the nationalist parties and the devolution legislation, amounted to a significant weakening of the Liberal bargaining position for the following season. Criticism of the agreement steadily mounted during the remainder of the year, fuelled by steadily worsening by-election results.

The crisis came over the question of the electoral system for direct election of the European Parliament, which votes by the Standing Committee, the Assembly and the Council had seen as a make-or-break issue for the pact. David Steel made it plain that he did not see the issue as being so important, thus both losing any chance there was of obliging the parliamentary Labour Party to give adequate support to proportional representation and turning the dispute into one between himself and his party rather than one between his party and the government.

The Liberal MPs decided not to withdraw from the agreement on 15 December 1977, the day following the Commons' defeat of proportional representation and the failure of a majority of Labour MPs to vote for it. This decision illustrates how clearly the power of political initiative lies with the parliamentary party in such a fast-moving situation. By 21 January 1978, when a Special Assembly met to consider the matter (despite the leader's wish that it should not be convened), it was realistically too late for that decision to be reopened. However, the non-renewal of the pact in the summer of 1978 became inevitable, despite Steel's original anticipation that it could have lasted into the 1978–9 parliamentary session.

The party considered its strategy for the following general election while the argument over the Lib–Lab agreement was being resolved.

The decisions to aim explicitly for the balance of power, to be prepared to work with either major party, and to make proportional representation the key to any such arrangement represented a new stance for the party; but these decisions were not taken without much heart-searching, and constitutional wrangling over the authority by which they had been decided and publicly announced in February 1978. They were put to the test in the 1979 general election. The delay in the election from October 1978, which Steel had assumed to be the date in all his planning, caused problems for the party. The memory of the Lib–Lab agreement, and its hoped-for appeal as a period of stability and a declining rate of inflation, faded steadily. In the post-agreement wait for the general election the Liberal MPs voted determinedly as part of the opposition in the House of Commons, but they could not easily find a role and nor did the Liberal Party get much publicity, with one agonising exception. That was the massively reported committal proceedings against its former leader, Jeremy Thorpe, on charges of incitement and conspiracy to murder; the problems caused by Mr Thorpe's determination to appear at the 1978 assembly, despite these charges, had overshadowed all other proceedings at it.

In the circumstances, the party remained at a low electoral ebb in the period before the Labour government fell on 28 March 1979. Its federalist philosophy, and the policies of the Scottish and Welsh Liberal parties, received severe setbacks in the devolution referendums in Scotland and Wales on 1 March 1979. Four by-elections held during this period showed a drop in the aggregate Liberal vote from 16 per cent to 7.9 per cent. The Liberal MPs helped to vote the Government out, consistent with their position in opposition, with no great confidence that a general election would suit their interest.

The day following the Government's fall gave the party its first really good news for years. A by-election occurred in Liverpool Edge Hill, the one constituency in the country where pursuit of the Community Politics strategy had built up an electoral base clearly strong enough to take a whole parliamentary constituency. The Liberal candidate, Mr David Alton, the 28-year-old chairman of Liverpool City Housing Committee, won the seat with a massive three-to-one majority.

From that point the Liberal campaign built up slowly but steadily towards an election result which showed that David Steel's approach evoked a considerable public response. The 14.1 per cent of the votes cast in Great Britain was the best Liberal poll outside the two 1974 elections since 1929 (though allowing for the number of seats fought, below the 1964 performance). It was dramatically better than the level of Liberal voting during 1975–8; in the seats just fought in by-elections the vote rose again from 7.9 per cent to 12.2 per cent, and in the local elections held on the same day as the general election, the Liberals did better than at any time since the 1973 local elections. The figures do not allow exact calculation; but it would seem that something of the order of a million people may have voted Liberal locally whilst on the same day choosing between a Callaghan and a Thatcher government. The BBC/Gallup election-day survey found that over a third of those who did not vote Liberal said they were 'fairly likely' to vote Liberal if they had 'thought the Liberals would win a lot more seats'. However, only 11 Liberal MPs were elected, though this was considerably better than the four or five who would have survived a strictly uniform movement of votes. The three who lost their seats suffered from local effects – Mr Thorpe's troubles seem to have lost his seat, and helped to lose that of his neighbouring Liberal MP, John Pardoe; in Montgomery growth of New Town voters plus a general upsurge in Conservative support in rural Wales ousted the Liberals from a seat held since 1880. In the remaining Liberal-held seats (including the Liverpool Edge Hill by-election gain) and in several constituencies where Liberals had come close to victory in 1974, the 1974 Liberal vote was maintained or improved; the party's appeal where it was locally credible was amply proved.

Yet David Steel had pitched his election message in terms of the need for a parliament without an overall majority, a 'People's Parliament', as he termed it. That did not happen; the Conservatives won a clear overall majority with only 44 per cent of the national vote. With a strong electoral base, the Liberal Party was set for a period of opposition to a Conservative government, which it strongly anticipated would bring it by-election gains. But its uncertainty over its role remained.

The election campaign had demonstrated that going for the balance of power, advocating co-operation between parties and electoral reform made a coherent and appealing message. But whether it would make such sense if the party started winning votes again on the 1972–3 by-election scale, and with the party's natural stance one of radical opposition to a Tory government, remains another matter.

Part II

The Scottish and Welsh National Parties

Part II

The Scottish and Welsh National Parties

4

The Scottish National Party

W. A. Roger Mullin

Increasing electoral support in recent years for the Scottish National Party (SNP) had created a major challenge, not only to the main UK parties operating in Scotland, but also to the legitimacy of the United Kingdom. Why, in an advanced industrial society, apparently with a long established and legitimated system of government, a nationalist party should emerge to threaten the established political order is a problem still awaiting a comprehensive answer. Whatever the reason, one thing is clear: the SNP has been able to mobilise the nationalist aspirations and discontents of the Scottish electorate to a remarkable degree, through a party structure and ideology which has proved able to attract more new political activists and to campaign more effectively than any other major party in Scotland in recent times.

Scottish nationalism and the SNP

The SNP came into being at a time in 1934, when the economic, political and intellectual legitimacy afforded the unitary state was being posed a growing, if yet small, nationalist challenge in Scotland; the reasons for this are conventionally attributed to circumstances and developments following the First World War. (Many of the most articulate advocates of Home Rule between the wars were, in fact, associated with the Labour movement.)[1]

Scotland was particularly affected by the post-war slump, because of overdependence on traditional heavy industries. This dependence had been increased during the war. Her industrial base was too old, too highly specialised and too lacking in newer technologies to maintain her relatively strong pre-war position. Relative economic decline within the UK coincided with growth in government intervention as the state was pressed, by growing public expectations, to play a more active role. Thus relative economic deprivation increased, as did the involvement of central government. In a Scotland which had retained its own church, educational system, legal system and local government after the parliamentary union of 1707, this extension of the role of central government had, perhaps, a more significant cultural impact than the original loss of independence in the eighteenth century, when parliamentary government had a much less important role.[2]

Economic circumstances after the First World War most obviously aided the Labour Party in recruiting and organising in largely industrialised areas with the help of an active trade unionism. The Labour Party remained weak, however, in some rural constituencies, particularly in the north of Scotland, where the levels of unionisation were low.

In the 1920s an intellectual nationalism began to develop as a result of the Scottish literary renaissance, led and inspired by nationalist and communist poet Hugh MacDiarmid. Consequently, a serious and intellectual concern for Scottish society was eventually to force its way on to the political agenda – although MacDiarmid himself was shunned by many early nationalists. The role of the intelligentsia in politics is often ignored, but the serious treatment of the idea of a Scottish state in the 1970s by a number of academics has proved an important step in legitimating this concept; for any party seeking major constitutional change must not only break down the legitimacy of the existing constitutional arrangements, but also convert people to its own proposals.

The First World War had also disrupted parliamentary progress on Scottish Home Rule. After a Scottish Home Rule bill proposed by Sir W. H. Conway of the Liberal Party was passed by 204 votes to 159 at the second reading in 1913, Asquith announced that his government would put through an act for Scottish Home Rule. The war made its postponement inevitable.

Post-war efforts were no more successful. In 1926 a Scottish

National Convention, sponsored by a Scottish Home Rule Association, was held, with members of all parties taking part. Dominion status for Scotland, within a Commonwealth of self-governing states, linked by the Crown, was accepted as the solution to the question of Scottish self-determination. Inspired by this, a Government of Scotland Bill was moved in 1927 by the Rev. James Barr and seconded by Tom Johnston (Labour). It was talked out by the Tories at the second reading.

Such failures, and the changing economic and intellectual climate, contributed to the establishment in 1928 of the National Party of Scotland. In 1932 right-wing nationalists formed the Scottish Party, and by 1934 the two nationalist parties had merged to form the Scottish National Party. To this day the influence of the 1926 Convention can be seen in the SNP's aims, which are in part 'Self government for Scotland – that is, the restoration of Scottish national sovereignty by the establishment of a democratic Scottish parliament within the Commonwealth' and the continuing acceptance of the British monarch as head of state.

The young nationalist party saw a need to distinguish Scottish nationalism from the violence associated with Irish nationalism. This helped establish the highly constitutional character of SNP politics, and explains the reluctance of SNP leaders until recently even to mention Ireland. This point is well demonstrated by an Irish journalist when relating his experience at one SNP conference: 'I recall asking the then press officer "What is your party's policy on Northern Ireland?" To which he replied all too appositely, "Jesus Christ!"'.

While making some early advances in recruitment, allowing dual membership, and viewing all party action as a possible means of success, the SNP had difficulty in establishing itself as a credible political alternative. The coming of the Second World War prevented the SNP holding a Convention similar to the one held in 1926. This was, in any case, a time of growing conflict within the party. Eventually a split occurred. In 1942 the annual conference elected Douglas Young as chairman, when he was out on bail pending appeal for having refused conscription by a British government. As a result John MacCormick, a founder member of the party, withdrew to establish the Scottish Convention. Although short-lived, it had some spectacular success in seeking all-party support. In 1949 it launched a 'Scottish Covenant', aimed at attracting support for a devolved parliament. The government failed to respond, despite the Covenant's 2 million signatures. In the meantime the SNP had had some success at by-elections, the high point being the election in April 1945 of Dr Robert McIntyre as MP for Motherwell. However, when the war-time truce and coalition ended, the SNP was able to contest only eight seats at the July 1945 general election. It failed to win any and saved only two deposits. In 1948 the SNP ended the dual membership principle, officially setting itself up as a full political and not merely constitutional rival of the other parties. This decision in its turn led to the withdrawal of some party activists, including Douglas Young. Post-war reconstruction needed strong government action. The public increasingly looked to government to solve the many social and economic problems of a war-disrupted society. This made the significant emergence of a nationalist party, increasingly critical of the centralising tendency of the state, a remote possibility.

Much as nationalists in Wales, outside the Blaid (Plaid Cymru), hurt that party, so nationalists in Scotland, outside the SNP, did little to improve the SNP's reputation. Events in the 1950s, such as the blowing up of postboxes because they were initialled E II R (Scotland never had an Elizabeth I) and the stealing of the Stone of Destiny, stigmatised nationalists in general as eccentrics or worse, and the SNP as politically irrelevant. Not surprisingly, the party's election performances throughout the 1950s were abysmal. By 1960 SNP membership was little more than 1000. The party was kept alive by the tenacity of a few branches and the work of some of its more active members. However, circumstances were about to change.

One of the most important changes in the long run may have been the change in intellectual climate. From abroad in the late 1950s and after began to be heard the strains of a new radical critique of some of the central features of the British state: large size, centralisation and bureaucracy. The earlier acceptance of the economics of scale, centralised decision-making and Keynesian economics was under challenge. The divergence between the affluent powerful large corporations and the poverty of many people's lives was very palpable in Scotland. Books such as Whyte's *The Organisation Man* and, later, Schumacher's *Small is Beautiful* were avidly read by a younger generation of Scots intellectuals, who, when they came to apply the new lessons to Scotland, became increasingly opposed to the large British state. Recognition of the relatively poor condition of the Scottish economy and its vulnerability to outside pressures supplied more fuel for criticism aimed at the status quo. The 'wind of change', too, sweeping across the face of the Commonwealth, brought with it a recognition of the rights of ex-colonies to independence, and of their feasibility as 'sovereign' states.[3] The loss of Empire led some Scots to question their own imperial status. Not all these Scots were attracted to the National Party's banner. Some of the most eloquent, such as Tom Nairn, were not. But the critiques of the British state and of Scotland's role in it, which Nairn and others developed, influenced the intellectual climate of Scotland and encouraged the National Party.

In Scotland the application of the new revulsion against all things large and growing vent itself on large foreign firms. Scotland became, in that period, particularly dependent on investment from abroad. The jobs were welcome but the dependence was not. In addition, the growing emphasis in the 1960s on regional policies, and the increasing number of government-sponsored reports into the economic and social conditions in Scotland, were of great significance. While aimed at finding real needs and applying remedies to major problems, thus increasing the integration of Scotland within the UK, the actual results of these official reports were different. On the one hand they pointed to the failure of successive governments to redress economic and social inequalities and injustices; on the other hand they strengthened the suspicion that the basis for correcting these regional imbalances depended upon regional explanation.

An early and important example was a report prepared, with government assistance, by the Scottish Council (Development and Industry) on the Scottish economy. Published in 1961, the report called for major policy initiatives aimed at creating a new, high-technology-based, industrial structure. It supported a massive expansion in educational investment and decentralisation of research and development. The chairman of the inquiry team, Sir John Toothill, was Managing Director of Ferranti – a new firm, which did have substantial research and development in Scotland. (A joint secretary to the inquiry team was John Donachy, a young economist. His father, a former Chairman of the STUC and a union official with the NUR, represented the old Scotland. In 1972 John Donachy joined the SNP and is now one of the party's parliamentary candidates.) The SNP gained credibility as a result of such reports and, in effect, was given a research department.

If the need for regional policy suggested the failure of central planning, the vulnerability of Scotland to external political interests was most dramatically emphasised by the siting of an American Polaris base on the Clyde in 1960, despite widespread popular protest – a decision still capable of raising the hackles of many Scots. The SNP benefited greatly from the anti-Polaris campaign. Indeed, an influential group of SNP National Executive members, and parliamentary candidates, were or are active members of the Campaign for Nuclear Disarmament (CND). In the Garscadden by-election of April 1978 the SNP candidate was also the pacifist Chairman of the Scottish CND. Growing discontent, particularly amongst the young, gave the SNP a potential source of growth. In the 1960s, aided by the new critique of large states and foreign firms, the SNP began to make some modest progress – particularly among the young.

Creation of the SNP electoral machine

Heartened at saving his deposit at a parliamentary by-election in Glasgow Bridgeton in 1961, Ian Macdonald gave up his career and devoted his energies full time to the SNP as its organiser. The organisation was to be built up around community-based branches. Indeed, the growth would have to be on the branches, because there were not, at that time, any constitutional arrangements for other sorts of local organisation, such as in parliamentary constituencies. By 1962, with membership around 2000, a by-election was fought by the party in West Lothian. This was one of the few areas where the SNP had active local branches. At the by-election the SNP, with William Wolfe the present Chairman as candidate, came second, with nearly 10,000 votes. Labour retained the seat. But second was an excellent performance for the party, and Macdonald was then establishing about two branches a month. The West Lothian success was a wonderful tonic.

In March 1963 the first-ever SNP constituency association was formed, in West Lothian. Setting a precedent, branches retained their major role within the party structure. The constituency association was entrusted with co-ordination of branch activity and election planning. But the branches remained largely responsible for the important functions of recruitment, fund-raising and the sending of delegates to the national forums within the party. Figure 2 shows the principal bodies and delegate routes within the SNP.

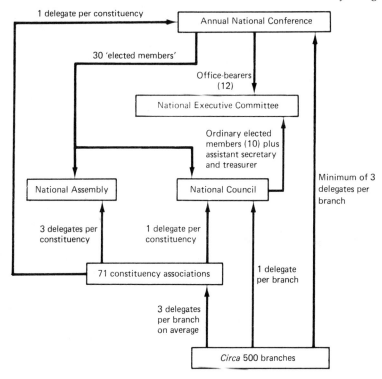

1 delegate per constituency → Annual National Conference

30 'elected members'

Office-bearers (12)

National Executive Committee

Ordinary elected members (10) plus assistant secretary and treasurer

National Assembly

National Council

Minimum of 3 delegates per branch

3 delegates per constituency

1 delegate per constituency

71 constituency associations

1 delegate per branch

3 delegates per branch on average

Circa 500 branches

NOTES

1. Annual Conference meets for three days in May.
2. Members of the NEC are automatically members of Conference, Council and Assembly.
3. The NEC meets once a month in full session and has twelve sub-committees.
4. National Council met four times in 1977.
5. National Assembly met six times in 1977.
6. Constituency associations normally meet once a month.
7. Branches normally meet once a month.
8. The party is served by ten full-time and three part-time staff in Edinburgh, and the parliamentary group has three full-time staff in London.
9. Seven MPs are also entitled to sit on the NEC.

FIGURE 2   *Principal bodies and delegate routes within the SNP*

Interaction between the party elite and branch activists is very frequent. With a comparatively small elite – an NEC of twenty-four and only seventy-one parliamentary candidates needed to cover all Scotland – strong personal ties and loyalties easily become established from top to bottom in the organisation.

Interaction does not merely take place within the formal party structure, but at the many social occasions organised by SNP branches. Since the party has no substantial 'outside' finance from big business or trade unions, a heavy programme of social activities is needed to finance its campaigns. Such local activities are made 'important' by inviting an MP, a party office bearer, or a candidate. As branch delegates account for the vast majority of those who elect the party's NEC and, through constituencies, select parliamentary candidates, it is not surprising that there is a considerable wooing of branches by members of the elite. Attendance at social events becomes mandatory.

Regular contact between members of the elite and many ordinary members has helped create a party 'communion' of sorts. Solidarity in the SNP develops as individuals encounter one another, recognise their common goal, and thence develop an enthusiasm in one another. Their patriotism becomes institutionalised.

While there are many divergences of opinion and different ideological attachments within the SNP, the overriding and very specific goal of an independent Scottish parliament has a crucial part to play in binding the party together. It may also be suggested that the very lack of achievement of national power helps keep the overriding goal free from blemish.

While most parties have local branches, SNP branches are systematically involved in all major party activities and have a considerable intensity of commitment. If participation and motivation within the SNP lessen in the future, as is quite possible if a Scottish parliament is established and the straighforward focus of party activity is lost, then the SNP may have to rely much more on its leadership to continue developing, or face the prospect of recession. The noticeable lack of strong leadership and centralised control which is welcomed by many party activists at present (encouraged by a distaste for presidential-style politics, increasingly identified with the Labour and Conservative Parties, and a fear of being seen to have a democratic party associated with any variety of nationalist 'Führer') may prove more of a handicap than help come independence or even devolution.

Throughout most of the 1960s the number of branches and members grew, although it is very difficult to be exact about membership figures. A minimum of twenty members with elected office bearers are needed before the SNP National Executive will give official branch recognition (in practice most branch memberships are considerably in excess of this figure). In 1966, when the SNP was in a particularly strong period of growth, the National Executive recognised 113 new branches, and in the first 4 months of 1967 sixty-three new branches.[4] This considerable growth was soon to be reflected in electoral success.

In the general election of 1966 the SNP, contesting twenty-three seats, polled 128,467 votes. It came second in three seats but won none. Not only was the party increasing in size, but the doubling of the SNP vote from the 1964 election, when fifteen seats were contested, indicated growing electoral support, too. By 1967 the SNP looked forward to contesting a parliamentary by-election in Glasgow Pollok. On 9 March, although coming third, the SNP polled 28.2 per cent of the vote in a five-cornered contest. In November 1967 another by-election was held at Hamilton in Lanarkshire. Thanks to a massive campaign, led by the candidate, the flamboyant Mrs Winnie Ewing, the SNP polled 46 per cent of the vote and won the previously safe Labour seat. Safe seats in a mainly two-party system were becoming a thing of the past. However, the SNP's new found ability to win elections led to new problems.

Electoral success and its effects

The local government elections of May 1968 gave the SNP its first opportunity to build on the success of Hamilton. The SNP won 105 council seats in a major electoral advance. However, some new SNP councillors had little previous political experience, not even much experience of the SNP. As a result, some resigned, others changed party, and yet others acted as independents, often clashing with fellow SNP councillors. The ensuing bad publicity did considerable damage to the SNP. Many branches folded up, and subsequent performances at local government election were poor when compared with the hopes generated by Hamilton and the May 1968 results. At the two parliamentary by-elections which occurred after Hamilton the SNP failed to win either Glasgow Gorbals or South Ayrshire. In the latter seat the MP elected was Mr Jim Sillars (now leader of the independence-seeking Scottish Labour Party), nicknamed the 'Hammer of the Scot Nats' because of a pamphlet, of which he was joint author, entitled 'Don't Butcher Scotland's Future'. It was typical of the attacks made on the SNP in the late 1960s. Scotland simply could not afford independence: she was too poor, too highly subsidised and too dependent on England. Economics was made the prime legitimating force for the existing state.

One aspect of Winnie Ewing's victory highlighted a significant deficiency of the SNP which activists were already aware of. The interest of the electorate and the media created a demand for information on the SNP's attitude to a whole range of policy questions. In 1962 Billy Wolfe had campaigned on the basis of a policy document drafted 15 years earlier. Party policy in the 1960s had depended very much on the enthusiasm of a few individuals. Their efforts were not enough. Therefore, at the 1967 Party Conference, a constitutional amendment to establish a National Assembly solely for policy and strategy debate was passed. It consists of parliamentary candidates, constituency delegates and the NEC. This body cannot establish party policy, but has to refer recommendations to Council or Conference to allow branch participation. It discusses reports from specialist committees and, although it has to refer its conclusions to a higher body, it has played the crucial role in shaping party policy. The Assembly's establishment was a further example of how increasing success had generated new demands and led to an expanded party network.

The creation of constituency parties and a National Assembly during the 1960s demonstrated that, while the party was less centralised than other parties, centralising influences were becoming stronger. If demands of government are ever placed upon the SNP in a Scottish parliament or Assembly, one suspects that these influences would be considerably strengthened. As elected representatives gather authority from the trappings of power and identify the need to have sufficient freedom to fulfil the decision-making demands of government, this could only be at the expense of grass-roots control.

Since the party has not had to face the rigours of operating a government as yet, it has, understandably, avoided some of the more painful decisions which a governing party has to make. This is particularly evident in its policy-making. Most of its policies are 'after independence' policies. They set out what an SNP government of an independent Scotland will do. Because they are so far removed from day-to-day life, these 'after independence' policies lack urgency. This makes it rather easy for the various interests in the party to agree to policies they do not really like. But if an Assembly is created, it will be necessary for the SNP to have specific urgent policies across a whole range of contentious social issues. When the party faces up to the need to write its first Assembly manifesto, it will have to make uncomfortable decisions which it has been able, so far, to avoid.

The traditional nature of political debate as it had developed in the 'two-party era' was now changing to accommodate the rise of the SNP. Mr Edward Heath, the Conservative Party leader, had at Perth in 1968 committed his party to support for a limited degree of devolution. The Labour government set up a Royal Commission on the Constitution headed by Lord Crowther, an anti-devolutionist economist (on Lord Crowther's death, a pro-devolutionist Scot, Lord Kilbrandon, took over). In its report of 1973 the Commission gave authoritative support to the principle of Scottish legislative control and proposed that a Scottish Assembly with limited powers be established.[5]

In the short term, increasing attacks on the SNP from an economic viewpoint, allied to the poor record of some SNP councillors, made the 1970 general election a greater ordeal for the SNP than might have been expected in early 1968. Nevertheless, the SNP contested sixty-five of the seventy-one seats in Scotland, and although Winnie Ewing failed to hold Hamilton, Donald Stewart, the present leader of the SNP in parliament, won the Western Isles from the Labour Party. The SNP's eyes turned northward after a period of concentrating on the central belt of Scotland. In total the SNP had but one victory, only nine second places and lost deposits in forty-three seats. However poor the performance seems, the SNP now had an established base in most Scottish constituencies. The party had learned the lessons of being too keen to contest local elections at all costs and, shamed by the charge of having no policies, had set policy-making machinery in motion.

Before its breakthrough in the late 1960s the party had had to adapt to the two-party system. One way it did this was by urging voters to 'lend us your vote'. The message meant that, while supporting the SNP to gain independence, traditional party allegiances could be reasserted once a Scottish parliament was established. However, the growing electoral success of the party in the late 1960s and increasing attention being paid to detailed policies led the SNP to believe:

1. that a third party could break up two-party dominance;
2. that, come independence, the SNP could reasonably aspire to power now that it was developing its own political programme;
3. that increasingly bitter attacks on the SNP by the other parties lessened any real prospect of political reconciliation come independence.

The discovery of oil off the Scottish coast in the early 1970s was crucial, however, in boosting the confidence of SNP activists in their ability to remain a major political force come independence. The nagging doubts which may have existed in some minds about the economic results of independence were soon dispelled.

It is over-simple, however, to attribute the rise of the SNP in the 1970s to oil alone. Before it ever became a major issue, the SNP in September 1971 at a by-election in the Stirling, Falkirk and Grangemouth constituency increased its vote from 14.3 per cent in the 1970 general election to 34.6 per cent, with former MP Dr Robert McIntyre as candidate. Just before the SNP launched the 'It's Scotland's Oil' campaign, a by-election at Dundee East saw it improve from 8.9 per cent in 1970 to 30.2 per cent, and another close second. Although by-elections tend to favour strong campaigning opposition parties like the SNP, the results did indicate a large potential vote in Scotland.

But the gulf between potential voters and a long-term mobilisation can be enormous. It was this gulf which was closed by the oil developments. In Scotland the economic arguments were trans-formed. For nationalists, oil supplied the economic base for the promises of industrial development and modernisation, which had a powerful popular appeal.

Launched in March 1973, the SNP's oil campaign caught the imagination of the party's activists. Before the end of the year branches had distributed over 1,000,000 leaflets entitled 'To London With Love', and follow-up leaflets by hundreds of thousands. The initial message was simply that an independent Scotland aided by oil revenues would not be poor. This reversed the 'Don't Butcher Scotland's Future' argument. Following on, an attempt was made to get a Scottish focus on oil (e.g. claiming a future Scottish government would lower the rate of exploitation, impose heavier taxes on oil companies, and have different priorities for the use of revenues – often in these instances looking towards Norway for examples of possible activities). The campaign had considerable effect. Recruitment quickened, branches became stronger and the SNP looked forward to two by-elections in November 1973. By a stroke of good luck for the SNP both were held on the same day, and the comparatively poor performance in taking only 18.9 per cent of the poll in the previously uncontested Conservative seat of Edinburgh North was over-shadowed by the spectacular victory of Margo MacDonald in Glasgow Govan, where the SNP improved from 10.3 per cent in 1970 to 41.9 per cent in taking a previously 'safe' Labour seat. Such success generated another intense wave of media interest. This time the SNP was more experienced, and with a very efficient headquarters staff put this rekindled interest to good effect.

The local government scene, too, was changing significantly if less spectacularly. It is clear from Table 4 that the SNP had been steadily withdrawing from participation in local government, and this was matched by a decline in their share of the votes. In 1973 this trend was

TABLE 4   *Local election summary: the performance of the SNP, 1969–73*

	1969	1970	1971	1972	1973
Candidates	303	214	139	120	95
Votes	198,000	121,000	75,000	58,000	55,000
Share (%)	26.7	17.4	15.9	14.2	21.0
City contestants (%)	26.1	14.0	10.6	8.2	13.8
Non-city contestants (%)	27.6	25.0	27.8	26.4	32.7
Seats defended	25	36	67	31	15
Seats held	14	11	25	16	12
Seats lost	11	25	42	15	3
Seats gained	29	4	5	4	6
Candidates elected	13	15	30	20	18

SOURCE: SNP Research Bulletin no. 6, May 1973.

reversed and an upturn was noticed. The SNP's research department summed up the 1973 position in the following terms:

Over the past four years, enthusiasm for local government elections among SNP members has undoubtedly waned ... Many SNP members undoubtedly came to regard local elections as an albatross round the party's neck with failure to sweep the boards at each year's local elections giving opponents the chance to write the SNP off, regardless of by-election successes and General Election prospects ... Now, however, this argument must be re-examined. The 1973 results show a marked and unmistakable improvement ... Next year sees the start of the new local government system, with elections for the new regional and district authorities. With a more positive approach there are prospects for the SNP doing very well indeed in these contests.[6]

Reorganised local government, with a two-tier structure involving large regional and district authorities, gave the SNP the opportunity to exploit its anti-centralist ideology and stress a need for community expression at local level. The party strongly opposed the newly reformed system. It sought, basically, to abolish the top regional tier. The party was now seeking change at local level under the same decentralist formula with which it attacked Westminster. Before the local elections were held in 1974, however, the SNP faced a general election in not altogether favourable circumstances.

With a 3-day week and miners' strike dominating the background to the February 1974 election, and with the near-presidential nature of the campaign as Heath and Wilson struggled for power, the SNP had some difficulty attracting the headlines. But the party was nevertheless able to launch the biggest election campaign in its history. The growing sophistication and expertise of party activists was put to good effect in the campaign – on the doorstep, in the pubs, at street-corner meetings, in car cavalcades, demonstrations and public meetings. This counteracted what appeared to party activists as their exclusion from much of the press, TV and radio coverage of the election.

The party contested all but one seat in Scotland. It won a 21.93 per cent share of the poll and, although losing Glasgow Govan, won seven seats, taking four seats from the Conservatives, two from Labour and retaining the former Labour seat of the Western Isles. Labour's share of the poll had fallen from 44.53 per cent in 1970 to 36.63 per cent. It won forty seats as against forty-four in 1970. The Conservative share fell from 37.9 per cent in winning twenty-three seats in 1970 to 32.93 per cent and twenty-one seats. The size of the SNP group in a 'hung' parliament meant that the SNP were now afforded greater access to TV and radio, and guaranteed substantial coverage in the Scottish press. It also meant that the SNP mattered in Westminster and that their enhanced credibility raised the prospect of further advance.

This success of the SNP nationally helped revive the party's performances in the May 1974 local government elections. With 269 candidates the SNP won sixty-two seats. Their share of the vote in seats contested was around 30 per cent. Come the general election of October 1974, the SNP was full of confidence, and the weakness of some local Labour and Conservative organisations added confidence to the forecast that another increase in electoral support and seats was likely. As it turned out, the SNP, for the first time contesting all seventy-one constituencies, won a further four seats from the Conservatives, held its own seven, came second in forty-two seats and took 30.44 per cent of votes cast. The Labour Party performed better than expected in SNP circles, with its share of the vote falling only slightly to 36.28 per cent. The Conservatives were the biggest losers and their share fell to 24.7 per cent. Four years after being written off by many people, the SNP had come back to a central place on the Scottish political stage. Furthermore, while it was possible to suggest in the late 1960s that, 'The politics of the SNP are not the politics of Gaeldom; their roots are in the Lowlands, not in the Celtic areas',[7] it was not possible to maintain this thesis any longer in the light of SNP victories in the Highlands and the fact that the SNP did not lose any deposits in October 1974, demonstrating a remarkable distribution of votes. The look north, which Donald Stewart's victory had encouraged, was proving of immense significance.

The new Scottish voter

What are the characteristics of SNP support? Does anything indicate that its basis of support is liable to pose a long-term challenge to the traditional parties, or is it merely a form of temporary protest vote? And what sort of outlook and ideological attachments does the SNP have which have been capable of attracting such a sizeable section of the electorate? Does the SNP really presage a new era in politics, or merely offer the same old mixture wrapped up in a tartan cover? These questions are not easily answered, particularly as the electorate still appears volatile, and as we still wait to see how the SNP will act in a Scottish Assembly or parliament. Parties in power are often forced to act differently than is suggested by party manifestos. Even in opposition in an Assembly the SNP will fulfil a quite different role than in Westminster. In an Assembly it will be able to aspire to power while being restrained from undermining the legitimacy of a Scottish legislature. Whether the SNP could handle such a situation is a matter of opinion at present. That said, there are some clues that the SNP is posing a long-term challenge to the traditional parties in Scotland on a number of fronts.

The picture is an extremely complicated one. The relatively poorer performance in working-class city seats than in rural or small-town-dominated seats is related to levels of unionisation and to past political allegiances. In Moray and Nairn, Banff, and East Aberdeen-shire – all won by the SNP in 1974 – substantial working-class populations are much less unionised than in city areas; and since the Labour Party had never been as strongly organised in such northern seats as elsewhere, it meant that until the SNP success in the 1970s the Conservatives had been winning these seats with the help of substantial working-class abstentions and votes. The SNP, whose belief in small-scale industry and small communities has a natural appeal to small-town workers, has been able to mobilise that vote, so aptly described as 'the silent voice of Scottish politics'.[8]

While the SNP did win eight former Conservative seats in 1974, it was with the substantial help of 'natural' anti-Conservatives as well as Conservative defection. Thus, in five of the eight seats in October 1974 the Labour candidates lost their deposits. Elsewhere the SNP seems to have benefited from an often non-unionised sector. In a study of the Clackmannan and East Stirling seat, which is 'occupationally a neat microcosm of Scottish society', V. J. Hanby found that 'In October 1974 the manual workers who voted SNP were over two-to-one non-unionised to unionised'.[9] Significantly, while one would expect the non-unionised voters to be less solidly Labour than the unionised voters, Hanby suggested that there were some signs (in 1976) of the SNP improving its lot amongst unionised workers as well.

Furthermore, in new towns – areas which often lack traditional community ties – the SNP made substantial progress. Thus new towns were SNP strongholds in the mid-1970s. These towns have been described as places where 'life [is] centred around home, family and television, with little involvement in any real "community"'. It is not suprising then that a party such as the SNP, which seeks to build a new thriving national community, does well amongst voters who have been physically torn from their old environment. The fact, too, that the SNP did not have to fight against traditional party ties, where no one said 'but this town has for generations voted . . .', made it that much easier for a new party to establish itself.

More generally, it has been argued that in the 1960s, as Britain moved into an era of bureaucratic growth, expansion in education and the development of new, high-technology industries (as the old industries moved into a period of massive recession), the old class-based nature of political allegiances came under some strain. As these developments have been related to a decline in industries with traditionally strong Labour ties, such as mining and railways, modern trends threatened the predictable nature of Labour's support. At the same time the growth in higher education (and the social sciences, in particular), and career opportunities in the social fields, produced a section of the middle class which would not give automatic support to the Conservatives. While *support* for the Labour and Conservative parties may have remained essentially class-based, it proved less solidly attached to its class party.

In Scotland there was the added dimension of the development of the 'branch factory' economy. For example, as C. Harvie has recently noted in relation to the growing number of American-controlled industries in Scotland: 'Between 1958 and 1968 they accounted for 30% of the employment created in Scotland ... by depending on American managerial techniques and personnel, the American firms restricted upward mobility, research and development, and graduate recruitment. Although they employed 87,730 in 1973 they took on only 250 graduates between 1965 and 1969.[10]

Scotland was increasingly dependent on production jobs in the industrial sector. Senior management posts and top scientific and technical positions were frequently centred outwith Scotland – within England or overseas. Upward occupational mobility was being restricted by nature of the changes taking place in Scotland's industrial life. We may speculate that changes in the industrial structure and education system are most likely to affect the political outlook of those experiencing such new conditions early in life. In Scotland these changes have made the young more amenable to an attractive national party. The indications are that the SNP is the major beneficiary of the changing society in Scotland, and that the party is proving itself sufficiently well organised and stable to make its sudden demise as a powerful force in Scottish politics highly unlikely in the foreseeable future. Both Scotland-wide opinion surveys and SNP-held constituency studies confirm that the SNP holds by far its largest support amongst voters under 35, while support amongst older age groups falls away substantially. Furthermore, it is noticeable that SNP support across occupational categories is much more uniform than either Labour or Conservative Party support.

The party's ideological appeal for the electorate in general is even more difficult to pin down. Indeed, as for all parties, followers will have many reasons for confessing support, but most will have no clear idea of party policy on many issues.

As disenchantment with traditional class-based parties has developed, since the 1950s, it has been attended by an antipathy towards the traditional rules of the game. Thus Swartz has noted that many activists are attracted to the SNP because they view it as more democratic than the traditional parties.[11] The party's rejection of creating a mini-Westminster in Scotland has attracted further sympathy. The party has promised more 'open' government, a one-chamber legislature, more power to backbenchers through US congressional-type committees and the implementation of the alternative-vote system of election.

The party advocates the decentralisation of much decision-making; but also favours strong interventionist powers being retained by central government (just how far the two are compatible is a moot point). Thus the party's industry policy states:

It is proposed that a Ministry of Development and Industry should be set up with a strongly decentralised structure of Area Development Offices charged with stimulating economic development appropriate to the needs of each area by means of a flexible, sensitive and discretionary incentive structure and with a special goal of radically increasing Scottish control over Scotland's industrial economy.[12]

Again, the SNP has a pragmatic view of some of the traditional points of division between the Labour and Conservative Parties, while leaning towards currently popular ideas about worker participation. As the industry policy adds with regard to the issue of public or private enterprise: 'The SNP has therefore no objection in principle to either private or public enterprise but believe that all contributions to the success of an enterprise including capital, expertise and labour, should receive a fair reward and have an effective voice in policy making.[13]

Certainly, the party's promise to change the rules and context of politics, and an attempt at breaking with traditional points of party division, appear to have been significant points of attraction for many, particularly among the younger SNP activists. Whether in power the SNP would usher in a real change in the manner of politics or whether present desires for change would prove forlorn, only time will tell.

Present dilemmas and future opportunities

However, all has not run smoothly. The SNP campaigned for a 'No' vote at the referendum on the EEC. All but two areas in Scotland voted 'Yes', overall the vote being 58 per cent 'Yes' and 42 per cent 'No' in Scotland compared to 67 per cent 'Yes' and 33 per cent 'No' throughout the UK. This has led to some hard thinking and not a few disagreements about the way in which the SNP should view the EEC in the future. Some argue that acceptance of independence within the EEC negates the separatist jibe and the threat of trading retaliation from England; Scotland could claim full member status and be a partner under the Common Market. Many consider the Irish to have performed well in the EEC, and this has led some SNP activists to reassure themselves that a small peripheral state need not be completely dominated within the EEC. If this reassurance is maintained (and let me stress that significant opposition exists to this argument), then the tactical advantages of membership may overcome some of the traditional hostility still felt by many activists.

It is the mere presence in Parliament of SNP MPs that poses the major threat to the traditional parties. The growing number of smaller parties represented in parliament, such as the SNP, is an indication of the declining support for the two main parties and for the traditional points of political division. Indeed, in one sense the scorn of both Labour and Conservative members further identifies the SNP as opposing the shared values of the old parties in the old system.

However, SNP MPs do not have the authority within their own party that the Labour, Conservative and Liberal MPs enjoy. In addition, 'emerging' parties have no safe seats. Thus, the SNP cannot guarantee the election of its leaders, and indeed some of the party's most influential figures remain outside parliament. Indications of this are easy to find. In Scotland it is often party office bearers who will make party political broadcasts and party spokesmen who will lead SNP campaigns. (For example, it was not the parliamentary spokesman on industry who led the SNP's steel campaign, but a party vice-president who was convenor of the SNP's action committee on steel.) MPs do have influence, of course – for example, a few have been important in moderating the attitude to the EEC, mainly Winnie Ewing, former member of the European parliament, and George Reid, former member of Council of Europe and the Western

European Union; but the fact that their centre of operation was outwith Scotland and is in a parliamentary system disliked by party activists has lessened their authority in the party. This is again emphasised by the decision of Douglas Henderson, MP, a former senior vice-chairman, to challenge Margo MacDonald for the post of senior vice-chairman at the party's 1977 Annual Conference. Mrs MacDonald won with a massive majority and, although many factors were involved, it is clear that the fact that she would be based in Scotland and not tied up in parliamentary affairs was a significant factor. The election also emphasised the desire of the party as a whole to avoid concentrating too much authority in any one part of the leadership. The operation of such informal 'checks and balances' contributes to the tension which exists between the National Executive and the parliamentary group

As mentioned at the beginning of this chapter, the SNP is strongly committed to constitutional procedures, and thus shuns any association with those who would pursue extra-constitutional means. Its main challenge comes at the electoral level, with the party's MPs charged with 'fighting for Scotland' in parliament but, as yet at least, not expected to disrupt parliamentary procedure or be obstructive. However, changes are afoot to broaden the SNP's opportunities for attacking the roles of the traditional parties.

For example, once EEC elections and the Scottish Assembly are established, it will be possible for the SNP to organise a campaign of squeezing out Westminster as a crucial level of government. Scotland will be relatively disadvantaged *vis-à-vis* other small nations within the EEC. She will not have direct representation on the Commission or Council of Ministers and only half the members of the European parliament allocated to other nations of comparable size. The SNP could therefore hope to show how Westminster obstructs Scotland from having effective international representation. Furthermore, if the SNP gains control of the Assembly, it could try to create an open, and effective, democratic structure of government. It could try to reform those areas under the Assembly's responsibility. Then, in any clash of interest between the Assembly and Westminster, the Scottish electorate might rise to the defence of the interests of the Assembly at the expense of Westminster. Such a strategy is optimistic. Parties in power often find it much more difficult to maintain public support than when in opposition. But this sort of optimism is increasingly popular within the SNP. Still, many hard-liners are worried that the party may be trapped by devolution. They fear that the very lack of power of the proposed Assembly, particularly in the economic and industrial fields, will prevent any SNP 'government' from being able to satisfy the oil-fuelled aspirations of the Scottish electorate. This could lead to disenchantment with the SNP, as just another party unable to fulfil its promises.

The SNP supported devolution as a step to independence; but even this strategy has its SNP opponents who feared that an Assembly would confuse the electorate and compromise the party leaders. In the late 1970s there had been increasingly open conflict within the SNP between the MPs, the NEC and the branches on this and many other issues. The inability of the MPs to use their number to compel concessions from the Labour minority government of 1977 and 1978 was obvious and frustrating. In general, the party in Scotland was more radical on social and economic issues than was the parliamentary group. The NEC and the branches had hoped for more direct democratic accountability of the MPs in their party than they saw in the other parties. For their part, the MPs increasingly demanded the right to act independently. Such conflict on economic issues blurred the SNP's image in Scotland and damaged its morale. Mrs Thatcher's right-wing promises when she led the Conservative opposition made the choice between her party and Labour all the clearer: the SNP could not come down on one side or the other.

These splits contributed to the SNP's loss of electoral support. The first sign of this came in March 1978, when the party failed to capture Garscadden in a by-election. Labour's candidates here, as in two subsequent by-elections in Hamilton and Berwick and East Lothian, were strong pro-devolution men. The SNP's defeats in these contests led many in the party to feel that Labour had stolen its clothes. Labour certainly stole SNP votes.

It was against this background that the SNP campaigned for a 'Yes' vote in the February 1979 devolution referendum campaign. Labour were badly split on the issue and the Conservatives were overwhelmingly in the 'No' camp. More people voted 'Yes' than 'No' (52 per cent to 48 per cent) but the result was so close that it was a considerable moral victory for the 'No' camp. The pro-devolutionists had argued in Parliament for devolution on the ground that the Scottish people were overwhelmingly in favour. The devolution referendum exhausted the SNP and the party's MPs voted with the Conservatives in a subsequent motion of no confidence in the Labour government when Mr Callaghan refused to implement the devolution legislation because the referendum result had been so close.

The subsequent general election in April and May of 1979 was, to some considerable extent, a re-run of 1970. Early SNP advances and threats were not followed through. The argument during the election was about UK economic policy, taxation and control of the unions. The SNP had no distinctive policies on these issues and the party was so demoralised by its defeats of the previous year that it hardly campaigned on a Scottish basis at all. Instead it ran a small campaign in each Scottish constituency. The SNP were bitterly aggrieved by the concentration that the press gave to the Liberal leader and the Liberal Party even though the SNP was much more popular than the Liberal Party in Scotland. In the end, the SNP's share of the vote was reduced to 17 per cent and it lost all but two of its parliamentary seats. Though this was a further blow to party standing, it still performed markedly better than it had in 1970 (when it won 10 per cent of the vote in Scotland) and it retains a considerable branch and constituency organisation.

It is perhaps ironic that the SNP supports reforming the method of election by introducing the alternative vote, while the Conservative and Labour Parties support the 'first-past-the-post' system, for this will make it considerably easier for the SNP to win a majority of seats in any future Assembly. SNP support for a change in electoral procedures emphasises its recognition that Scotland is likely to be a multi-party country for some time to come. The SNP appreciates that a volatile Scottish electorate, faced with at least four parties under a 'first-past-the-post' system, would make elections too much of a lottery and too unstable a base for a new legislature. On the other hand, the present electoral system makes the SNP dream of winning a mandate for independence – 36 seats – more credible. But whatever happens during the next few parliaments, one thing seems clear: Scottish politics are changing fast, and however much some may regret the passing of the two-party competition of the 1950s, the SNP has forced its way into the centre of the arena and there it will remain.

5

Plaid Cymru: the Welsh National Party

Denis Balsom

Nationalism has long been a force in Welsh politics, and since 1925 its cause has been most actively articulated by Plaid Cymru. The party's message, however, made little impact in the wider context of British politics until its dramatic victory in the Carmarthen by-election in July 1966. From that date Plaid Cymru has maintained a vigorous public presence in Wales, but has failed to match the spectacular growth and achievements of its Scottish counterpart – the Scottish National Party.

Nationalist parties vary greatly and can be difficult to locate upon a left–right ideological spectrum. Plaid Cymru's philosophy is an amalgam of conservatism and radicalism,[1] the precise mixture of which has varied over its lifespan as a party. Plaid Cymru's early development was dominated by Saunders Lewis, the Welsh *littérateur*, who may still be regarded as the philosophical father of the party. Yet the party of Saunders Lewis in the 1920s and 1930s is very different from modern Plaid Cymru. Butt Philip notes: 'It is clear that the Welsh Nationalist Party was at the outset essentially intellectual and moral in outlook, and socially conservative. Its principal concerns were the Welsh language, the Welsh identity, and Christianity in Wales.'[2]

This initial outlook followed in a logical progression from that of nineteenth-century Welsh Liberalism. The great Liberal Ministries had passed a great deal of legislation designed to protect the distinctive Welsh way of life, but their achievements had fallen short of the ultimate goal of Welsh radicalism – Home Rule. Plaid Cymru emerged after the First World War to continue this struggle, at a time when the experience of war had thrown into sharp relief the continuing threat to traditional Welsh values and society. Plaid Cymru's philosophy has always reflected a basic humanitarianism, be it in protecting the Welsh language and culture, or in promoting progressive economic policies for the ailing Welsh economy. It is this strange mixture of cultural conservatism and innovative Social Democracy that gives Plaid Cymru its particular hue and its place in contemporary Welsh politics.

Electoral development

The party's first electoral foray was in the 1929 General Election in the Caernarfonshire constituency. The Rev Lewis Valentine polled 609 votes (1.6 per cent); two years later Professor J. E. Daniel was able to increase the Plaid Cymru vote there to 1136 (3 per cent). In 1931 Plaid Cymru also contested the more 'natural' constituency of the University of Wales. Since the party's inception it had been rooted in the university colleges, and within the academic community the appeal of Plaid Cymru's nationalism might have made great inroads; but Saunders Lewis, the leading party figure, could only run second to the Liberal candidate with 914 votes (29.1 per cent). Plaid Cymru policy at this time was heavily orientated towards cultural and linguistic nationalism. The writings of Saunders Lewis indicate the specific philosophical direction of the party; and the events that led up to, and followed on from, Plaid Cymru's most conspicuous direct action – the burning of the bombing school at Penyberth – indicate its practical implementation.

The pre-eminence of cultural concerns for Plaid Cymru was clearly out of place throughout the economic and social turmoils of the inter-war years. Writing in 1937, Professor Daniel suggested: 'It is in the poetry of Taliesin and Dafydd Nanmor, in the ruling conceptions of the ancient laws of Wales, far more than in Special Areas Acts or Five Year programmes that the salvation of Wales is to be found.'[3] Amongst the unemployed of South Wales such a prescription must have appeared very inadequate. The first sign that the party could adopt a more pragmatic line came during two by-election campaigns

in 1945. As the period was still officially covered by the war-time
electoral truce, Plaid Cymru had an opportunity to poll well. The
principal issue of the campaign was the post-war reconstruction of the
Welsh economy, and Plaid Cymru pursued this point to the exclusion
of linguistic and cultural concerns. This marked a significant depar-
ture. Butt Philip notes 'The ease with which the Blaid adapted its
platform to meet the situation was indicative of the future developments in the party . . .'[4]

Gwynfor Evans also assumed the leadership of the party in 1945. A
total contrast to Saunders Lewis, Evans appeared a much likelier
candidate to lead Plaid Cymru to the forefront of Welsh politics.

The late 1940s and early 1950s saw Plaid Cymru involved in two
public campaigns. Firstly, it organised a mass petition advocating
equal validity for the English and Welsh languages, and, secondly,
took part in the Parliament for Wales Campaign. This latter campaign, modelled upon the Scottish Covenant, collected 250,000 signatures between 1954 and 1956. Both campaigns were non-partisan in
the sense that support was drawn from a broad spectrum of the
electorate, and were successful in terms of the number of signatures
gained on the petitions. The Parliament for Wales Campaign suffered, however, from poor support amongst MPs; only six out of the
thirty-six supported S. O. Davies' Parliament for Wales Bill, and this
undoubtedly enabled the government to ignore the petition. The
experience of these public campaigns seems to have reinforced Plaid
Cymru's commitment to working alone and through conventional
electoral politics.

In 1950 the party fought seven seats, retained its deposit in
Caernarfon and only just failed to do so in Merioneth. The 1951
election saw only four Plaid Cymru candidates, the reduction being
due to financial difficulties incurred during the 1950 campaign. Since
1951 the party has fought every by-election in Wales with considerably better results than in the corresponding general-election campaigns in the same constituencies.[5] This build-up of successes at
by-elections and a larger share of the vote in 1955 led to an expectation of greater success in 1959. This expectation was further heightened by the great demonstration of popular opinion hostile to the
flooding of Cwm Tryweryn to form a reservoir serving Merseyside.

Although twenty candidates were put into the field in 1959, the
hoped-for breakthrough never came. This disappointment contributed to internal tension, the outcome of which was a major reorgan-

isation and some shift in emphasis on major policy issues. These developments in Plaid Cymru need to be seen against the backdrop of British party politics at that time. The Labour Party had been denied electoral success since 1951, the clashes between the Bevanites and the leadership had reverberated throughout the 1950s, and the Clause IV debate had broached the whole question of the party rank and file's relationship with the parliamentary elite. These issues could not be overlooked in Wales, for not only were many of the leading personalities Welshmen, but the party relied heavily upon its support in Wales during times of Conservative government. Plaid Cymru's reassessment reflected these changes and offered a more rational, pragmatic approach to its electoral prospects.

Within Plaid Cymru there emerged a younger, more radical group, which sought to promote the party in industrial South Wales as well as in the traditional Welsh-speaking areas of the North and West. They were much more concerned about economic and social matters than their predecessors, and strove to de-emphasise, but not abandon, the party's commitment to the culture and language. These trends generated considerable divisions within the party, but Plaid Cymru's development and subsequent transformation into a more radical Social Democratic party undoubtedly grew from this basic realignment on policy issues.[6] The process was also aided by the formation of *Cymdeithas Yr Iaith Gymraeg* (The Welsh Language Society). This group was formed at a Plaid Cymru summer school, but drew its inspiration from a radio lecture given by Saunders Lewis entitled *Tynged yr Iaith* (The Fate of the Language). In his lecture Saunders Lewis maintained that the preservation of the language was of higher priority than the pursuit of self-government. Moreover, he emphasised that the language issue must be used as a political weapon regardless of whether it brought self-government in its wake:

> To revive the Welsh language in Wales is nothing less than a revolution. Success can only come through revolutionary methods. Perhaps the language would bring self-government in its wake; I cannot tell. The language is more important than self-government. In my opinion, if we were to have any sort of self-government for Wales before the Welsh language is recognised and used as an official language in all the administration of state and local authority in the Welsh areas of our country, it would never attain official status, and the doom of the language would come more quickly than it will come under English Government.[7]

The implications and consequences of Saunders Lewis's lecture were of profound importance to Plaid Cymru. The formation of *Cymdeithas Yr Iaith* meant that the party's role as guardian of the culture and language was now shared; and, moreover, *Cymdeithas* could mount the militant unconventional action deemed necessary to make the language a political issue. In turn the South Wales Social Democrats within the party were able to claim a higher priority for their programmes and initiatives because the language issue was being fought elsewhere. Another important factor which eased pressure on Plaid Cymru was *Cymdeithas'* policy of blatantly breaking the law.[8] Plaid Cymru's obvious lack of electoral success, and its impotence in cases such as Tryweryn, had led to some pressure to abandon its wholly constitutional approach and take up direct action, even violence. The advocates of such action were always defeated in the Annual Conferences, but the fact that such pressures could be diffused by the activities of *Cymdeithas* undoubtedly helped to contain this potentially dangerous situation for Plaid Cymru.

The two organisations moved along, sometimes in parallel, sometimes interwoven and sometimes at odds until about 1970. There were moments of embarrassment for Plaid Cymru when the sons and daughters of prominent members appeared in court; equally, there was frustration for *Cymdeithas* in what they saw as a devaluation of the language issue in Plaid Cymru's programme. The general elections of 1964 and 1966 had again proved disappointing for Plaid Cymru. Its total vote had declined from its 1959 level, and no seat looked winnable. There had also been the humiliation of Elystan Morgan's victory for Labour in Cardigan in 1966 only a few months after he had resigned from Plaid Cymru following his defeat for the Vice-presidency. Yet within four months of the 1966 election, party morale was totally transformed by Gwynfor Evans' capture of the Carmarthen seat.

It is impossible to overestimate the psychological lift given to the party by the Carmarthen success. Plaid Cymru assumed an importance in national politics far in excess of that warranted by a party with one MP. Gwynfor Evans became the 'Member for Wales', as had the first Liberal MP of an earlier radical generation, and the House of Commons gave Plaid Cymru a perfect forum from which to promote its case. In his first period as an MP Gwynfor Evans exploited this opportunity, and put down hundreds of questions to the Government. Parliamentary activities automatically generate publicity and, particularly in Wales, the regionally based media are quick to exploit any aspect of 'Welsh affairs'. It seems too, that the experience of Westminster made Plaid Cymru aware of some of its own shortcomings. In particular, Gwynfor Evans appeared to broaden his outlook and concentrate upon the economic affairs that were the principal concern of the party as a whole. The requirement of 'servicing' an MP at Westminster created difficulties the party had not faced before, and gave rise to an important development – the formation of the Research Group. This group contained many of the party's 'Young Lions', and within the next three years was to dominate policy making within the party.

The cumulative effect of these developments, together with the massive recruitment that followed the Carmarthen victory, put the party into the foreground of Welsh politics. As a political machine, Plaid Cymru developed to a fine art the by-election 'Blitzkrieg' – intensive campaigning with mass canvasses, motorcades and jingles. This technique was demonstrated during the by-election campaigns in Rhondda West and Caerphilly. Here, in areas that had been bastions of Labour strength, Plaid Cymru demonstrated its ability to win over the Labour voters. But, on the basis of subsequent election results in these constituencies, it is difficult to avoid the conclusion that the by-election breakthroughs failed to make a lasting impression. It may be, however, that by-elections serve the more important functions of providing a stimulant, breaking traditional loyalties and creating party organisations. As such, the long-term effects of these results may be seen over a number of years rather than in comparison with the next set of election results. In the short term, however, the political initiative appeared to have passed to Plaid Cymru, which was in effect determining the agenda of Welsh politics, whilst the other parties struggled to produce a response to this new threat.

The Investiture of the Prince of Wales in 1969 created an interesting dilemma within Plaid Cymru. The event proved to be immensely popular amongst the population of Wales, and thus Plaid Cymru could hardly criticise it too fiercely; equally their traditional ideology prevented them from joining the festivities. This ambiguity may have slowed the momentum that Plaid Cymru had established in the aftermath of the Carmarthen by-election. The 1970 election thus became the crucial test to see whether or not Plaid Cymru had the potential to fulfil its promise and ambitions.

At that election Plaid Cymru gained over 175,000 votes – 11.5 per cent of the poll. This represented its best-ever performance, and yet the results were still seen by many to be a major disappointment. Gwynfor Evans lost his seat at Carmarthen and the Labour majorities were restored to something approaching their former magnitude in the Rhondda and Caerphilly. The election post-mortems produced recriminations, and much attention focused upon the role of *Cymdeithas Yr Iaith*. The Society's concerted activity and public demonstrations had, it was claimed, seriously damaged the image and credibility of the party. Indeed, Gwynfor Evans' daughter, Meinir, had been sent to prison as the result of one *Cymdeithas* demonstration. Perhaps, too, the Investiture, by emphasising the Union and the monarchy, had weakened the party's public standing to a greater extent than had been imagined. Even worse perhaps was the possibility that the party's recent successes in the 1966–70 period had merely been a protest phenomenon and a reaction to a very unpopular Labour government.

The anticlimax of the 1970 election was quickly relieved by Plaid Cymru's success in the Merthyr Tydfil by-election. The 1970 general election result had demonstrated Plaid Cymru's poor standing in the constituency, and the traditional by-election phenomenon of an anti-government swing would no longer be of advantage to Plaid Cymru, but might go instead to the Labour Party. Plaid Cymru conducted a lively campaign, and, though denied victory, demonstrated their continuing ability to compete with Labour in Labour's own traditional territory – the solidly working-class valley seats.

The early 1970s thus remained a frustrating time for Plaid Cymru. Its greatest asset, an MP, had been lost; and there was no further series of by-elections to maintain its 'bandwagon' advance, as there had been in the late 1960s. Its record in local government elections remained patchy, though success at such levels fails to capture the public's imagination in the same way as parliamentary contests. But Cymdeithas Yr Iaith continued to dominate the language issue, thus allowing Plaid Cymru to concentrate upon substantive social and economic issues.

The comparatively sudden announcement of the February 1974 election presented Plaid Cymru with a difficult situation. Mr Heath appeared determined to fight the election on the issue of the unions versus the government. Such an issue offered little prospect for Plaid Cymru; it was not closely identified with either side, and although the party had hoped to extend its support in South Wales, such an issue was likely to polarise opinion in communities where organised

Labour is traditionally so strong. Potential defectors from the Labour
Party thus faced an even greater crisis of conscience. Countering this
difficulty was the fact that the Labour Party had yet to re-establish
itself fully, and recover from the unpopularity it had gained during its
period of office. The by-elections held during the Heath administration had shown a considerable swing away from the government, but
the Labour Party had not been the beneficiary – the usual perk of
opposition status.[9]

The results for February 1974 again showed mixed fortunes for
Plaid Cymru; it won its first ever Parliamentary seats at a general
election, Caernarfon and Merioneth, but Gwynfor Evans failed by
three votes to recapture Carmarthen. Elsewhere, however, little
progress was made; in the seats of the famous by-election campaigns –
Caerphilly, Rhondda and Merthyr – further ground was lost to the
Labour Party. The total vote was less than in 1970, at 171,374, 10.7
per cent of the poll. The election of the two MPs from Gwynedd
masked what might have been interpreted as worrying signs in the
results. The subsequent election in October 1974 produced similar
results. Again the circumstances were perhaps not to Plaid Cymru's
best advantage – a minority Labour government appealing for a
mandate to continue in office. A traditional Labour area such as
South Wales could hardly let such a call go unheeded. The results
showed a consolidation of Plaid Cymru's position, with Gwynfor
Evans being elected for Carmarthen after a massive effort by the party
in the constituency. This success, together with increased majorities
for the MPs in Caernarfon and Merioneth, again perhaps masked
worrying results and trends elsewhere.

There can be no doubt, however, that with the elections of 1974
Plaid Cymru finally 'arrived'. The years of minority government up
to the election of 1979 gave all the small parties enhanced status. Yet
the suspicion remains that Plaid Cymru's successes have been built
upon shallow foundations. The events of early 1979 demonstrated
this fallibility only too well. On 1 March, St David's Day, the
referendum was held on whether or not the provisions of the Wales
Act, the Government's proposals for devolution to Wales, should be
implemented. Plaid Cymru, after some initial misgivings, campaigned vigorously for a 'Yes' vote. The pro-Assembly lobby consisted of the official Labour Party, the Wales TUC, the Liberals and
Plaid Cymru. As in the EEC referendum campaign, Plaid Cymru
benefited greatly from this common front.[10] Yet, in many areas, the
'Yes' campaign was totally dependent upon local nationalist strength

and organisation. The result of the referendum, a 'No' vote of some 80 per cent of the poll, was a crushing defeat. Plaid Cymru blamed the lack of commitment of some of their allies, whilst others blamed the failure upon suspicion of the nationalists' motives. In any event, development towards any form of self-determination in Wales was put back many years.

A direct consequence of the devolution referenda in Wales and Scotland was the fall of the Labour government in March. The resultant general election was scheduled to coincide with the district council elections on 3 May; a synchronisation that did not augur well for Plaid Cymru. In 1976 the party had made substantial gains in the local government elections, winning control of Merthyr Borough Council and forming the largest party on the Rhymney Valley Council.[11] These results were both the product of assiduous party work and the customary mid-term reaction to the party of government. 1979 did not proffer such good omens. The Labour Party had bitterly resented the loss of control of these Valley authorities and fought a long campaign to discredit the new administrations. Also, the parallel general election campaign emphasised national issues at the expense of local concerns, increased the turn-out on election day and generally strengthened the Labour Party's hand. All these factors were borne out in the results; in Merthyr alone, Plaid Cymru lost some fourteen seats to the Labour Party.

The general election also presented Plaid Cymru with a great challenge. Their small parliamentary group had controversially supported the government in the crucial confidence debate on 29 March. For the first time they could defend their record in terms of real achievements and concessions wrung from the government. The party contested all 36 seats, including Cardiff West held by the Speaker, and in the event polled some 130,000 votes – 8.1 per cent of the poll. It was their poorest election result since 1966. Merioneth and Caernarfon were retained but Gwynfor Evans lost Carmarthen to the Labour Party. Elsewhere, the party lost further ground in South Wales and has yet to prove its ability to poll consistently outside the strongly Welsh-speaking areas of rural Wales.

Plaid Cymru has thus established itself as part of the Welsh electoral scene, yet its experience suggests that its goals will never be achieved through the ballot box. If the focus of political competition was ever shifted to a wholly Welsh tier of government then Plaid Cymru might compete equally, and more successfully, with the other parties. Whilst electoral competition and success remain focused on

Westminster there would appear to be little long-term hope of competing with the powerful attraction of national British political parties in an increasingly integrated community.

Party ideology

Plaid Cymru is a self-confessed nationalist party, but such a label does not provide an exact enough description of the ideological direction of the party to allow one to make intuitive assumptions as to its motives and ambitions. As the literature on nationalism indicates, the term has been used to justify a multitude of causes and movements. Definitions abound; but their components can be reduced to rather simpler elements. These elements include the loyalty of an individual to some social or political group, be it family, tribe, nation, state or race; the idea that collectivity perceives itself as a nation, distinct from all others; and the personnel required to mobilise the idea as a political force, be this through an elite, a class or a genuine mass movement.

The particular thrust of Welsh nationalism as expressed by Plaid Cymru can be placed within such a broad definition of nationalism. The concept of loyalty is complex: Birch suggests that group loyalty can be focused upon language and culture, obviously relevant in the Welsh case; but more normally (and perhaps more potently), 'based on a feeling of social unity that has developed over many centuries, although . . . peoples [may be] of varied ethnic origin and follow more than one religion'.[12] Such feelings are perhaps not foremost in the minds of most Welshmen. The idea, that Wales is a nation, is also not universally held. Birch notes that the concept of nationhood involves both social relationships and political beliefs and institutions, but most realistically 'is a society which either enjoys statehood or formerly enjoyed statehood or aspires to statehood'.[13] In the Welsh case only the last condition can be satisfied, and then only in the minds of a small percentage of the population. The final element requires the mobilisation of a nationalist movement; here, too, the Welsh position is ambiguous. Plaid Cymru cannot claim to have a monopoly on the affiliation of those claiming to be nationalistically inclined. It has, however, in more recent times been the most successful group articulating the nationalist cause. Plaid Cymru is not a mass party, and it is doubtful whether it ever will be. Because of these ambiguities, many of the basic issues along which nationalist opinion might consolidate are divisive within Wales – none more so than the Welsh language, an article of faith for Plaid Cymru yet spoken by only one-fifth of the population. It is upon such fragmented foundations that Plaid Cymru has attempted to build its electoral strength, and to date with only mixed success.

The Plaid Cymru membership card pledges those joining the party to pursue three objectives:

1. to secure self-government for Wales;
2. to safeguard the culture, language, traditions and economic life in Wales;
3. to secure for Wales the right to become a member of the United Nations.

In pursuit of these objectives the party has also adopted other basic elements in its ideology. The party is constitutional, decentralist, co-operative, Social Democratic and non-violent, and the pursuit of self-government is sought within these parameters. It is these factors that give Plaid Cymru's nationalist ideology its distinctive character; it is these factors also that Plaid Cymru wishes to promote to overcome a long-standing 'British' reaction to nationalism. Hence Gwynfor Evans writes: 'It has been something of a tragedy for Wales that fascists and imperialists and racialists should virtually have taken over the word nationalist by the time Plaid Cymru had begun to campaign to any purpose.'[14] And elswhere:

> . . . the evils attributed by anti-nationalists to nationalism are more properly attributable to imperialism. . . . The heart of the kind of nationalism found in Northern Europe is the effort 'fully to develop the nation's moral and material resources' – which was Masaryk's description of nationalism. This responsible development of the cultural economic life in a historic community is a far cry from imperialism. . . . The one cherishes the life of the community, the other exalts the power of the state.[15]

Central to the party's pursuit of nationalism is the concept of non-violence. The creed of non-violence was adopted by Saunders Lewis in the party's first-ever document, and is constantly being reiterated by Gwynfor Evans: 'If I thought violence could ever be justified in the pursuit of any social objective it would be to secure

freedom and full nationhood for Wales . . . But even this noble cause
. . . does not . . . justify the use of violence.'[16]

Plaid Cymru ideology maintains that it was the pursuit of material-
ism (often itself violent) that deprived the ancient nations of their
freedom; and that only a return to a state of greater moral and
spiritual awareness can regain for Wales her freedom. It is freedom
that Saunders Lewis wanted rather than independence:

> . . . let us not ask for independence for Wales. Not because it is
> impractial, but because it is not worth having . . . it is materialistic
> and cruel, leading to violence, oppression and ideas already proved
> to be bad. The age of empires is fast passing, and afterwards there
> will be no meaning or value in independence. Europe will return to
> its place when the countries recognise they are all subjects and
> dependent. If this does not come to be, Wales for her part may be
> content to recognise the supremacy of England. That is not the
> greatest evil. Let us recall what it was like between the thirteenth
> and sixteenth centuries. Today we too can build a Welsh civiliza-
> tion without independence.[17]

If this view appears naïve and romantic it is notable that similar
sentiments still appear in some of Plaid Cymru's more recent works.
Saunders Lewis himself has admitted that the struggle for freedom
may provoke violence, but he maintains, in neo-Gandhian fashion,
that those who suffer must be the Welsh freedom fighters.[18]

This rather sophisticated argument developed by Saunders Lewis
and Gwynfor Evans, of freedom not independence and a return to the
spiritual values and the precepts of Christianity, is somehow uncon-
vincing as a political ideology. Its ideal society extols the virtues that
are accredited to the Welsh language and culture:

> Where Welsh is alive and vigorous, there you will find flourishing
> local eisteddfodau, literary meetings, reading classes, singing
> schools and an admirable interest in literature and music. And
> wherever Welsh declines, and the English way of life and language
> replace it, there these things degenerate, and one finds football
> matches, races, billiards clubs and the cinema, and if there is any
> class at all held under the aegis of the colleges, it will more than
> likely be a class in economics.[19]

Yet from its earliest days Plaid Cymru has acknowledged the

essential interdependence of the nation states, and its call for freedom within a 'Britannic Confederation' reflects this philosophy as well as the reality of the electorate's fear of independence. The input of a more practial political theory can be traced especially to Dr D. J. Davies. Just as Saunders Lewis spoke principally of the cultural side of Welsh nationalism, D. J. Davies produced the party policies on economic and industrial matters.[20] This focus automatically confronted Plaid Cymru with the problems and concerns of industrial South Wales and to those of Welshmen who spoke no Welsh. D. J. Davies was a declared socialist and this strain of thought, with its emphasis upon co-operative democracy, has always remained central within the party.

The realities of the political contest have had their effect upon the ideology of the party. It has been noted how the language issue has sometimes been 'dropped' at by-elections; an increasing pragmatism has also been noted. Rather than being seen as a compromise with first principles, this flexibility is perhaps a sign of political maturity. At a time of increasing political violence throughout the world and through a period of escalation in the general norms of protest, Plaid Cymru has clung to its commitment to non-violence. Moreover, the party has remained wholly constitutional in outlook since Gwynfor Evans took over the presidency in 1945. Before that date the party had been associated with a major incident of illegal direct action that both helped and hindered its embryonic development. In 1936 Saunders Lewis, the Rev Lewis Valentine and D. J. Williams set fire to the RAF Bombing School of Penyberth on the Lleyn peninsula. The incident was carefully staged to avoid any danger to human life and the three party members, though claiming to be acting solely as individuals, duly gave themselves up at Pwllheli Police Station. Their subsequent trial focused attention upon the party and the nationalist cause; the number of applications for membership increased markedly, yet there can be little doubt that the action also set many minds against the 'National Party of Wales'.

Saunders Lewis used the trial as a platform from which to propagate his personal ideology. There was considerable sympathy for the substance of the protest but not for its form. In selecting the Lleyn for its bombing school, central government had shown remarkable insensitivity to local opinion. The first trial in Caernarfon was inconclusive; it was then transferred, amidst much protest, to the Old Bailey, where the three were found guilty, committed to Wormwood Scrubs and to pride of place in party mythology.

Given this spectacular antecedent, it is even more surprising that Plaid Cymru has kept to the constitutional path. There have been incidents of violence, explosions, even deaths in the name of Welsh nationalism since that time, but Plaid Cymru has always dissociated itself from those concerned. In doing so, the party has laid itself open to the charge of inactivity and impotence. John Jenkins, a convicted extremist wrote:

> ... the leaders of Plaid Cymru are prepared to accept the loss of Wales itself as the price for their respectability. They seem to believe that because what they want is right and what their opponents want is wrong, that they will automatically get it. I would suggest that they put the Bible down and study their history books, particularly the British Empire parts. Even their Biblical knowledge is very biased and partisan – had they made rather less of Job, then I would not have had to make more of David.[21]

In particular, the flooding of the Tryweryn valley in the 1950s created particular pressures for Plaid Cymru. In the face of almost total opposition from within Wales, the scheme was pushed through by government. Nothing seemed to illustrate Plaid Cymru's impotence more greatly, and there followed a series of explosions on the site.

The establishment of *Cymdeithas Yr Iaith* in 1962 placed Plaid Cymru in a similar dilemma. The members of *Cymdeithas* were committed to break the law in their pursuit of more equitable linguistic policies. Initially *Cymdeithas* appeared fairly close to Plaid Cymru, but after 1969 and the escalation in their protest methods the connection became increasingly embarrassing for the party. And yet, in its attraction for young people and for those less committed to the constitutional road, there can be no doubt that *Cymdeithas* provided a 'safety-valve' for pressures that would have increased within Plaid Cymru.

Traditionally, Plaid Cymru ideology could be described as Christian, non-violent, and culturally and linguistically orientated. Their opponents have often been able to label them 'teachers, preachers and poets'; a new wave of Plaid Cymru leaders and activists, however, has altered the ideological thrust somewhat. The influence achieved by the Research Group in the late 1960s was instrumental here. The election of Plaid Cymru's first MP in 1966 served to concentrate the collective mind of the party, and far more policy studies were initiated. Foremost of these was the economic plan published in 1970. In formulating these policies the natural focus of attention had been the small, successful nations of Europe, such as Switzerland and the Scandinavian countries. There was also the influence of Leopold Kohr and Ernst Schumacher, extolling the virtues of intermediate economies and the view that 'small is beautiful'.[22] The section of the party most attracted by these theories can be termed 'modernist', and this section has come to play an increasingly important role in the party.

Thus Plaid Cymru today would present itself as a 'radical' party, and as such follows in a long Welsh (Liberal) tradition; it is humanitarian, even socialistic. Its nationalism is thus open, flexible and modern in standing as a bulwark against the growing evils of 'bigness', be it in the form of the state or of the large corporations, yet traditional in its defence of the Welsh culture and language. The electoral situation in Wales has perhaps given a greater thrust to the 'left' of the party, in that votes have had to be won from Labour, yet the party remains broadly consensual around the aims of the movement rather than strictly ideological.

Party organisation

Plaid Cymru is a firm believer in the value of good political organisation. For many years its day-to-day strategy has meant maintaining a public presence out of all proportion to its true size and influence. This strategy was sustained in the country at large by the diligence of the early Plaid Cymru officials. As the party has grown stronger, so the organisation has expanded and currently represents the most advanced and sophisticated political machine operating in Wales.

The basic unit of party organisation is the *Cangen* (branch), of which there are some 350. The minimum membership of a branch is twenty, and its primary function is the raising of funds for the party's national effort. Delegates from the various branches constitute the membership of the *Y Gynhadledd* (the conference), the highest authority within the party. The key level of party organisation, however, is the *Pwyllgor Etholaeth* (constituency committee). Plaid Cymru maintains constituency organisations in all thirty-six parliamentary divisions of Wales, whereas the concentration of branches is less even and less well distributed. The most important function at constituency level is campaigning at parliamentary elections, and, as the party is committed to contesting all Welsh seats, this task has acted as an organisational catalyst in areas of weakness. To organise and co-ordinate its attack upon local government, Plaid Cymru maintains eight provincial councils (*Cyngor Talaith*). The effectiveness of these bodies varies across the country, but constitutionally their position is fairly powerful; should four of the regional representatives oppose a motion at National Executive Council level, they constitute an automatic veto.

At national level there are three significant party bodies – the National Executive Council (*Pwyllgor Gwaith Cenedlaethol*), the National Council (*Cyngor Cenedlaethol*) and the Conference. The Conference maintains the absolute policy-making function, whilst the National Council is responsible for the implementation of conference decisions, deciding policy when Conference is not in session, and to allow lengthier policy debates than are feasible at the Annual Conference. The remaining National Executive Council is the heart of the party. The executive is in charge of the whole organisation of the party and its committees act on the resolutions of Conference or the National Council.

The formality of the constitution needs to be placed in the context of everyday events and the *de facto* working of the party. There is no doubt that, for much of the party's history, the only effective body was the National Executive Committee; 'due to the limited supply of political experience power became heavily concentrated in the NEC'.[23] The party in the country was largely a revenue-raising organisation to support the political work of the Executive and the Central Office.

The great change came with Plaid Cymru's electoral breakthrough in the late 1960s. Subsequently, new branches, particularly in South Wales, began playing a more prominent political role. Once branches began fighting local elections, they made the transition from being providers of resources to being consumers of resources. Of course this was only the case when the candidate stood in the party's name. The long-standing tradition in North and West Wales has been for local councillors to stand as Independents without any overt party support. Indeed, quite well known members of Plaid Cymru, such as W. R. P. George (Caernarfonshire) and H. H. Roberts (Cardiganshire), have been very active as local council leaders, but always as Independents. The recent local election results confirm this trend for the rural areas to be dominated by Independents. This division between the South, North and West clearly created some tension within the party, and Tanner notes the more overt political involvement of the South Wales branches in using the Annual Conference. There has been perhaps a slight correcting of this position in recent years, with very active political groups emerging in the North West (especially the groups associated with Dafydd Iwan and *Tai Gwynedd*).

The role of selecting parliamentary candidates gives the constituency committees an important position, and, more importantly, a considerable responsibility. Since 1970, when the party first fought all the Welsh seats, this function has given purpose to constituency committees in even the most unpromising seats. This policy of fighting on a broad front has not always been unanimously accepted and, indeed, has committed the party to some rather undistinguished candidates. In February 1974 the Swansea West constituency nominated Derrick Hearne as candidate; he polled 3.6 per cent of the vote but subsequent to the election published a volume of his 'political thought'.[24] The content of this book, together with his role as a 'military adviser' for a Middle Eastern state, led to considerable embarrassment for the party, and was only resolved when the NEC expelled Hearne, even though they had, presumably, endorsed his candidature a few months earlier.

The concentration of comparatively few individuals in the upper echelons of the party has been seen as a weakness in Plaid Cymru, and the creation of the *Talaith* Councils, with their powerful position on the executive, was perhaps a conscious attempt to broaden the base of the executive and of the leadership in general. The National Executive Committee remains powerful in the absence of a large parliamentary party or Assembly party. Should either of these groups materialise, then one might expect tension to emerge between the NEC and these external groupings of the party. The National Council also appears to live somewhat in the shadow of the NEC, though its constitutional functions certainly give it an important role in policymaking. In 1976 the Annual Report noted that the NC had debated devolution, education, and industrial democracy. Indeed, a special paper on education was presented to Conference that year, and industrial democracy was a major issue on the agenda. The devolution debate provides an interesting example of the position of the National Council. When the major White Paper was published in 1975, the Plaid Cymru MPs at Westminster gave a characteristically cautious welcome. On their return to Wales at the weekend the National Council discussed the issue and resolved to oppose the White Paper, which the MPs then did.

A recent innovation has been the creation of three sub-committees of the NEC: Strategy and Policy, Finance and Organisation, and Liaison. The Liaison Committee is especially interesting, as it acknowledges the need for the various wings of the party – parliamentary, those in local government, and the central party organisation – to keep in close contact and to maintain as far as possible a common front on policy. In particular, some of the leading councillors have felt the dilemma of working, at a time of decreasing local expenditure, to maintain and protect a system with which they fundamentally disagree. As the party gets closer to the points of real power, these problems can only increase, but the committee has not been a success.

The constitutional figurehead of the party, the Annual Conference, is, as in other parties, a managed affair. Its function is primarily that of an annual rally rather than a policy-making forum. The programme is very tightly packed; interventions from the platform carry great weight; and the whole proceedings are dominated by comparatively few individuals – the NEC and the leaders of the half dozen leading constituency committees. The Conference is given extensive coverage on Welsh television, a factor that may inhibit lively and heated debate.

To conclude this section on organisation, the picture that emerges is of a centralised party structure where real influence lies in the hands of relatively few people. In the past, events conspired to force Plaid Cymru to operate in this manner to preserve the image of a truly 'national' party. Now that this status has been achieved, the old methods and traditions are perhaps unsuitable, and efforts are now being made to decentralise the party organisation. Yet because of its strong central bodies, the party is able to maintain a very vigorous public presence and exert an influence out of all proportion to its size, electoral strength or current electoral potential. The Central Office now employs nineteen full-time officials. These are deployed at the main office and around the country. The party has also managed to mobilise considerable financial support. In the summer of 1977 an appeal was launched for £45,000 to purchase a new headquarters in Cardiff. The money was raised by October, 80 per cent having been collected in the first six weeks of the appeal. The party income and expenditure accounts show a heavy dependence upon the annual St

David's Day Appeal to cover the increasing day-to-day costs of the party; in 1976 this Appeal raised some £40,000. Plaid Cymru confonts its opponents in Wales with considerable professionalism and a campaigning ability that belies its small size.

The party in action

The Plaid Cymru parliamentary group has never had an opportunity to play a very important role at Westminster. Gwynfor Evans sat alone for the 1966–70 period, he lost his seat in February 1974 but rejoined Dafydd Elis Thomas and Dafydd Wigley in the October 1974–9 Parliament. The last election saw the party reduced to two members again, which together with the two members re-elected for the SNP may revive ideas of greater co-operation between the two parties. Plaid Cymru MPs have always been noted for their diligence, frequently asking more questions than any other member in a session. They have also generally supported the Labour government on policy questions as well as in the crucial divisions that sustained the Callaghan minority government until March 1979. Yet none of the MPs has ever appeared to be at home in the Palace of Westminster. The loss of the Welsh Assembly came as a great blow, for all three would have preferred to seek election to a body in Cardiff. Plaid Cymru's experience in London has brought success as a pressure group, and to secure particular demands the MPs quickly developed the Westminster skills of vote-trading and bargaining. Yet London can never be the focus of the party's activities and the MPs remain fairly isolated, the Parliamentary Research Officer being based in Cardiff and the MPs having only the support of their joint secretary. Ideologically Plaid Cymru needs consciously to reject the institution of Westminster. Winning parliamentary elections is not the prime goal of most committed activists – it is a necessary stage in the pursuit of their higher objectives. Westminster and Whitehall are not the fount of their ambitions – as they are for politicians from the major parties – but the source of their denial. Plaid Cymru has always accepted that the road to a Welsh state would be a very long one. The interim danger is that MPs and other elected officials become neutered and institutionalised by the routines and conventions of political bodies with which they ultimately have little affinity.

The presence of Plaid Cymru at Westminster must be equated with its goal of a self-governing Wales. Although the party has fought

elections since its inception, the role of those elected in bringing about
the ultimate aim has remained unspecified. The example of Sinn Fein
suggested that elected members should boycott Westminster and sit
in exile, though this would sacrifice the obvious short-term gains of
publicity and a participatory role in national affairs. The essential
danger remains that in becoming caught up in day-to-day events the
elected representatives would lose sight of their eventual aim. Party
policy remains the following: 'As soon as the people of Wales decide,
by giving Plaid Cymru a majority of seats and votes in a general
election, that they want a Parliament of their own, the Plaid Cymru
parliamentary party in Westminster will introduce before the House
of Commons a Parliament for Wales Bill.'[25] This rather simple
scenario belies the intense hostility that such a measure would
engender. A more realistic strategy sees the eventual release from
Westminster coming through those bodies controlled by Plaid Cymru
increasingly acting *ultra vires*. In any event Plaid Cymru appears to be
some way from having to face the decision of forcing the break with
Westminster.

In local government the party's performance has been rather
mixed. It has had only limited experience, though since 1976 it has
controlled Merthyr District Council and has been the largest group in
the Rhymney Valley.[26] In the North and West, despite an increased
effort to get candidates to declare themselves, the Independent
tradition is still strong. This has not diluted Plaid Cymru's influence
on these councils, and until very recently has probably helped. The
best example is in Gwynedd, where all council proceedings are
bilingual, simultaneous translation facilities are available, and great
emphasis is placed upon the Welsh language and education. When
Gwynedd Education Committee met to decide how to spend money
allocated to mark the Queen's Silver Jubilee, it decided, rather than
issuing Jubilee crowns and mugs, or even nationalistic atlases or
history books, as many counties did, to mark the occasion by hiring
six additional Welsh-language teachers.

In South Wales the party's emphasis is upon 'good government'.
Plaid Cymru councillors have tried to develop a name as effective
representatives, and the long running local government corruption
cases, involving many Labour councillors, have not harmed Plaid
Cymru's advance.[27] The party has been acutely conscious of the risks
of campaigning at local government level. At a time of financial
stringency and cut-backs in services, the controlling party has diffi-

culty in demonstrating its ability, and a poor record in the eyes of the local electorate may damage its long-term prospects. In an attempt to combat this potential trouble, the Merthyr Council, led by Emrys Roberts, has developed several programmes designed to offer an alternative strategy for resource-starved councils. In housing the council 'sponsored' and encouraged the creation of many new Housing Associations, for which public money was still available when the Council Housing Account was frozen. Similarly the Council has initiated its own advance factory schemes and utilised the Job Creation Scheme in efforts to make use of all possible sources of income.

A recurrent problem has been the lack of experienced political personnel. This has been demonstrated most acutely at local government level, where many inexperienced and unlikely candidates have suddenly found themselves elected councillors. Mistakes made are vigorously exploited by the Labour Party. When Plaid Cymru has fought on an 'end corruption' ticket, it is very embarrassing to find a Blaid councillor on the Housing Committee allocating himself a council house, as happened in Merthyr. Yet local government must remain an essential proving ground for prospective parliamentary candidates and for establishing the party's credibility in administration.

Plaid Cymru had hoped that the great forum for future political debate and activity in Wales would have been the Welsh Assembly. Although many in the party were uncertain as to the degree of support that should be given to the government's proposals in the referendum campaign, none doubted the political capital to be exploited in the Cardiff Assembly had it been established. Plaid Cymru can successfully compete at a Wales level; it is in the context of national British politics that its inability to match the major parties is most exposed. At by-elections, Plaid Cymru has challenged both the size and longevity of established traditions and succeeded because the focus is essentially local. At general elections, however, the principal campaign is fought in the media between the two major parties and their leading personalities. Most of Wales is not distinct or isolated enough for this wave of homogenising forces to be resisted.

The defeat of the Assembly proposals, the loss of control in the local authorities and their general decline in the 1979 general election raise fundamental questions for Plaid Cymru. The goal at Westminster had been to secure a Welsh Assembly, but the referendum has dashed all hopes of this for many years. The experience of local government administration, whilst useful to the party, has also proved thankless. Voting habits in local elections tend to be of a cyclical nature and not necessarily accumulative. The problem thus remains of how to sustain the party and, in broader terms, the nationalist movement in unsympathetic times. It is to this problem that Plaid Cymru must address itself; for some activists the necessity of a political response to the decline of the language is cause enough to continue. For others, and in the long term it is the essential majority, the realisation of real political power remains the crucial means of sustaining their nationalism.

Conclusions

For much of its history Plaid Cymru can perhaps best be described as having been a pressure group, promoting the Welsh language, emphasising Welsh consciousness and generally safeguarding the conscience of the nation. Since 1966, however, the party has developed in a more genuinely political sense, and the decline of the two-party system within the UK as a whole has given the party added significance. Yet it is still possible to view it as a house of cards with very little substance. The pattern of the party's performance at the 1979 general election shows the overall weakness of the electoral position; polls of over 20 per cent were only achieved in four constituencies. Yet the party's public presence is far more significant; Plaid Cymru believes in good organisation, it tends to outmanoeuvre its opponents in the field, and its large, full-time staff is extremely capable and professional.

Major problems remain, however. The language, the most obvious badge of Welshness and the most common correlate of Plaid Cymru voting, is still a divisive issue amongst much of the Welsh electorate. Even so, there appears to be something of a revival of the language within the party. This seems to be a product of several factors. The availability of simultaneous translation facilities at Conference and at other large gatherings has reversed an increasing trend for internal party affairs to be conducted through the English language. There is a generation of activists who were very active in *Cymdeithas yr Iaith* at an earlier stage in their political careers re-emerging within the party. The third element would appear to be based on the popular view of what Plaid Cymru stands for: the language is the one issue readily identified with the party, so that it is useless to play down the language in a tactical sense, because the fine distinction would be lost on the electorate anyway. Private polls have also revealed a latent sympathy for the language amongst many English monoglot Welshmen. This is a finding which does not appear to have deterred Leo Abse, and other Labour politicians, from using the threat of linguistic discrimination as a stick to beat Plaid Cymru with. The activities of Cymdeithas yr Iaith also complicate the picture. Gwynfor Evans has publicly stated that its campaigns cost him his seat in 1970, but perhaps now the public can clearly distinguish between the two groups, and Plaid Cymru's own position on the language issue can be promoted positively without fear of it being counter-productive.

The position of Gwynfor Evans as President also requires some comment. Gwynfor has been President since 1945 and is very much the father of the Party. The remainder of the leadership is comparatively young and reflects a fairly broad ideological spectrum, cohesion being maintained by Gwynfor's unifying presence. As the party has grown, he has consciously shed much of the organisational responsibility of day-to-day affairs and has, at least once, attempted to retire. That move was resisted in 1975 and he has subsequently been re-elected for a further two years, but it can be expected that he will retire in 1979. The constitution was amended in 1975 to provide for an Honorary Presidency, to which Gwynfor will doubtless be elected. His successor as President will be an ordinary elected official and no way a replacement in terms of the role that Gwynfor fulfils. A new President would be part of an integrated leadership. Plaid Cymru will, however, have lost the active involvement of their one major figure, a person respected throughout Wales by a body of opinion far broader than that which supports Plaid Cymru. This facet of Gwynfor Evans' leadership will be irreplaceable; his legacy must surely be, however, that the party has now achieved the dynamic necessary for progress and growth and will never have to depend upon one man again.

The final word ought to be about future prospects. In parliamentary terms the future looks bleak; unless there is a major realignment of partisanship in South Wales, the Labour Party would seem secure for many years.[28] In the North and West of Wales the seats currently held by Plaid Cymru appear relatively safe, but there are few additional constituencies which might be termed good prospects.

Much will depend upon Plaid Cymru's success in district and county council elections, and increasing their presence in local government. Without the discipline of electing representatives and of actual administration, the party could quickly revert to its role of keeper of the national conscience and guardian of the language.

Part III

The Extra-Parliamentary Parties

6

The Marxist Left [1]

Peter Mair

Electoral disenchantment with the major parties does not in itself imply greater political opportunities for the Marxist left. Unlike, say, the Liberals, the left is not simply an alternative party (or parties) which can hope to exploit any disintegration in the two-party system. Rather, the Marxist left represents another system of politics, ideologically and in some cases organisationally divorced from the political culture of British liberal democracy. To transfer one's political loyalty from Labour to the Liberals is not the same as transferring from Labour to the Marxist left. Whereas the former may involve little more than a change in voting preference, the latter suggests a commitment to a wholly different style of politics, and involves favouring a group or party which organises its support in a qualitatively different fashion to that of 'conventional' or 'within-system' parties. Anti-system parties are, by definition, extraneous to conventional politics: to abandon conventional politics and to support an anti-system party is thus to undergo a much more serious change than is implied by the transfer of loyalties from one conventional party to another.

But the decline of the two-party system is relevant in so far as it is interpreted by many people of the left to signify a much more general political decay, and a crisis in the regime which could eventually lead the working class to reject reformism and embrace revolutionary politics. Particularly pertinent is the 'waning of opposition' between the two parties, Labour and Conservative. The fact that it was a

Labour administration which presided over widespread unemployment and the cuts in public expenditure was seen by the left as encouraging working-class disillusion with reformism in general, and with Labour in particular. That Labour's vote had fallen from 40.3 per cent of the electorate in 1950 to just 28 per cent in May 1979 was seen as further evidence of a growing disillusion, and suggested to the left that there existed a real possibility for the growth of a revolutionary socialist alternative. Other factors also contributed to the growing optimism of the Marxist left: the student movement of the late 1960s, the growing feminist militancy, the extended political awareness of ethnic and other social minorities, and the increased militancy of rank and file trade unionists have all been important. Equally significant has been the impetus for mobilisation provided by the growth in the National Front. This last factor has been influential in two ways: firstly, there is a perceived need to organise to combat the Front, and, secondly, as an anti-system group, the growth in support for the Front has indicated a substantial body of opinion rejecting conventional politics – this in itself suggests the presence of a potential constituency for anti-system groups of the left.

Attempting to mobilise anti-system opposition is never an easy task. Attempting to mobilise such opposition where the system opposed enjoys a wide degree of respect and legitimacy is almost impossible. In particular, the traditionally consensual politics of Britain allow little scope for parties which seek to undermine the regime. Yet the last decade has seen a major *relative* growth in support for anti-system politics in Britain. While the National Front provides the most obvious example of such growth, certain groups on the Marxist left have also increased in both size and influence, though this increase is accompanied by a steady decline in the support for Britain's traditionally dominant Marxist party, the Communist Party of Great Britain (CPGB). Even with this relative growth, however, the Marxist left appears insignificant when compared with Labour, the Conservatives or even the Liberals. The CPGB, which, despite its decline, remains the largest party to the left of Labour, has only some 25,000 members. The second largest group on the left, the Socialist Workers Party (SWP), has only 4600 members, while the International Marxist Group (IMG), the third group with which we are concerned here, has barely 800.

As a general rule, it is possible to establish links between the size of a political group and the intensity and commitment with which its members experience their politics. A party which counts its adherents in the millions will inevitably contain a large proportion of members who betray little concern for the nuances of an articulate and consistent political ideology. Conversely, a group such as the IMG is almost wholly composed of 'ideologues', each of whom has developed a carefully constructed and highly articulate system of beliefs. Each such ideologue is deeply committed to his particular group's goals. This is particularly so in the case of the IMG and SWP, and is evidenced in the members' willingness not only to remain but also to be extremely active in groups which exert but little influence on the mainstream of British political and economic life.

The combined effect of their numerical weakness, the intensity of their politics and the deep commitment of their members leads such groups to develop two noteworthy characteristics. Firstly, they become introverted to the extent that they devote an immense amount of energy to attacking, bitterly, those other groups to whom they can relate most easily, i.e. one another. The subsequent internecine strife which occurs within the immensely fragmented revolutionary left frequently surprises observers who might otherwise expect their shared Marxism to justify these groups uniting in opposition to the centre and right of British politics. Such confusion is understandable: for instance, despite the economic crisis, falling living standards and the growing support for the National Front, a document submitted for consideration at the 1978 Conference of the normally conciliatory IMG suggested that 'the most globally unfavourable development for the revolutionary left in the last period has been the evolution of the International Socialists/Socialist Workers Party'.[2] This introverted sectarianism is very much a product of the isolation of the Marxist left. It is interesting to note that when they enter the external, i.e. conventional political environment, most directly, such as when contesting local or parliamentary elections, left groups lay most stress on the need to achieve revolutionary unity.

The second relevant characteristic which such groups develop is the tendency to exert political pressure through vicarious means. In a situation where a revolutionary group is particularly weak, it frequently adopts the tactic of 'entryism', i.e. discreetly joining a larger and more influential, though less radical, party.

The decision to 'enter' a party is generally taken only in specific circumstances; put simply, the reason for entryism is both to identify and encourage the potentially revolutionary members within the entered party with the intention of either recruiting those members to one's own organisation or forcing a split between left and right within the entered party in order to win the former to revolutionary politics. Similarly, the left seeks to exert influence in other organisations of the working class, particularly trade unions, and in such autonomous protest groups as the women's movement and the gay liberation movement. While entryism is partly a product of the isolation of the left, and the need to gain influence vicariously, it is also prompted by questions of revolutionary strategy. As Marxist revolutionary organisations, each group on the left emphasises the need to centralise all protests against the state, the need to politicise and revolutionise such protests, and the need to make it clear to those protesting that their grievance is part of a wider, more generalised class struggle. Thus they eschew the scission between political and civil society, seeking to exert influence in a wide range of areas other than simply in formal political life.

The past decade has seen a diminished emphasis on the entrist tactic among the groups on the Marxist left, as well as a movement away from the more indirect means of exerting political influence. This results from the growing optimism on the left about the prospects of revolutionary politics in Britain. The various left groups have begun to stress their independent and direct intervention in the political and economic process. While this optimism is partly the result of the student movement, the women's movement, rank and file activity and the Ulster conflict, it is also partly due to what is seen to be a crisis of the major parties and, in particular, to the declining support for the Labour Party. This has led the left to see an opportunity to increase its influence within the working class. Specifically, it has led to the transformation of the International Socialists into the Socialist Workers Party, and to the new, and increasingly successful IMG-sponsored Socialist Unity campaign, which seeks a regrouping of the Marxist left and the creation of a unified revolutionary organisation. Both the SWP and Socialist Unity hope to nominate as many as fifty candidates each in future general elections; this, together with the regular CPGB nominations, could mean as many as 150 candidates from the revolutionary left at these elections. While it remains difficult to estimate the electoral impact such a development might have, it is evidence of a more militant and politically ambitious Marxism than has been seen in Britain for decades.

The context

Writing on Britain in 1854, Karl Marx noted that 'in no other country . . . [has] the war between the two classes that constitute modern society assumed so colossal dimensions and features so distinct and palpable'. Because of the sheer starkness of this conflict, and the unique absence of substantial intermediate social groups which might detract from the importance of the Capital–Labour opposition, he argued that 'the working classes of Great Britain, before all others, are competent and called for to act as leaders in the great movement that must finally result in the absolute emancipation of labour'.[3]

Now, more than a century later, Britain is noteworthy among other European countries for the marked absence of Marxist actors on the political stage. Far from taking the lead in the international struggle against capitalism, as Marx hoped it would, British Socialism displays a degree of quiescence almost without parallel in the rest of Western Europe. This is immediately evident in the extent of electoral support for Marxist parties: in France, for instance, the Communist Party receives some 20 per cent of the popular vote; in Italy the figure is 30 per cent; while in Denmark parties to the left of the Social Democrats can expect a combined total of 10 per cent. In Britain, on the other hand, the CPGB has never exceeded 0.4 per cent, while in the last three elections it has averaged only 0.1 per cent. Even in those countries in Europe where the far left is now noticeably weak, e.g. Belgium, the Netherlands and Germany, Marxist parties have won more than 10 per cent of the poll on occasion.[4] It is only really in Ireland, Britain's nearest neighbour, that the parties to the left of the Social Democrats have been as politically negligible. In Ireland, however, where even Social Democracy maintains but a minority following, radical politics have traditionally been channelled into republicanism rather than socialism, and consequently the absence of a significant Marxist tradition is less striking than is the case in Britain.

The British working class is heir to a legacy which has persistently militated against the mass adoption of radical politics. The absence of a sharp cleavage between the landed interests and the emergent bourgeoisie at the time of the Industrial Revolution, and the *rapprochement* and eventual fusion between these two groups, prevented the emergence of a revolutionary tradition which could itself have encouraged a radical conflict between the working class and the bourgeoisie. In place of the generalised European pattern of confrontation, the old landed interests of Britain and the developing middle class came to terms with one another's existence, and while conflicting over parliamentary reform in 1832 and the repeal of the Corn Laws in 1846, entered into a symbiotic relationship with one another to produce an essentially single and unified ruling class. The shared, or rather fused, culture of this new social bloc created a 'bourgeois ideology [which was] in essence a containment and rejection of the class-struggle'.[5] Thus, in Britain 'a supine bourgeoisie produced a subordinate proletariat. It handed on no impulse of liberation, no revolutionary ideas, no universal language'.[6]

But despite the fusion of landed and bourgeois interests in Britain, the crisis of the Industrial Revolution itself could have laid the foundations for a radical working-class political tradition. Rapid economic growth and change is frequently the harbinger of radical politics in so far as it involves the severing of traditional social ties, the internal displacement of population and the need to adapt to dramatic cultural and institutional innovations. Certainly the social and economic changes in the first century of the Industrial Revolution stimulated the vigorous protests of Luddism, Owenism and Chartism. But, however militant they were, the strategic inadequacy of these movements ensured their eventual defeat and/or collapse, and by the time that Marxism had developed an articulate socialist theory which could have served the radicalism of the early British working class, the impetus for militancy had abated. At that stage the 'destabilising' period of the Industrial Revolution had passed, and the working class was beginning to enjoy the material benefits of the world's leading industrial economy. Commenting on the absence of a separate working-class party in Britain seven years after the extension of the franchise, Engels found it 'understandable in a country in which the working class has shared more than anywhere else in the advantages of the immense expansion of its large-scale industry'.[7]

Thus the working-class political tradition which did finally emerge in Britain was essentially 'trade-unionist' or 'corporatist' in character, emphasising reform within the society while eschewing the prospect of posing a revolutionary challenge to that society. When the need was felt to form a separate working-class party, it was prompted, significantly, by the need which was felt to protect the interests of the trade unions at parliamentary level; and despite the socialist constitution which that party, Labour, adopted in 1918, it never sought to challenge the basis of the prevailing social order within which it operated. As one radical critic put it in 1972, 'the Labour Party remains, in practice, what it has always been – a party of modest social reform in a capitalist system within whose confines it is ever more firmly and by now irrevocably rooted'.[8]

Even by European standards the British political environment is particularly hostile to Marxism. The politics of the left are monopolised by the Labour Party, and the impact of more left-wing groups has, to say the least of it, been quite negligible. Symptomatic of this is the almost total lack of reference to the oldest and most firmly established of Britain's Marxist protagonists, the CPGB, in any of the standard textbooks on British politics. But if the present party and political system is indeed in flux, and if voters are willing to consider alternatives to the traditional major parties, then the parties and groups of the Marxist left deserve consideration. The remainder of this chapter will be devoted to a brief examination of the background, structure and strategies of the relevant protagonists.[9]

The protagonists

The Communist Party of Great Britain

In March 1919, almost two years after the Russian Revolution, the Bolsheviks inaugurated the Comintern (the Communist, or Third, International), an organisation designed to supersede the Social-Democratic Second International, to co-ordinate the international struggle for socialism, and to emphasise the need for 'subordinating the interests of the movement in each country to the common interest of the international revolution'.[10] In response to Lenin's call for the establishment of national communist parties, a number of small left-wing groups in Britain amalgamated in 1920 to form the CPGB. These groups included the British Socialist Party and substantial sections of the Socialist Labour Party. Shortly after its formation the CPGB applied for affiliation to the Labour Party, but was rejected. Following further attempts to affiliate, and following the election of a Communist on the official Labour ticket in the general election of 1922, Labour decided in 1924 to preclude CPGB members from being nominated as Labour candidates in future elections. The following year the party excluded CPGB members from its constituency branches. Despite its attempts to establish close links with Labour, the CPGB gained an expanding support base as the only apparent left-wing alternative to Labour. For the first fifteen years of its existence its membership fluctuated around 5000, jumping to 11,000 in 1936, the year the Spanish Civil War began. From there it continued to grow, reaching a peak of 56,000 in 1942.

The dissolution of the Comintern in 1943, accompanied later by the growing moves among European Communist Parties towards 'polycentrism', i.e. the pursuit of individual 'national roads' to social-ism as opposed to the subordination of national strategy to the needs of the international revolution, precipitated the publication in 1951 of the CPGB's *British Road to Socialism*. This, with some minor amend-ments in 1952, 1958 and 1968, was to remain the policy of the party until 1977, when the CPGB began discussion of a modified program-me, published as the *British Road to Socialism – Draft* in February of that year, and extensively debated at the party's 35th National

TABLE 5   *Electoral support for the Communist Party, 1922–79*

	Number of candidates	Number of votes	Votes per candidate
1922	5	33637	6727
1923	4	39448	9862
1924	8	55346	6918
1929	25	50634	2025
1931	26	74824	2878
1935	2	27117	13559
1945	21	102780	4894
1950	100	91765	918
1951	10	21640	2164
1955	17	33144	1950
1959	18	30896	1716
1964	36	46442	1290
1966	57	62092	1089
1970	58	37970	655
1974 (Feb)	44	32743	744
1974 (Oct)	29	17426	601
1979	38	15958	419
1983	35	11596	331

SOURCES: F. W. S. Craig, *British Parliamentary Election Statistics, 1918–70* (Chichester, 1971); F. W. S. Craig, *Britain Votes 1: Parliamentary Election Results, 1974–77* (Chichester, 1977).

Congress in November. The party which debated the new programme was, however, but a pale reflection of that of earlier days.
Membership stood at only 25,293, compared with 28,519 at the time
of the 34th Congress in 1975, and compared with the peak of 56,000 in
1942. The party's daily paper, *Morning Star*, had an average circulation of only 36,572 in the second half of 1977, compared with 38,533 in
the earlier part of the year, and compared to the peak circulation of its
predecessor, the *Daily Worker*, of 122,788 in 1947. The decline of the
party is such as to lead two recent commentators to suggest that,
while the original edition of the *British Road to Socialism* sold some
200,000 copies, sales of the new draft will only amount to barely 10 per
cent of that figure.[11] The decay of the party is also evident in its
diminishing electoral support, as can be seen in Table 5. In pre-war
elections, for example, the average CPGB candidate won 3088 votes;
in the first five post-war elections this average was reduced to 1688,
and in the five most recent elections it has been reduced even further –
to only 701.

Socialist Workers Party

Even allowing for its decline in both membership and support, the
CPGB remains the largest group to the left of Labour. With some
4600 members, the SWP, formerly the International Socialists (IS), is
modest by comparison. Though the SWP paper, *Socialist Worker*,
claims a circulation of some 30,000, equivalent to that of the *Morning
Star*, the *Worker* appears only on a weekly basis. But the SWP's impact
is greater than these cold statistics might imply. In the first place,
SWP strategy enables the party to maintain a much more public and
militant profile than that of its larger rival (see below). Secondly, in
sharp contrast to the declining CPGB, the SWP has grown rapidly in
the last few years, having increased its membership by some 50 per
cent since 1976.

The roots of the SWP can be traced back to 1944, when the
Trotskyist Workers International League and the Revolutionary
Socialist League, the then British section of the Fourth International,
fused to form the Revolutionary Communist Party (RCP) – see
Figure 3. In 1947 a minority tendency within the RCP, led by Gerry
Healy, 'entered' the Labour Party, to be joined there two years later
by the rump of the RCP. Known variously as 'the Club', and 'the
Group' (as an entrist organisation it did not maintain a formal name),

it expelled a section of its members in 1951. Known as the Socialist Review Group after their journal *Socialist Review*, this section rejected the standard Trotskyist position on the USSR. Orthodox Trotskyism argues that, despite its 'degeneration' under Stalin, the USSR remains fundamentally a workers' state and, as such, should be defended by socialists. The SRG opposed this position, arguing instead in favour of a 'state capitalist' theory of Russia, and insisting that it was basically no different from the Western imperialist powers. Thus, for instance, it refused to take up the cause of North Korea during the 1950–53 Korean War, a policy which led to its expulsion from 'the Club' in 1951.

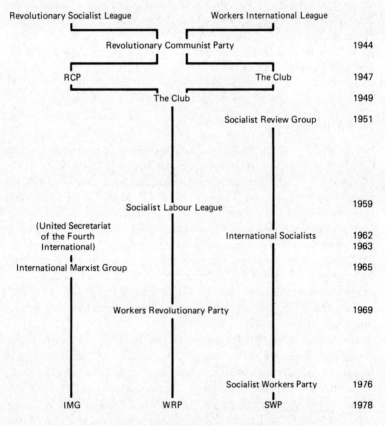

FIGURE 3   *An organisational genealogy of British Trotskyism*

SOURCE: Adapted from Paul Thompson and Guy Lewis, *The Revolution Unfinished? A Critique of Trotskyism* (Big Flame, 1977).

In 1962 the SRG regrouped as the International Socialists, maintaining its original position on the USSR, and basing its strategy on the mobilisation of independent rank and file militancy within the working class. Abandoning its tactic of working within the Labour Party in the mid-1960s, the IS slowly grew as an independent grouping, and eventually transformed itself into the Socialist Workers Party at the end of 1976. At the same time it began to nominate candidates in by-elections but its record has been quite unimpressive so far. In Newcastle and in Walsall in November 1976 the party gained only 184 (1.8 per cent) and 574 (1.5 per cent) votes respectively. In Stetchford in March 1977 it won only 377 (1.1 per cent) votes, and in Ladywood the following August it won only 152 (1.1 per cent). Despite this, however, the SWP continues to emphasise the importance of electoral intervention, and intends to nominate sufficient candidates at forthcoming elections to enable it to gain free TV time for political broadcasts.[12]

The International Marxist Group

As has been noted above, the SWP traces its organisational roots to the then British section of the Fourth International (FI). The FI was established by Leon Trotsky in 1938, with the intention of superseding the Stalinist Third International (Comintern) in much the same way as the latter had sought to supersede its predecessor. The FI came into being in the wake of the growth of Fascism in Europe, and was prompted by the failure of the Comintern to organise adequately the struggle against this new, and particularly sustained assault on the working class. The founding document of the FI attacked the failure of leadership, referred to 'the definite passing of the Comintern to the side of bourgeois order, its cynically counter-revolutionary role throughout the world', and proclaimed that 'the chief obstacle in the path of transforming the pre-revolutionary into a revolutionary state is the opportunist character of proletarian leadership'.[13] In further opposition both to Stalinism and the parties of the Comintern the FI also urged the overthrow of the increasingly bureaucratised regime in the USSR, which, it argued, was hastening the prospect of the restoration of capitalism in Russia and which demonstrated, both theoretically and practically, the inadequacy of the theory of 'socialism in one country'.

Fifteen years after its foundation the FI split into two separate organisations, the International Committee of the FI and the International Secretariat of the FI, both of which reunited as the United Secretariat in 1963. It is this body, the USFI, which currently maintains the IMG as its British section. Not all the various national sections which had been involved in the split agreed to affiliate to the new USFI. In Britain, for instance, the Socialist Labour League, heir to 'the Club' and currently organised as the Workers Revolutionary Party, refused to recognise the authority of the new organisation. Thus, for a period in the mid-1960s, the USFI maintained no British section.

The IMG itself was formed in 1965 by a group of former CPGB members who had left that party in 1956. They were originally loosely organised around their paper, *The Week*, and their decision to form the IMG was quickly followed by their adoption as the official British section of the USFI. From its inception the IMG was almost wholly involved in entryism into the Labour Party. During the late 1960s, however, it acquired a more public profile through involvement in the student movement and such offshoots as the Vietnam Solidarity Campaign. At the same time it reached a wider audience through its participation in the publications *Black Dwarf* and *Red Mole*. Since 1972 the IMG, in line with developments within the USFI itself, has been playing a more independent role, advocating the development of a 'class struggle left wing', and urging the regrouping of the Marxist left into a unified revolutionary organisation. In terms of membership it is the smallest of the groups discussed here, having only some 800, though this is partly due to its lack of emphasis on 'party building' as such, and the rather strict control it maintains over the type of member recruited. The group's weekly paper, *Socialist Challenge*, currently sells approximately 8000 copies, and the paper's editor, Tariq Ali, estimates that some 1500 people are either 'very sympathetic' to their strategy or are organised in '*Socialist Challenge* support groups'.

At first sight, the size of the IMG – small by even the standards of the Marxist left in Britain – would seem to render it unsuitable for inclusion in this discussion. In practice, however, the current activities of the group mark it out as a potentially significant force on the left. As a result of its new strategy in the 1970s, the IMG has been in the forefront of the Socialist Unity campaign, an 'embryonic united front' designed to reduce the fragmentation of the left. To date, the campaign has drawn the support of Big Flame and other groups and individuals on the left, including a number of former members of

IS/SWP. *Socialist Challenge*, which is designed to promote Socialist Unity, has already almost doubled the circulation of the explicitly IMG-oriented *Red Weekly*. If, as shall be suggested later, the fragmentation of the left is one of the major factors preventing its growth, then the increasing strength of Socialist Unity offers perhaps the most likely chance that the left has of encroaching into the territory of the two-party system. In the Ladywood by-election, for instance, in August 1977, the first time Socialist Unity *per se* appeared at the polls, its candidate won 3.4 per cent of the poll, almost four times that of the SWP candidate. By way of contrast, the purely IMG candidate in the Stetchford by-election the previous March won only 1.4 per cent.[14]

Organisation

For revolutionary Marxists, 'politics and organisation are inseparably connected . . . the organisational form of the revolutionary party flows from the nature of its programme'.[15] All three of the groups with which we are concerned here exhibit an immense concern with the necessity to develop a structure appropriate to their revolutionary programmes. All three claim to practise the Leninist organisational principle of 'democratic centralism', i.e. maintaining the ability to act quickly and cohesively, while at the same time permitting the maximum degree of intra-party democracy.

As such, each of the groups has a strong executive arm, which facilitates the efficient mobilisation of the entire organisation as the need arises. In the case of the CPGB the executive functions are shared between an Executive Committee, elected at the biannual Congress of the party, and a Political Committee, which meets weekly, and which is in charge of the day-to-day implementation of EC decisions. The EC itself, which meets every two months, 'has full responsibility for the direction and control of current policy . . . [and the] power to decide new policy where events made this necessary'.[16]

In the case of the SWP the executive arm is known as the Central Committee, which, having been elected at the Annual National Conference, is given responsibility for day-to-day organisation and, where necessary, to adopt new policies. In the event of major policy changes, however, the Central Committee may summon a meeting of the Party Council for consultation. The Party Council is itself composed of representatives of the party's 'district aggregates', i.e. meetings of all SWP branches in a particular area or district. The Central

Committee also maintains regular liaison with the party's National Advisory Committee, a body elected by the National Conference, and containing corporate representation from the various areas of SWP activity, e.g. socialist feminists, the anti-racist campaign and the right to work campaign.

The executive functions of the IMG are, like those of the CPGB, shared between two bodies – the National Committee (NC), which is elected by the National Conference (meeting about every eighteen months), and the Political Committee, which is largely composed of all the full-time organisers, and which meets on a weekly basis. The NC meets quarterly, and is given wide scope to develop policy. Most recently, for instance, the decision to organise the Socialist Unity campaign was taken by the NC. Within the broader international structure, the IMG is represented at both the World Congress of the USFI – meeting every four years – and on the organisation's International Executive Committee. Both the IMG and the SWP also have committees which deal with matters of internal party discipline: in both cases the body is known as the Control Commission.

In many respects the executive organisation of the Marxist left does not vary significantly from that of the more conventional parties. In other organisational matters, however, the left is unique. This is particularly evident in the case of the IMG, and the individual fashion in which it structures its internal democracy affords an opportunity to demonstrate quite clearly the distinction between such groups and the larger mass parties of the political mainstream. Within the IMG, and within the USFI itself, members have the opportunity to organise 'tendencies' and 'factions'. 'Tendencies' represent specific political positions developed within the context of an acceptance of the group's overall programme, but which are not shared by the membership as a whole. 'Tendencies' might arise, for instance, where there are conflicting tactical alternatives suggested within the group. Individuals are encouraged to bring such differences into public debate within the organisation, but are also obliged to dissolve the 'tendency' once the issue has been finally settled by the group as a whole. The delegate structure of the IMG is also organised in such a way as to facilitate the representation of 'tendencies': thus the delegates to National Conference from the Regional Aggregates are elected in proportion to the support the various 'tendencies' have received at these Aggregates. A similar proportional representation exists in the election of the NC, though here the largest 'tendency', even if only a plurality, is guaranteed an overall majority of NC seats in order to ensure the maintenance of a stable majority on that body. 'Factions' represent a more serious source of opposition, in so far as they are formed by a minority grouping within the organisation which is based on real programmatic differences. The creation of a 'faction' thus means 'that a state of emergency and a life or death struggle is signalled for the organisation'.[17] As such, the ultimate goal of a 'faction' is to overthrow the existing leadership.

The reasoning behind this encouragement of the expression of intra-party opposition is based on the need to preserve the often fragile unity of the group. Given the intensity with which revolutionary Marxists experience their politics, and given the seriousness with which they view theoretical, strategic and even tactical disputes, the failure to allow such disputes expression could, and does, lead to splinters and breakaways. While in larger parties with their emphasis on electoral success, unity is sustained partly through the fear that a splinter or breakaway would find itself isolated in the political wilderness, this is not a factor which is really relevant to the small groups on the far left. As they are already essentially isolated and lacking in political influence, a breakaway loses very little by establishing an independent organisation.

The CPGB is less tolerant of internal opposition than is the IMG, and discourages the formation of 'factions' within its ranks: 'a faction means the splitting of the Party, the establishment of a competing centre of political leadership, the establishment of loyalties other than party loyalty . . . factions are dangerous'.[18] While permitting its members to inform the upper reaches of the party of their criticisms, the CPGB does not allow critics in these upper reaches to mobilise sections of the membership in their favour. In short, the flow of internal opposition is permitted in one direction of the party only. The SWP is also less tolerant of internal opposition, permitting 'factions' to be organised only during the three months preceding the National Conference.[19]

The contrast in the approach to internal party democracy in the IMG on the one hand, and the CPGB and SWP on the other, is symptomatic of their respective views of their own organisations. Both the CPGB and SWP regard themselves as fully constituted revolutionary parties, whereas the IMG sees itself as a current, though a major one, in a future unified revolutionary organisation. Hence the IMG emphasises its compatibility with other groups and individuals on the left, and does so partly by allowing quite a diversity of opinion within its own ranks. As such, it is somewhat more organisationally amorphous than either the CPGB or SWP, each of which stresses its own particular growth as an existing party.

The organisation of Marxist parties differs from that of their more conventional opponents in two other important respects, namely the branch structure and the role and function of party members. In common with other Western democracies Britain maintains a formal distinction between civil and political society, between *homo civicus* and *homo politicus*. Symbolically, this distinction can be seen in the inability to practise the most common form of political participation – the act of voting – in one's work place. At another level, the culture (and most British workers) eschew the use of industrial or commercial power as a means of directly raising purely political demands. Thus, for instance, Harold Wilson could seek to undermine support for the seamen's strike in 1966 by questioning the motives of some of the strike-leaders – 'this tightly knit group of politically motivated men who, as the last General Election showed, utterly failed to secure acceptance of their views by the British electorate'.[20]

Marxism rejects this separation as spurious, and the branch organisation of Marxist parties reflects this perspective. The CPGB, for instance, maintains three types of branches – geographic, student and factory – and lays particular emphasis on the latter: 'wherever possible it is desirable that our members should be organised in branches in their particular place of work. The factories are at the centre of the class struggle. Our Party is seriously concerned to increase the number of factory branches and the proportion of the membership organised in this way'.[21] This practice is in sharp contrast to that of the conventional parties, which tend to organise their branches in mainly geographic terms. In the case of Labour, for instance, there exists a sharp division between the political side of the party, represented by the constituency associations, and the industrial side, represented by the trade unions, and any attempt by the former to organise the latter would be seen as an unjustified encroachment on the territory of the unions. The Scottish National Party, however, does attempt to organise politically in factories and other places of work.

The SWP also encourages the formation of factory branches, as well as the organisation of industrial branches, i.e. the coming together of all SWP members in a particular industrial sector. Parallel to this, the party forms 'fractions', which are groups of members in particular trade unions. These meet annually in a National Union Fraction, which has a separate Executive Committee, and which elects delegates to National Conference. The IMG, however, eschews the formation of factory branches, though this is partly due to sheer logistics: with less than 1000 members, it is doubtful whether the group could sustain other than simple geographic branches.

In the role assigned to party members, the left is also unique. To be a member of the CPGB, the SWP and the IMG, and particularly in the case of the latter two, involves more than simply attending infrequent meetings, organising occasional social gatherings and canvassing at election time. In other words, by comparison with other parties, members of Marxist groups are expected to be activists – very active activists. CPGB members for instance, are expected to be not only active in their unions and party branches, but also to sell the *Morning Star* and 'improve their political knowledge and their understanding of Marxism–Leninism'.[22] SWP members must attend meetings regularly, be active in their unions, sell the *Socialist Worker* and, in the case of white-collar workers, for instance, 'be a better than average timekeeper . . . the best attender at . . . union meetings . . . [and] should not get involved in supervision'.[23] A proposal to the IMG's 1978 National Conference suggested that IMG members should be obliged to attend local organisational and educational meetings 'on a regular and disciplined basis', and, where necessary, 'each member should submit, when requested, reports on her or his area of work, theoretical reading, and the results of contact work'. Finally, it is suggested that IMG members wishing to change their place of work or residence should inform the group, which would then offer advice as to the most suitable area to which to transfer.[24] The IMG also emphasises the selling of the *Socialist Challenge*, and vets prospective members before their full acceptance into the organisation: for a period of some six months the prospective member is treated as a 'candidate', i.e. probationary, member, during which period he or she is both educated and tested by the group.

All Marxist groups in Britain, regardless of size, place immense emphasis on the production and distribution of political literature. This literature includes theoretical journals, the emphasis on which is symptomatic of the intense concern for ideological development, and newspapers, the emphasis on which is symptomatic of the isolation of the left from the mainstream of political life. Such papers are one of the few means by which a revolutionary group can communicate with a wider audience. As a broad generalisation, it is probably true to say that the less influential and conspicuous a party or group, the greater the emphasis it will place on its newspaper as a means of political communication. Thus, for example, the production and distribution of the *Socialist Worker* by the SWP is much more relevant to that group than, say, the production and distribution of *Labour Weekly* is for the Labour Party. Newspapers are a technique for getting the group's message across to a wider audience: *Socialist Challenge*, for instance, sells almost ten times as many copies as the IMG has members, while the *Socialist Worker*'s circulation of almost 30,000 dwarfs the SWP's 4600 membership.

To appreciate the organisational specificity of the revolutionary left fully, it is necessary to understand the role of the revolutionary party. The stress laid on newspapers, for instance, is explicable not only in terms of the isolation of the left – though this is important – but also in terms of the perceived need to politicise and situate the everyday experience of the working class. In a word, such newspapers are agitational. Both the branch structure and the role of members in the groups on the left are also intimately bound up with the theory of the revolutionary party, predicated as it is upon the need for 'proletarian self-emancipation',[25] with the movement to revolution stemming from the interaction of socialist theory with the day-to-day experience of the working class in confrontation with employers, managers, the state, etc. Tangentially, we may note that the renewed optimism of the British left in the 1970s has partly resulted from the growing evidence of such rank and file militancy. As can be seen from Table 6, the number of working days lost through stoppages increased from less than 5 million in 1968 to almost 30 million in 1972; and, while this trend has been reversed since then, the proportion of days lost through *unofficial* stoppages has increased. Unofficial stoppages are particularly welcomed by certain sections of the British left in so far as they express an extreme form of shop-floor militancy. Between 1972 and 1977, with the one exception of 1974 (when the number of days lost through overall stoppages increased by over 100 per cent), the number lost through unofficial stoppages increased steadily from 24 per cent to 87 per cent.

The revolutionary party, the vanguard of the working class, tries to involve itself intimately in such conflicts, linking up the otherwise fragmented and isolated oppositions, politicising the protagonists, situating the conflicts within the broader perspective of the class struggle, and educating itself strategically through its own experience. Such a party naturally rejects the conventional emphasis on electoralism, and refuses to confine itself within the formal political

TABLE 6   *Industrial disputes, 1968–77*

	1968	1969	1970	1971	1972	1973	1974	1975	1976	1977*
Number of working days lost through stoppages (thousands)	4690	6846	10980	13551	23909	7197	14750	6012	3284	9985
% of working days lost which were lost through unofficial stoppages	53	76	70	26	24	72	52	81	86	87

*Figures for 1977 are provisional, and those for unofficial stoppages refer only to the first 10 months of 1977.

SOURCE: *Department of Employment Gazette*, February 1978.

arena; rather, it seeks to extend its influence in trade unions, women's groups and other areas where oppressed sectors confront the polity. From this derives the need to establish branches in factories and industries, and fractions in unions. From this also derives the need for the member to work actively, and to develop a rigorous grasp of revolutionary theory: in a sense, the member stands proxy for the party, and without his or her efforts and theoretical ability the party cannot politicise the people with whom this member works. This, of course, is the broad strategy of the revolutionary party and, to a greater or lesser extent, all three groups accept these basic principles. But there are sharp differences between them, and it is to a closer examination of their individual strategies that we shall now turn.

Strategies

The Labour Party is the majority working-class party in Britain, and the commitment of workers to Labour, and hence to reformism, is seen by the left as the major obstacle in the development of the revolutionary consciousness. While opposing Labour, neither the CPGB, the SWP nor the IMG can afford to ignore it; indeed it is from their recognition of working-class loyalty to Labour, and from their respective views on how best to surmount this problem, that the logic of the strategy adopted by the various Marxist groups can best be derived.

None of the groups on the left seek to deny the importance of Labour. In a recent interview, for instance, the General Secretary of the CPGB argued that 'anyone who "writes off" the Labour Party, the party of the working class, not recognising its vital role in present and future political affairs in Britain, is making a fatal error'.[26] The IMG, though reluctantly, also emphasises Labour's crucial position, in so far as 'the workers see it as the only mass alternative to the Tory Party. We can attempt to change this position, but we should not attempt to deny that it exists, however subjectively painful and irksome it might appear.'[27] The SWP·in its turn regrets 'workers' illusions in Labour reformism', but takes comfort from the party's declining electoral fortunes and by emphasising that 'their loyalty to Labour is residual, continuing to exist because they do not see an alternative'.[28] Of the three groups, the SWP seems the most optimistic about the chances of detaching the majority of the working class from the grip of the Labour Party. This characteristic can be related to the relatively *sui generis* development of the International Social-ists/Socialist Workers Party, which, despite its earlier links with Trotskyism, is not formally part of an international socialist move-ment. By contrast, both the CPGB and the IMG are self-consciously protagonists in a larger, international and organisationally continu-ous revolutionary tradition. This leads these groups to situate their respective relationships to the Labour Party within the context of Communist or Trotskyist confrontations with Social Democratic parties in other countries and at other historical periods. This, in turn, leads both the CPGB and the IMG to place more emphasis on the political importance of reformism as a force in working-class politics than is suggested by the more isolationist SWP.

The approach of the CPGB to the Labour Party is at once the most straightforward and easily summarised of the three groups discussed here. Briefly, the party 'does not . . . seek to replace the Labour Party as a federal party of the working class, but rather . . . see[s] a much more influential Communist Party as crucial to the future of the Labour Party itself'.[29] In effect, the strategy of the CPGB is to use itself as an external force pressurising Labour into more socialist policies. Recognising the existence of both a right and a left within the larger party, the CPGB seeks to strengthen the influence of the latter and to weaken the grip of reformism at all levels within the Labour movement. This will be achieved through CPGB influence in trade unions and thus, indirectly, in the Labour Party itself, and by achieving a degree of electoral success sufficient to demonstrate wide support for socialist politics. As the influence of the left grows in Labour, the party will move closer to the CPGB, eventually leading to a situation where all anti-Communist bans and proscriptions within the larger party are removed, and the trade unions will be free to elect delegates to the Labour Party regardless of the political affiliations of those elected. The resultant Labour–CPGB unity will try to provide a movement with sufficient strength to implement socialism in Britain. Socialism might be won through parliament, though a parliament with a democratised state machine (e.g. civil service, armed forces, etc.); and, while government might enter into a closer, though unspecified, relationship with the Labour movement outside parliament, the ultimate authority of parliament will be neither challenged nor abridged. Nor will the right of other parties to contest elections be forbidden, even those parties hostile to socialism.

Following the publication of the draft version of the new *British Road to Socialism*, *The Times* concluded that

> . . . it is a much more realistic purpose [for the CPGB] to seek the extension of left-wing influence within the trade unions and the Labour Party. That is where the main Communist threat lies at this time, and the threat is all the greater because it is not confined to the Communists. Indeed the different Trotskyite groups are in all probability now a greater menace . . .[30]

One can only assume that within the term 'Trotskyite' *The Times* included the non-Trotskyist SWP as well as the Trotskyist IMG, and certainly the strategy of both groups is much more publicly militant than that of the CPGB.

The SWP does not consider that socialism can be achieved through a more left-wing Labour Party: 'it is extremely unlikely, though not impossible, that socialists could capture control of the Labour Party. But to put one's energies into doing so is a complete waste of time. The only time the Labour Party could be captured would be at a time of massive struggles when it would be irrelevant'.[31] Unlike the CPGB, and unlike even the IMG, both of which emphasise the strength of reformism within the working class, the SWP argues that the links between Labour and the working class are tenuous. While Labour is the only political organisation to which the majority of workers give their loyalty, this support is essentially negative. It continues only in so far as 'workers do not yet have faith in their own ability to transform society by collective action . . . the job is to build up faith in collective action'.[32] The real arena for the SWP is the shop floor, among rank-and-file workers *qua* workers. The act of voting, and the alternatives offered by purely electoral parties, are no substitute for rank-and-file militancy, where demands are raised by workers without reference to the Labour Party. In fact, argues the SWP, the last decade has seen the locus for 'the struggle for "reforms" shifted from parliament to the trade unions . . . It was shop-floor "do-it-yourself" reformism that won concessions through collective action, and not parliamentary legislation'. Hence, 'the industrial struggle [is] the main field of *political* activity'.[33]

The SWP focus on the self-reliant militancy of rank-and-file workers leads the group to disregard parliament as a source of change, and its decision to participate in electoral politics is only inspired by the opportunity it affords to gain publicity, by the ability to demonstrate that there is an alternative to Labour, and by the likelihood of recruiting new members through an electoral campaign. But this is an essentially secondary activity, and support for and involvement in rank-and-file struggles is seen as the most effective means of advancing the cause of revolutionary politics. Not only does the SWP encourage workers to place less reliance on the Labour Party, it also encourages them to challenge the existing trade-union leadership. This leadership, it argues, is both divorced from the experience of rank-and-file workers and reformist in character, and therefore should not be fully trusted to seek the implementation of demands; rather, workers should trust and use only their indigenous militancy. In short, the emphasis is on 'self-emancipation' in a very literal sense.

The IMG, like the SWP, believes that socialism can only be

achieved if the working class can be torn away from Labour: 'a mass party will only arise when there is a political breach, a break inside the mass organisations of the workers' movement'. Like the SWP, it sees its main task as preparing the ground for such a rupture, though it is at this point that the approaches of the two groups diverge. The IMG continually stresses that the struggle against reformism must be fought politically: rather than create a rank-and-file movement which seeks to circumvent the existing *organisations* of the working class, the IMG strives for the development of a broad alliance of the left which can combat the *politics* of the existing leadership. While accepting that trade-union leaders become isolated from the experience of the ordinary workers, and that 'virtually all trade union leaders, albeit in different forms, become prisoners of the bureaucratic apparatus on whose behalf they exercise power within the union', they do not exclude the possibility that these leaders may be won over occasionally to militant positions, nor do they exclude the possibility of revolutionaries uniting in *action* with these leaders. What the IMG finds lacking in the SWP approach is the latter's tendency to tackle reformism and bureaucracy on a largely organisational, as opposed to political, basis. For the IMG, 'left social democracy and its ideas [have] to be encountered before they [can] be combated and defeated'.[34] The IMG also differentiates itself from the SWP by emphasising its *transitional* programme and by criticising the SWP for failing to bridge the gap between its minimal programme for socialism, as represented by short-term demands in strikes, protests, etc., and its maximum programme, as represented by rhetoric and ideological polemics.

IMG current strategy is devoted to developing Socialist Unity in both the unions and in the electoral arena. In the former the intention is 'to struggle for building the broadest possible rank and file organisations against class collaboration and *politically* independent of the trade union bureaucracy'.[35] In electoral politics success will demonstrate that there is an alternative to reformism. This in turn will encourage the left to mobilise within the Labour Party, forcing a split in that party and so enabling the formation of a mass revolutionary organisation. Thus, like the SWP, the IMG views electoral politics as simply a means to an end, rather than an end in itself. A secondary activity, it is designed to bolster and encourage a more substantial mobilisation of the working class towards the revolutionary overthrow of the state itself.

If Socialist Unity, or indeed the SWP, is to have any degree of success in electoral terms, then some pact will have to be agreed between the two groups. One major factor militating against such an agreement, however, and preventing more substantial moves towards unity on the Marxist left, lies in the different perspectives which each group has of its own role. While the SWP, for instance, is prepared to engage in unified action in certain circumstances, particularly with the CPGB, to whom it has already made such proposals, as an already constituted party it regards the future revolutionary politics in Britain as being intimately bound up with its own particular future as an organisation. Thus long-term unity will only be considered by the SWP in terms of other groups coming under its specific aegis. Yet this perspective of the SWP may be changing; a recent assessment of the organisation by its Central Committee suggested that the group had some 'negative features', i.e. 'a growth of triumphalism and organisa-tion sectarianism, a contempt among sections of the cadre for the non-SWP left', and further argued for the need to involve the SWP in general discussion with the rest of the Marxist left.[36] As a constituted party, the CPGB is in a similar position to the SWP, and again stresses the link between the future of revolutionary politics in Britain and its own organisational future. But, even apart from this factor, the sheer numerical superiority of the CPGB *vis-à-vis* the SWP and the IMG, and its conciliatory attitude to the Labour Party, would seem to render it an unlikely partner in any future fusion of the Marxist left. Of the three groups, the IMG is the most vociferous in its advocacy of unity and/or a regrouping: not having constituted itself as a party, it is less concerned than the SWP or CPGB with its own specifically organisational future, and envisages the emergence of a unified revolutionary organisation of which it itself would be but a current.

Conclusions

Any attempt to explain the relative weakness of the Marxist left in contemporary Britain must clearly emphasise the absence of a radical socialist tradition. But even allowing for this, other factors must also be considered. Part of the reason must, of course, lie in the immense fragmentation of the left. No single group has been able to emerge to monopolise the leftist response to the recent social and economic crisis of the 1970s. Rather, this response has either been dissipated over a plethora of small parties, groups and sects, or simply not exploited in the absence of any clearly dominant single organisation. For potential recruits to the revolutionary left, the fractionalism and confusion which exists within organised Marxism in Britain must, to say the least of it, be extremely discouraging. In this sense the 'rationalisation' promised by Socialist Unity offers perhaps the most likely foundation for the growth of the revolutionary left since the initial momentum of the late 1960s.

A second, and potentially much more significant, factor preventing the growth of the left is its very style of politics. Ideologically anti-system, Marxist groups also tend to be organisationally anti-system in that they reject electoralism, attempt to politicise what are normally seen to be non-political spheres of activity, and in that they expect a degree of commitment and support from their members and adherents which is markedly greater than that expected by conventional parties. While, say, the Scottish National Party seeks an important change in the UK constitution, it does not face the obstacles confronted by groups of the left in so far as its support is organised in a fashion comprehensible to its potential supporters, i.e. while having an anti-system ideology, the SNP remains organisationally 'within-system'. To paraphrase L. P. Hartley, Marxist politics is a foreign country: they do things differently there. In this sense a communication gap exists between the politics of the left and the politics of the mainstream, and yet support for the former can grow only through recruitment from the latter. Overcoming such a communication gap has been the traditional goal of the revolutionary left since the emergence of socialism. In practice, it has been overcome through a translation of the left's ideological message into a communicable form, e.g. through an emphasis on electoralism, on parliamentary socialism, etc. In practice also, such a translation has frequently meant the eschewing of much of the left's revolutionary purpose, as the experience of European Social Democracy and, latterly, of 'Eurocommunism' demonstrates. The existence of this communication gap may also explain the sectarian concern which groups on the left betray for one another: unable to converse politically with the adherents of conventional politics, they are frequently reduced to communicating, however bitterly, with each other.

As long as this communication gap exists between the Marxist left and conventional politics, then the outlook for Marxists in Britain must remain pessimistic. Nevertheless, the decision of both the SWP and Socialist Unity to enter the electoral arena, however reluctantly and cautiously, may enable them to communicate their message to a wider audience. Certainly the fact that the electorate has abandoned the traditional parties to the extent it now has means that the political system is potentially much more receptive to the anti-system politics of the Marxist left than has been the case in any other period in recent memory.

7

The National Front

Martin Walker

The National Front (NF) was formed during a series of negotiations in the winter of 1966–7 between the leaders of three small parties and pressure groups: the League of Empire Loyalists, the British National Party, and the Racial Preservation Scoiety. In the following year it absorbed into its thin ranks another party, the Greater Britain Movement. The NF came into official being on 7 February 1967, and it claimed 2500 members. On paper, this was a reasonable figure. In fact, active (and subscribing) members were fewer than 1200.

Of the groups which made up the NF, the League of Empire Loyalists was less a party than a right-wing Conservative pressure group held together by its charismatic leader, the first chairman of the NF, A. K. Chesterton. Chesterton had been a Fascist under Sir Oswald Mosley in the 1930s, editing the Fascist party journal, *The Blackshirt*. Chesterton's view of the world was shaped by his theory of a vast Zionist conspiracy, joining together Wall Street capitalism and Moscow Communism. He believed these were both the work of Jews, whose object was to overthrow the British Empire and achieve world domination. This theory still underpins the ideology of the NF.[1] But Chesterton's own gifts as a writer and propagandist made him into a rallying point during the 1950s for many right-wing Conservatives who objected to the liberal conservatism of party leaders like Macmillan and Butler. Chesterton's staunch defence of the British Empire, and his hostility to the Welfare State, attracted traditional Conservatives, while his Fascist credentials and his conspiracy theory attracted a number of young National Socialists, who could, in post-war Britain, find little other outlet for their politics.

Another of the British groups which made up the NF was the British National Party (BNP). It had been formed in February 1960, in the wake of the race riots in Notting Hill. Its leaders were two graduates of Chesterton's League of Empire Loyalists: John Bean and John Tyndall. They were joined by Colin Jordan, who had formed the frankly Nazi 'White Defence League' during the riots. The BNP later split, with Jordan and Tyndall going on to found the tiny National Socialist Movement, whose paramilitary activities won them prison sentences. Bean's BNP developed into a more conventional political group. Based mainly in areas of high immigration, it stood in elections as the defender of white communities and white property values. In Southall in 1964 Bean won 9 per cent of the vote. During the same election, in Birmingham Smethwick, the offical Conservative candidate Peter Griffith won the hitherto safe Labour seat, against the national trend, in a campaign which was marked by the slogan 'If you want a nigger for a neighbour; vote Labour'.

The final group which combined with the others to form the NF was the Racial Preservation Society. It was a well financed blanket organisation for a number of anti-immigration bodies in the Midlands and the South-East which sprang up in the wake of the Smethwick election. It believed in white racial superiority, and, like the League of Empire Loyalists and the British National Party, was bitterly anti-Communist and more discreetly anti-Semitic.

The coalition of these movements into the National Front was prompted partly by the declaration of UDI in Rhodesia. This was seen as marking the final British abandonment of the Empire and the white kith and kin in Rhodesia. Other factors leading to the coalition were the financial insecurity of the LEL and BNP, the crushing Labour victory in the 1966 general election, and the emergence of a bi-partisan Labour–Conservative policy on coloured immigration. That policy, of increasingly severe controls on the numbers of immigrants, with mild legislation against racial discrimination in Britain, was undermined by the solitary campaign of a Conservative Shadow Minister, Enoch Powell, against coloured immigration.

The National Front remained a tiny sect, trying, in the words of Martin Webster, now the NF national organiser, 'to kick our way into the headlines', but to little effect.[2] The political backgrounds of men like Tyndall and Webster, and the often published photographs of them wearing Nazi uniforms, turned away many sympathisers. But Powell's refusal to build a political movement around himself left the way open for the NF to mobilise around the anti-immigration senti-ments which Powell had stimulated. In their first electoral trial, in the general election of 1970, the NF fielded only ten candidates, and gathered a puny total of 6000 votes. Much of the blame rested with the lack-lustre, because ageing, leadership of Chesterton, who was al-ways dubious of Tyndall's strategy, and necessary tactics, of turning the NF into a mass movement. Chesterton was replaced by John O'Brien, a compromise candidate on whom the warring factions of the NF could agree, and under his leadership the NF made little further headway.

The breakthrough came in 1972, with the decision of Idi Amin of Uganda to expel his Asian community. The British Conservative government under Edward Heath honourably agreed to welcome them to Britain. After a split in the NF, Tyndall succeeded O'Brien as leader. The new leader galvanised the tiny NF into heady months of protest activity, winning a number of converts from the right wing of the Conservative Party, particularly its anti-immigrant Monday Club. The NF began to grow in number and in quality of members. The momentum was maintained with a 16 per cent vote at the West Bromwich by-election in May 1973, for which the NF had brought canvassers and party workers from all over the country.

With the sole objective of getting free TV time for party political broadcasts, the NF decided to spend all its financial reserves on fighting fifty parliamentary seats in the February 1974 general elec-tion. (Fifty seats was the threshold for free TV time.) With fifty-four candidates, the NF won 76,000 votes and enough national publicity for the far left parties to see them as an important threat. From 1974 to the present every NF march or demonstration has seen organised left opposition, usually with violence, mass arrests and enormous publici-ty. In the October 1974 election the NF fielded ninety candidates and won 113,000 votes, establishing themselves firmly on the political map. Increasingly, their voting strength was seen to be located in the deprived inner cities, which bore the brunt of the social costs of mass immigration.

By October 1974 the NF was going through another leadership crisis. The Conservative politicians who had joined the NF after the Ugandan Asian campaign were more politically experienced, and apparently more 'respectable', than Tyndall and Webster. Inevitably, they began to challenge Tyndall for the leadership, and in October John Kingsley-Read, a former Conservative official from Blackburn, took over the chairmanship.

The NF's fortunes slumped during the internal battles of 1975, with Tyndall mobilising his own supporters, many of them friends and loyal stalwarts from the old Nazi party, against the Populists, as the other .faction were called. The bitter and embarrassing rows developed into a split, with Kingsley-Read and his supporters leaving to form the rival National Party (NP), and Tyndall and his supporters left in charge of the NF. By this time the NF had grown to some 20,000 members, the bulk of them recruited since the Ugandan Asians' arrival. And the bulk of them knew Tyndall best and stayed with his faction. Kingsley-Read's group tended to be branch and regional officials. Few of them were able to carry their rank-and-file members with them into the NP. The NP had collapsed as a political force by the end of 1976.

During that year, which saw five racial deaths and an ugly climate of racial violence, the NF was able, under Tyndall's energetic leadership, to exploit a series of related political issues. When Asians were expelled from the African republic of Malawi, it was Tyndall's NF which won headlines with demonstrations, public marches and rallies. The rallies attracted left opposition and the TV cameras, and more of the publicity on which the NF thrived.

Then, too, the party began to benefit from the lessons it had learned from its old Conservative members. These members, now removed into the defunct NP, had taught the NF the value of political organisation at branch and constituency level. This lesson was applied in local elections. In Leicester, in 1976, the NF won almost 50,000 votes on a complex voting system of three-member constituencies. The NF fielded 176 candidates around the country; 80 of them won more than 10 per cent of the vote. In 1977, in the GLC elections in London, the NF pushed the Liberal party into fourth place in inner London, winning 119,000 votes. The NF won 235,000 votes around the country.

The growing electoral success of the NF attracted the concern of trade unions and the Labour Party, but they remained – for the time being – unwilling to follow the violent tactics of the far left groups, whose avowed policy of 'Smash the Nazi Front' appeared to be anti-Police, and therefore counter-productive. Attempts by numbers of leading political organisations, in particular by the Board of

Deputies of British Jews, to establish an all-party and non-extremist opposition to the NF foundered on the rocks of Conservative suspicion and universal fear of association with the Marxist left.

The NF by this time had evolved a systematic party programme, whose central policy remained an end to all coloured immigration and compulsory repatriation of all non-whites. The policy went on to argue that blacks should not have jobs while whites were unemployed, nor homes while whites were homeless. It called for racial segregation in schools. NF policy on the trade unions called for their abolition, and replacement by industrial unions; for mandatory arbitration and secret ballots before strikes. Internationally, the NF policy called for total support for the whites of Rhodesia and South Africa, a withdrawal from the EEC and from NATO, massive rearmament and much greater defence budget. It also called for the progressive dismantling of the Welfare State. In John Tyndall's words: 'For able-bodied people in the prime of life there should be the inducement to rely much less on the Welfare State and much more on personal initiative and hard work.'[3]

The National Front and its members

The National Front is like no other political party in Britain. Although it fights elections, wages political campaigns, and seeks membership and power like other parties, there are a number of vital reasons which makes loyalty to it different in kind, rather than degree, from conventional political allegiance. In part this is a direct result of the success of the NF's opponents in labelling the party as a loathsome graveyard echo of the old Nazism. The act of allegiance to the NF has become, therefore, a simultaneous act of wilful defiance of the democratic consensus. This argument should not be pushed too far. A bare 20 years ago, in Britain and the USA, the act of allegiance to the Communist Party involved a similar, conscious act of removing oneself from the national consensus. Parties which are seen by the consensus as 'extremist' will always face this hurdle.

But in the case of the NF the problem is compounded by the NF's deliberate attack upon the principle of rationality. Extremist parties of the left are at pains to stress, no matter how much they practise 'democratic centralism', that they are at the root democratic, and, above all, that their ideology is based upon logic and rationality. The

NF spurns rationality. As the NF leader, John Tyndall, expressed it in his pamphlet *Six Principles of British Nationalism*:

> It is the single minded emphasis on intellect for its own sake, and its resultant tendency to reduce all vital questions of existence down to a flat, uninspired pseudo-rationale, that atrophies the much more potent factors of instinct and will which move great and vigorous races and which ultimately determine history.[4]

Tyndall expanded this philosophy, and applied it explicitly to membership of the NF in an article in his own magazine, *Spearhead*, in the issue of September 1974:

> I believe that most people have been won over to our movement in the most committed and active sense of the term by a deep personal compulsion to be involved in our work, which may be influenced by duty or self-interest or both to a degree, but which is mainly stimulated by some mystical, emotive power within us that compels allegiance, by an appeal to forces within the human character which defy rational analysis.[5]

This goes a great deal further than the hoary old claim made so frequently by Emmanuel (now Lord) Shinwell at successive Labour Party conferences that 'The Labour Movement is a Crusade or it is nothing'. Membership of the NF involves a series of obligations and responsibilities which stem from its beginnings as a tiny sect.

A. K. Chesterton, the Front's first leader, told the NF's inaugural conference that 'The NF must become an elite.'[6] He tended to see the NF as a pressure group, rather than as a potential mass movement, and was never happy at the way the young firebrands of the 1960s, such as John Tyndall and Martin Webster, insisted that the NF's sights be set on a mass membership, a nation-wide and popular movement. As Chesterton put it, in a spirit of morose compromise in his magazine *Candour* in June 1967: 'Ideally we should seek to recruit only the dedicated elite, but we do not live in an ideal world and must make the best use of the material at our disposal'.

One of the reasons for Tyndall's emergence among the leadership of the NF after 1972, in spite of his embarrassing past as a leading member of the openly Nazi 'National Socialist Movement' and his two prison sentences, was his long campaign to maintain the qualitative advantages of a tiny, elite movement while the NF expanded and won the quantitative advantage of greater membership. It was a theme for which Tyndall campaigned tirelessly, not in public and even less in print, but which he hammered home at the NF's internal debates and functions. A classic example comes from his address to a NF leadership training seminar on 15 July 1973. He was speaking to a group of handpicked recruits, who were to go on to become branch and group organisers for the NF: 'Our job is not just to win sympathisers, but to win activists,' he told them. 'Not just to get people to agree with us, but to get them to work and if necessary, to fight for us.'[7]

He went on to reiterate his arguments against reason, and for emotion as the NF's inspiration:

> There is a unique quality of enthusiasm in the NF that an appeal to reason alone could not possibly create. We are not ashamed to appeal to people's feelings and to utilise those feelings in spurring them on to ever greater efforts.... Reason may play its part in deciding people as to what is the right course, but the forces that spur them into action ... to go into the night working for a cause with no prospect of personal reward, are entirely forces of feelings of emotion.... In the last analysis, reason simply builds on a foundation that feeling supplies in the first place.[8]

These obligations were clearly delineated into financial contributions, propaganda and organisational work. In 1974, during the first period of Tyndall's leadership, the NF's National Directorate had as a primary function the monitoring of the activities of each branch of the NF and its obligations. Minimum targets for each branch included:

the buying and distribution of 3000 leaflets per week
selling 100 copies of *Spearhead* each month
selling 300 copies of *Britain First*, the then irregularly issued broadsheet
fighting at least one council election each year.[9]

This involved a minimum branch contribution to HQ of £480 a year. The targets were progressively raised, so that by the summer of 1974 each local NF group had to fulfil what had once been the branch obligation of fighting a council election each year. Nor were these weekly and monthly targets the limit of the members' expected endeavours. In the course of 1974, with its two general elections, at which 154 NF candidates stood (and lost their deposits), the NF's turnover was £104,000, according to the annual report of the Treasurer, Carl Lane. At the time the best estimates of NF membership (which are not published) were about 20,000, although many of these had allowed their annual contributions to lapse. At all branch and group meetings, at all public rallies and election meetings, collections were taken. The pro-Ulster march in September 1974, for example, raised £607, and the annual Remembrance Day rally of that year took a collection which just topped £1000.

But raising money was only one area of activity. The magazines and leaflets which the branches must buy must equally be delivered, and all the NF groups and Branches are now told to organise at least one evening of leafletting a week. Because of the controversial nature of the NF, leafletters do not work alone, but in groups of three, one to deliver the material through the letter boxes, and two more as escorts. The NF's own annual reports have claimed that 4 million leaflets were delivered in 1972–3, mainly on the subject of the arrival of the Ugandan Asians, and a further 5 million in 1974. It is through tactics such as leafletting, in groups, that the NF encourages its members to see the party as a focus for a social, as well as a political, commitment. In rather the same way that the Young Conservatives were once a national joke as a marriage bureau, the NF assiduously holds dances, social evenings, and parties, and even the regular political meetings are usually held in the upstairs rooms of pubs. A duplicated recruiting sheet used by the Wood Green (London) branch in 1974 carried the slogan 'You're never alone with the NF'.[10]

The pattern continues with another major NF tactic: that of street-selling their newspapers and publications. In part because of the unwillingness of most retail outlets to stock the NF publications, such as *National Front News* and *Spearhead*, and in part because of the opportunities for personal canvassing and for constant presence on the streets, the bulk of the sales are made on street corners. In parts of south and east London, and in Leicester, these pitches have become predictable scenes of left–NF violence, with rival sellers bringing up reinforcements to defend their own pitches, and challenge their opponents. There is a *camaraderie* factor here, which is difficult to define. Members who go on escort duty – the NF's own phrase – with the street-sellers know that they are likely to face physical violence, and yet be guaranteed support. Personal observation of the Brick Lane street-sellers in the East End suggests that these occasions either start or finish in a public house – when they do not finish in a Magistrates' Court.

Since 1974, the NF has established a structure for these militants, called the Honour Guard. On the major marches they are the young men who carry the forest of Union Jack flags. They wear, almost as a uniform, Army-style combat jackets emblazoned with miniature Union Jacks. They make a fetish of their toughness. Indeed, on a BBC Panorama programme in November 1977, Martin Webster, the NF's National Activities Organiser, claimed that the NF was deliberately recruiting soccer hooligans, and suggested that their violence was simply frustrated nationalism, which could find an effective focus in the NF. The official NF view is that the organised hostility of the left leaves the NF with little option but to take defensive precautions. The NF's opponents retort that the bulk of the work of the NF thugs is done not on defensive duty in public, but in vicious racial attacks late at night.

The immediate question, for the purposes of this chapter, is what effect this quasi-military organisation has upon the character of the NF as a party. It certainly separates it from the mainstream of British political life. The established parties certainly have no such parallel groups. It is only fair to note that the parties of the far left have, more discreetly, organised similar groups of young toughs, whose main target is the NF. One of these parties now renamed the Socialist Workers Party, once had a marching song with the refrain 'We are the I.S. boot boys'.[11] The difference about the NF's militants is that the theology and leadership of the party specifically call for shows of strength, for the panoply or parades and marches, for the image of virility which goes with the Honour Guard.

Tyndall put the issues bluntly to a private NF meeting in Tunbridge Wells in July 1975, when he was campaigning hard against the 'moderate' wing of the NF Populists, who were later to break off to form the ill-fated National Party: 'We have got to dedicate ourselves to producing, as we used to do, young men who are tough and hard. Not only young men with the knowledge and crafts to survive in the modern world, but the physical stamina, the character and the will to survive.'[12] Writing in the September 1975 issue of *Spearhead*, he returned to one of his constant themes, his belief in the enormous psychological impact of the NF marches: 'I believe that our great marches, with drums and flags and banners, have a hypnotic effect on the public and an immense effect in solidifying the allegiance of our followers.' Again quoting from his address to the NF leadership training group in July 1975, we find the same theme:

> It is always a necessary part of political psychology to seek to show strength. That is why at certain intervals of the year we concentrate our forces together by transporting people hundreds of miles by coach. We have got to show strength to the public and to our own people.

Tyndall's explicit approval of the NF strategy of marches, banners, 'young men who are tough and hard', sits unhappily with the bland explanations of the NF's official spokesmen that the party was forced to rely on public marches and demonstrations in its early days because it found no other way of getting publicity; or that it was forced to recruit the Honour Guard as a legitimate measure of self-defence against attacks from the left. It was at that Tunbridge Wells meeting that Tyndall encapsulated the distinctive feature of the NF – the emotionalism, the wilful brutalism, the way in which the NF positively flaunts the contempt it feels for the democratic-humanitarian consensus: 'The day that our followers lose their capacity to hate will be the day that they lose their power and their will to achieve anything worthwhile at all.'

The electoral appeal of the National Front

This fundamental difference in character between the NF and the other British political parties and movements is central to an under-standing of the NF's nature. Moreover, it may also be central to an understanding of the NF's growing electoral appeal, at a time when British voters are increasingly refusing to vote. In 1950 83.9 per cent of the electorate voted. By the 1970s the percentage of voters had dropped to 72 per cent (1970 and October 1974). The decline in turnout at local elections was even more marked.

Not only were electors not bothering to vote, they were also breaking away from their traditional loyalties to the two great parties. In every post-war election until 1974 the Labour and Conservative

Parties had collected at least 87.5 per cent, and usually well over 90 per cent, of the votes cast. But in 1970 the combined share of the vote fell to 75.4 per cent, and fell even further to 75.2 per cent in October 1974. The Liberals and Scottish Nationalists shared the great majority of the shifting votes, but the NF's 113,000 votes of October 1974 and 189,000 votes in 1979 were a part of this underlying change of British voting habits.

It is both easy and tempting to conclude that British voters were saying to Labour and Conservative, 'A plague on both your houses', and even 'A plague on your whole electoral system'. Such a hypothesis would be premature; there is too little evidence to tell. But this hypothesis clearly underpins the electoral strategy of the NF. Tyndall had spelt out the grand design in his pamphlet *Six Principles of British Nationalism*. He called for:

> Not merely a new type of political party but entirely new types of men to take over the nation's destinies ... Given the character, image and psychology of Conservative and Labour Parties, such a prospect seems remote. Long standing class divisions, however irrational, do not appear as if they can be reconciled by the traditional followers of one attaching themselves to the other. Such a reconciliation could only be achieved by a synthesis of both elements in a new political movement which by tradition was identified with neither one class nor the other ... This is the object of Nationalists in Britain: a new party of the character that can capture a majority following from both sides of the present political spectrum.[13]

In short, Tyndall was calling for the destruction of the two-party system. The subsequent tactics of the NF have shown this strategy in action, attacking the class loyalties and institutions which underpin the two main parties. This carries the vital tactical implication that any attempt to infiltrate political institutions was not to be done solely to take over the institution but (a less ambitious and easier task) to disrupt it to the point where its traditional role of reinforcing the class or party system was undermined. For example, NF policy in the trade unions, as expressed by Tyndall in *Spearhead* in February 1974, is 'To do what the Tories have not done and cannot do; to fight the Left on its own ground in the Unions'.

Growth of NF influence in the trade unions weakens Labour

without giving the Conservatives an advantage. For example, the NF in 1977 claimed more than 100 members and two elected shop stewards in the Rathbone Place depot of the Post Office in Central London, which has some 1600 employees. The NF did not mobilise this support in the dispute at the Grunwick factory in that year, when the fate of the strike depended upon whether or not the postal workers would refuse to deliver mail to Grunwick's. The defence of the Grunwick management had been assumed by the right wing of the Conservative Party. The NF decided not to get involved in the dispute, arguing that it was 'Not in itself of great historical importance ... one gang of Asian Trotskyites trying to force another lot of Asian immigrants to stop working or join a trade union'.[14] In short, the NF will not mobilise its growing influence in the unions where the result might be to gain a victory for the Conservatives. Equally, the NF did not use its strength in the Postal Workers Union to support the Labour Party's line over the Grunwick dispute, even though the strike had assumed considerable symbolic importance for the whole trade union movement in 1977.

Similarly, the formation of the NF Students' Association did not have to envisage eventual control of any students' unions. Its very presence, tiny and feeble as it was, served to disrupt the two-party system, as left-wing and right-wing students joined to work together against the NF. In the autumn of 1977 efforts were made to establish an all-party Joint Committee Against Racism, which was to have included Labour, Conservative and Liberal Parties, the Churches, the Board of Deputies of British Jews, the immigrants' organisations and the National Union of Students. The scheme appeared guaranteed of Conservative support, through the involvement of Conservative Students. The vice-chairman of the Conservative Party, Mr John Moore, MP, was to have been the Joint Committee's co-chairman, along with the Labour MP Miss Joan Lestor. This effort to have an all-party, non-extremist coalition against the NF collapsed, two days before its inaugural meeting, when the Conservative leader Mrs Margaret Thatcher informed Mr Moore that neither he nor the Conservatives could affiliate to the new body, even though her own deputy leader, Mr William Whitelaw, had already given his blessing to the scheme. The National Front was delighted. Had the Joint Committee gone ahead, the NF was prepared with a campaign which would stress that Labour and Conservatives were Tweedledum and Tweedledee, and the NF was the only real alternative. When the

scheme collapsed, with a great deal of bitterness inside the Conservative Party, and with a gulf between Conservative Student organisations and the party leadership, the NF were able to claim another
success.

The classic advantage the NF obtains by placing itself outside the
two-party system is the freedom to make, and quickly abandon,
short-term political alliances with groups inside the political mainstream. For example, in the wake of the arrival of the Ugandan Asian
refugees in 1972 the NF worked closely with the Monday Club, an
anti-immigration pressure group inside the Conservative Party. NF
members helped to steward some of the Monday Club public meetings which protested against the arrivals of the refugees, and NF
members were specifically instructed by the Front leadership to
'swamp' all such meetings with NF banners and leaflets. The result
was a steady erosion of traditional Conservative support into the NF.
At the Uxbridge by-election in December 1972 the local Monday
Club leadership encouraged its members to campaign for the NF
candidate. The Uxbridge leader of the Club was to be but one of a
number of leading Clubbers who later joined the NF. The list
included such Conservative parliamentary candidates as Roy Painter
in Tottenham, such constituency officials as John Kingsley-Read of
Blackburn (later to be a chairman of the NF), and such national
officials as the Club's Midlands Organiser Peter Dawson. 'The
defection of rank and file members of the Club into the NF is as
inevitable as windfalls from an apple tree in autumn,' Martin
Webster wrote in *Spearhead* in May 1973.

But the right-wing of the Conservatives was not the NF's only
recruiting ground. As Tyndall had put it in *Spearhead* as early as
February 1971: 'The Right will always be weak so long as it is based
predominantly on white collar support.' The opportunity to win
recruits from the working class came in 1974, with the bitter confrontation between the Conservative government and the National Union
of Miners, which led to a 3-day week, a national state of emergency
and a general election. The NF supported the miners' strike, and their
pay claim. But at that same time the NF's official policy on trade
unions called for powers to imprison without trial any union leader
'who sought to sabotage the national recovery'. The NF's policy also
calls for the abolition of the current unions, and their replacement by
individual unions for all the workers of each industry – a classic facet
of Mussolini's theory of the Corporate State.

But in 1974 the NF worked tirelessly at winning ground inside the trade unions. At strike after strike–at the Tate and Lyle dispute in London's East End, at the Mansfield Hosiery dispute, at the Imperial Typewriters strike – the NF organised support marches, and demonstrations in support of the strikers – so long as they were white. The two thrusts of the NF argument in the trade unions were spelled out, the first by Philip Gannaway, NF candidate in Bristol and a shop steward in the ETU: 'It is imperative as nationalist trade union members we prove to our fellow workers that we really care about every aspect of their welfare, that our policies embrace what is best in the interests of Britain's future, regardless of class and social status.'[15] The second thrust was exemplified in the report sent to HQ on the NF's successful role in the strike at Imperial Typewriters by Antony Reed-Herbert, leader of the NF in Leicester and a member of the National Directorate:

> The industrial action by Britons at Imperial is a racial struggle ... the struggle of a united British people fighting to preserve their freedom and identity against the forces of communism and international capitalism which seek to destroy the British nation and which use as their tool the immigrant minorities placed by them in our midst.

Reed-Herbert went on to explain how the NF was able to capitalise on the growing concern within the trade union movement over the multi-national corporations: 'The NF has made British workers see just how much their real bosses, the plutocrats of international capitalism snug in their office penthouse suites 3,000 miles across the Atlantic, care for British interests and the concerns of British workpeople.'[16]

In short, the NF has a coherent strategy of undermining the class and institutional reinforcements of the two-party system, and has scored a number of tactical successes to that end. It should, however, be noted that the NF has expended at least as much energy on campaigns with different objectives, which have had considerably less success. Specifically, the NF's attempts to secure a political base in Ulster, and to win votes in Britain by their staunchly pro-Unionist policy on Ulster, have been an almost complete failure. The NF interested itself in Ulster for three main reasons. The first was that a bi-partisan policy over the Ulster crisis was quickly reached by both

Labour and Conservative Parties in the course of 1969–71 – a bi-partisan policy of seeking a political solution and overcoming the terrorist threat to public order. The NF hoped to capitalise on this unity of the two parties, and to win Unionist support in Ulster by championing their cause. Above all, the NF hoped that its extreme 'law and order' stance, bringing back the death penalty and demanding that 'the IRA be smashed', would win British votes. For a number of reasons, the most important being that the UDA, the main Unionist militant body, refused to have any connection with the NF, the money and effort and demonstrations the NF organised were largely wasted. By 1975 the NF appeared to have accepted this defeat and chosen to cut its losses. As a result, the Ulster problem has almost disappeared from NF journals and campaign leaflets.

The NF was also unable, in the period 1971 to 1975, to capitalise upon its staunch hostility to British entry to the EEC. During 1972 the NF's public statements on the EEC became increasingly hysterical in their hostility to the Common Market, culminating in the issue of *Spearhead* in November of 1972, which called on members to 'Obstruct, disorganise and sabotage the working of the Bureaucracy as much as you possibly can . . . Defy the law, be prepared to go to prison too as a gesture of defiance against the imposition of foreign laws on Britain'.

This was no isolated example of mania. The following month, at the largest indoor rally the NF had then held, at Church Hall, Westminster, Tyndall told the meeting: 'The man who signs the Treaty of Rome on January 1 will put himself in the same bracket of history as those who at the end of the war were hung as collaborators.'[17]

The NF then expended little more energy on its anti-EEC policy until 1975, the year of the British referendum on whether or not the country should stay inside the Common Market. The other political groups, parties, and trade unions that were campaigning for Britain to leave the EEC rejected the NF's repeated and determined requests to join that campaign. The NF's attempts at organising its own anti-EEC rallies were destroyed by organised opposition by extreme left groups. There were mass arrests in Glasgow, Oxford and Islington. More than 120 Labour-controlled councils announced that they would refuse to hire out halls to the NF, and the party was reduced to making hostile demonstrations at meetings of the National Referendum Campaign, the coalition for anti-EEC groups, complaining that it was not being allowed in. It had been yet another dismal failure for the NF – but one which may yet be redeemed. The NF is now the only political party in Britain committed to withdrawal from the EEC. There is still a substantial, and perhaps growing, anti-EEC sentiment in the electorate. Intelligent exploitation of the issue by the NF could be an advantage, but there is little evidence that any of the NF's undoubted political acumen has yet been focused on the issue, which remains one of emotionalism and visceral nationalism for the NF leadership.

It is important to recognise the degree to which the NF suffers from its own incompetence. Like extreme right (and, for that matter, left) parties throughout the world, the NF has suffered, in the 10 years of its life, from damaging internal splits, which have often had as much to do with personal rivalries as with genuine differences of ideology. There have been two major splits of the NF membership. The first was in 1972, when the then chairman, John O'Brien, left the party with half of its ruling national directorate, claiming that the Front had been infiltrated by a neo-Nazi group led by John Tyndall and Martin Webster. Little more was heard of O'Brien and his fellow-defectors. In 1975–6 a similar split took place, and again the Front chairman, John Kingsley-Read, with almost half the ruling directorate, left the Front and established a rival National Party, which won two council seats in Kingsley-Read's home town of Blackburn, and had other pockets of support. By the end of 1976 it had collapsed. After each of the splits, John Tyndall emerged as leader, helped each time by his control of the main NF magazine *Spearhead*, by his control of the party's membership lists (which meant that the Front's bewildered membership received only Tyndall's version of events) and by Tyndall's insistence each time that the splitters were 'moderates' who would dilute the NF's uncompromising nationalism.

Left-wing observers, and in particular David Edgar, the play-wright, have seen the second of these splits as a parallel to Adolf Hitler's Night of the Long Knives of 1934, when the 'socialists' of the National Socialist German Workers Party were massacred. He sees, not without reason, the NF's ideology as a 1970s' British version of Hitlerism, and the populist faction which split away from the NF as the political reincarnation of the Nazi Party radicals, such as Röhm and the Strasser brothers. The view rests heavily upon one article in *Spearhead* in December 1975, written by Richard Verrall, a trusted follower of Tyndall. Attacking the Populist faction, Verrall wrote:

'The emergence of these ideas within the NF represents the perennial heresy of Nationalist politics; it was preached before ... by the Strasser faction of the early Nazi Party. It is Marxism in the guise of Nationalism.'

Tyndall had no such theoretical interpretations. For him the whole affair was very simple: he attacked his critics in a pamphlet titled 'Misfits, Inadequates, Failures Ltd', and described them as 'people who can be seen to belong to a thoroughly unprepossessing type ... there is a moronic set of the jaw and a sullen and shifty look in the eyes'.[18]

This tendency to split, when seen in the light of the NF's campaign failures, illustrates the NF's essentially amateur grasp of politics. The alarm that the NF's publicity and electoral successes began to inspire in 1977, particularly in the Labour Party and the trade unions, tended to obscure the NF's own internal weaknesses. The success of the NF in winning traditional Labour votes among the white working class of the deprived inner-city areas in 1976 and 1977 was widely accepted at face value. C. T. Husbands, in *New Society*, was one of the few voices to question whether the growing NF inner-city vote was not simply a protest vote – an angry response against the entrenched Labour councils and their bureaucracy.[19] Husbands suggested that this might be a classic protest vote of the kind the Liberals had won (and quickly lost) in the 1960s, and not some sinister white working-class move towards racism and Nazism. The evidence is still unclear, although the NF's vote in the inner-city areas of London's East End grew through two general and three local government elections, which suggests a certain continuity. But what is clear is that the NF leadership did not realise until very late that the inner cities were becoming their electoral stronghold, and there is no evidence to show that the NF planned an inner-city electoral breakthrough, nor that the leadership had the kind of ideological perspective or political intelligence to expect it.

In October 1974 the NF fielded thirty-six candidates in London and won 4 per cent of the vote. They were sufficiently satisfied by this result, and particularly by their performance in Hackney South and Shoreditch (9.4 per cent), to decide to concentrate on this area.

In the 1977 local elections this strategy was confirmed when the NF won 19.6 per cent of the vote in the Hackney South constituency.

Thus encouraged the Front put up candidates in eighty-eight of London's ninety-two seats in the 1979 general election. The 2 per cent of the vote they won in these seats was a considerable setback even if they won 8.3 per cent in their Hackney South and Shoreditch redoubt, where John Tyndall was the Front's candidate. This drop in Front support in its heartland may well be temporary, however, and may well have been caused by the Conservative Party's success – easier to achieve while in opposition than while in government – in signalling that it too favoured repatriation of black immigrants. Certainly the Conservative Party scored impressive gains in the East End of London.

Much of the East End, particularly in the areas of Hoxton and Shoreditch, looks as though the Luftwaffe was bombing it last week. It is an urban wasteland, pocked by high-rise tower blocks of public housing into which the white working class has been 'decanted' – the planners' word – after slum-clearance programmes. The traditional sense of working-class community in the streets was undermined when the streets were cleared by the (Labour-) council bulldozers. The sense of work-force solidarity was undermined when the docks, and the dockers, were moved down-river, and by the progressive deindustrialisation of the inner city. These are the low-employment, low-earning areas, and because they are cheap, they are the areas where immigrants have tended to congregate. Naturally enough, the immigrants bring their shops, their churches and their own community into the shattered relics of the working-class white culture which once thrived there. The more one studies the process, the more one is surprised that the NF's level of vote has so far only reached 20 per cent. The entrenched local Labour Parties and Labour councils have only themselves to blame for the 'protest' votes of their electors.

The local Labour leadership has responded in two ways to the process. One has been to borrow the NF's own weapons. When Newham council changed its system of allocating council houses, the Housing Committee chairman, Councillor William Watts, told the press: 'One of the reasons for the rethink is the influx of Asians. In five years we would have been doing nothing but giving homes to Asians.' The other Labour strategy was to appeal to central government. The Labour leader of Lewisham council said: 'We have to impress on the Government that to avoid racial violence, we will have to increase public spending in this kind of deprived urban area. This has now become a national priority which must override even the spending controls of the financial recession.'[20]

Neither of these policies addressed themselves to the fundamental political problem of East and South-east London, which was that the NF was an organised political party moving into a political vacuum. Labour's traditional control of the East End had been so secure for so long that the political machine atrophied, particularly when deindustrialisation removed much of the trade-union base. In 1950 and 1951 more than 80 per cent of East and South-east Londoners voted. By 1974 the proportion of people bothering to vote was between 51.6 per cent, Newham NW, and 64.4. per cent, Woolwich East.[21] Labour Party membership, which had topped 1 million in Britain in 1950, was below 300,000 in 1976, and membership had declined most steeply in inner-city seats. In strong Labour areas, such as the mining regions of Durham or the London docks, the Labour Party and the trade union had traditionally been more than the dominant political forces in the community; they had also been key vehicles of education, of recreation, of social life. By the 1970s the Labour organisations in the inner cities had begun to look like rotten boroughs. By comparison, as we have seen, the NF branches deliberately combined their political work with a social, recreational appeal.

It is significant that this growing NF appeal in the inner cities has come at a time of economic recession, with unemployment rising to 1,500,000, and successive cuts in public expenditure reducing the money available to improve the housing, the health care, education and social services available to deprived areas. We do not have to look to alarmist comparisons with Weimar Germany to see that traditional working-class support for Labour in these circumstances will be under severe pressure. But the importance of the economic crisis for the NF's own propaganda does raise the question of the economic future.. And even the optimists, who see North Sea oil prosperity as the answer to Britain's social and economic problems, have not explained how the capital-intensive (and consequently low-employment) development of oil and related petro-chemical industries will reduce the kind of mass structural unemployment which Britain now suffers from.

The future of the NF is not at all easy to predict. The party is now nationally established. It has a coherent series of policies on the major issues and an effective party organisation that can reach into some 300 of Britain's 635 constituencies. It is not yet genuinely British. In spite of sporadic attempts to establish bases in Scotland and Ulster, it is still basically an *English* party; and, indeed, there are significant ways in which it can be seen as an English response to the same kind of pressures which have helped to bring about the growth of Welsh and Scottish Nationalism. But striking as the rising curve of NF votes may be, it is worth remembering that proportional representation in multi-member constituencies of the size used for STV would not have given the NF any seats at a parliamentary nor in a GLC election. Under the Blake Commission's suggested additional member system of PR (which inserts a 5 per cent barrier but above that is more generous to small parties) the NF would on its 1977 county council performance win four parliamentary seats in Greater London, and probably four more in the West Midlands. This is small beer in psephological terms.[21] The NF has already shown, at the West Bromwich by-election of May 1973, that it can mobilise its national support into effective *blitz* canvassing teams to fight one constituency. The NF may feel that the advantages of having one MP, and using the privileged platform of the House of Commons as a showcase, would be worth the effort.[22] Certainly the NSDAP used the German Reichstag as a showcase for its policies, for its attacks upon its opponents, and for expressing its contempt for the Reichstag as a 'talking-shop'. But the French Poujadiste movement began to collapse when it won parliamentary seats.

A parliamentary presence for the NF would present the party with a number of options, not all of them attractive. If the British electorate continues to withhold a clear mandate from either of the two major parties, as it did in the two 1974 general elections, then the time may come when the NF MP or MPs may be courted for their votes in some kind of *de facto* coalition. This would present the NF with the same kind of dilemma as the one which tore at the Liberal Party during its 'pact' with the Labour Government in 1977–8. Much would depend on the calibre of any NF candidates elected to the Commons, their capacity as public speakers, as campaigners, and, most of all, their capacity to secure the essentially volatile vote which put them in parliament by becoming a classically 'good constituency MP'.

But it is useful to bear in mind this perspective of the NF's possible future as we look at the movement in 1979. We are, after all, observing a party that is still dynamic, still with a very much shorter pedigree and more disparate tradition than the SNP or Plaid Cymru, let alone the Labour, Liberal and Conservative Parties. It is also a party which grew without institutional roots, in the sense that the Labour Party grew out of the trade unions, or the Conservatives long depended on their connections with the various 'interests' of Church, universities, and the landed interest. The NF was born without any such natural constituency or source of funds. It is essentially rootless, and, because of this, depends upon a rising tide of votes. In so far as it is a vehicle for protest votes, there must be continuing fuel for protest, and an apparent return from that protest. The NF depends now, as much as it did in its earliest days, upon regular publicity, the morale-boost of growing success, of a rising number of votes. And this means, of course, that the NF's future depends, quite dramatically, upon the continuing erosion of the traditional stability of the two-party system.

Part IV

The Northern Irish Parties

8

The Northern Irish Parties: the Background

Sarah Nelson

Constitutionally, Northern Ireland is part of the United Kingdom. Yet the politics of the province have been different in some fundamental ways from British politics; so, traditionally, has been its two-party system. Historically, the parties did not share a basic loyalty to the state itself; on the contrary, their main division was over whether the Northern Ireland regime should exist at all. The Unionists stoutly defended the Border and the British link: the Nationalists demanded Irish unification. Secondly, the electorate was divided on religious rather than class lines – most Protestants voted for the Unionist Party, most Catholics for the Nationalist Party. Thirdly, stability did not result from competitiveness or the alternation of parties in government. Such stability – or stagnation – as existed resulted from the fact that the Protestants were in a permanent two-thirds majority. Fourthly, the parties did not see themselves as national groups competing for the 'middle-ground' vote among all sections of the population. Parties stood for one religious community, made no attempt to win votes from the other, and had little faith that such an attempt would succeed. There was no 'middle-ground' to appeal to anyway – what little existed voted for third parties, such as the Northern Ireland Labour Party.

The political culture was also very different from the British one. Despite many important differences between Protestant and Catholic ideology, both religious communities tended to share certain political values. First, the constitutional issue took priority over socio-economic issues, except for short periods and in exceptional circumstances. People were divided over non-compromisable issues; hence politics had many of the characteristics of a zero-sum game. Refusal to compromise was synonymous with honesty and integrity, compromise with weakness, treachery and appeasement. Each side was expected to work 'for its own': while people complained about discrimination and Catholics felt it to be a serious injustice, people expected it to happen as a normal part of political life. It was difficult for many to imagine that if Catholics gained some benefit Protestants would not lose one, and vice versa.

Most political outcomes were highly predictable: Stormont was less a real debating chamber than a gladiatorial arena for the ritual restatement of old positions. When the vote was taken in the House, the Unionists always won. Few constituencies were marginal: many seats remained uncontested for decades. Most people in politics behaved as they were expected to – this may have been boring, but it lent important reassurance in a society riddled with so many tensions and divisions. Political careers did not tend to attract the intelligent or unconventional while the rewards for those who joined third parties were low. Many people (especially the professional middle class) opted out of politics, and lamented the bigotry of politicians from a safe distance; others emigrated, and some felt deeply alienated, a few sufficiently to prefer the gun to politics.

Terence O'Neill, who became Prime Minister in 1963, challenged many of the traditional rules and assumptions we have described; so did the Catholic civil rights movement. O'Neill saw the future stability of Northern Ireland in the reconciliation of Catholics to the Northern Ireland regime and to Unionist party government. He spoke for a growing number of middle-class Protestants who felt hampered and embarrassed by the old rigidities. They wanted to develop good economic relationships with Britain, Eire and foreign countries, attract investment, and modernise the economy. They looked to a future in the EEC and saw themselves as Europeans rather than as Ulstermen. O'Neill was thus turning many traditional values upside down – implying that some Catholics could be 'loyal' and trusted, that material values were more important than non-material ones, that both religious groups could be economic and political winners in the 'game'. Moderation became a virtue rather than a vice, ambition and efficiency were new gods, parochialism (or local pride) was shameful rather than praiseworthy.

At the same time a growing number of Catholics were tiring of the sterile, conservative, anti-partitionist politics of the old Nationalist Party, which had brought them few benefits. A new Catholic middle class was growing up under the impetus of the Welfare State. They were readier than their predecessors to relegate to second place the old demand of Irish unity, and to accept existing realities if they gained equal participation within the state. Such people played a key role in the new Civil Rights movement; they called for 'full British rights, full British standards' and an end to the discrimination which crippled their attempts to participate in the system. They were prepared to be conciliated if the necessary reforms were passed by the government.

Thus the reassuring predictability of politics was eroded: some Catholics were suddenly calling for British standards rather than Irish unity, some Protestants were openly courting Catholic support. More extreme elements were instantly stirred to protest. Traditional republicans and nationalists felt their leaders were 'selling out' on their principles. Staunch Protestants felt likewise, and believed that a treacherous Prime Minister was attempting to conciliate Catholics who neither would nor could be conciliated. The stage was set for intensified strains between each religious community, and divisions within them. Catholic expectations were raised about real reform, which O'Neill was either unable or unwilling to meet. Protestant suspicions, and fears about their constitutional future, were heightened and articulated by politicians like William Craig or Ian Paisley. These uncertainties were not confined to bigoted or extreme Protestants, just as impatience and frustration was not confined to extreme Catholics. The impact of O'Neillism and the Civil Rights movement was far-reaching.

On the party system the immediate effect was to split the traditionally dominant Ulster Unionist Party. The splinter groups and new parties which emerged during the conflict (such as Vanguard and the Democratic Unionists) have been fighting within the Protestant 'camp' over two major issues. The first concerns the extent of conciliation which should be offered Catholics within Northern Ireland, and across the border (the Irish Republic). The second concerns the attitude to be adopted to Westminster's demands after Britain became an active party to the conflict with the arrival of the British army in 1969. Protestant groups have divided on whether they should obey, question or actively oppose the British government's constitutional proposals for the province.

While the Unionist Party fragmented, an opposite process took place among the anti-partitionist parties: the new Social Democratic and Labour Party became electorally dominant within the Catholic community. This party has combined an ultimate aspiration towards Irish unity with a social-democratic economic policy, and demands for Catholic accommodation within the existing regime through participation in government. Republican groups have competed with it for electoral (and other forms of) support. While these groups have disagreed internally on socio-economic policy, on the attitude to be taken to the Protestant population, and on the political stages necessary before Irish unity can be achieved, they have seen the formation of an Irish republic of thirty-two counties as the major goal, and have accused the SDLP of collusion and appeasement.

Recent history has shown that the parties can be grouped into three broad political tendencies: pro-union, centre and anti-partition. Further, despite the rise and fall in individual party fortunes, electoral support for these tendencies has remained remarkably stable.

The *pro-union* tendency has encompassed the major Protestant party, the Ulster Unionist Party, and its splinter parties. Fragmentation within this tendency reached its height in 1974 when at least five Protestant parties were competing for the Protestant vote. The *centre tendency* was filled, before 1969, by the Liberal and Labour Parties, and to some extent by the O'Neillite wing of the Unionist Party. Since 1970, however, the political centre has become synonymous with the Alliance Party. This is a predominantly middle-class grouping which has consistently called for participation in government by Protestants and Catholics and equal opportunities for all citizens of Northern Ireland. It has supported the Union on the ground that this reflects a majority wish in Ulster, but has also called for closer, more co-operative links with the Irish republic. The Alliance Party has been able to attract only 10–15 per cent of the vote at elections.

The *anti-partition tendency* has seen some consolidation since 1969; the traditional vehicle for Catholic aspirations, the Nationalist Party, has become moribund and has been replaced by the SDLP. The traditional republican groupings which periodically competed with the Nationalists have remained, under different labels, but have failed to make any serious electoral challenge to the SDLP.

Recent trends in the province have indicated that the number of parties receiving any significant electoral support has been reduced to four: the Ulster Unionist Party and Ian Paisley's Democratic Unionist Party, representing the pro-union tendency; the Alliance Party, representing the centre tendency; and the Social Democratic and Labour Party representing the anti-partition tendency.

It will be seen that the kinds of issue which have absorbed Ulster parties in recent years have been markedly different from those dominating the attention of British parties. Their own centre of attention has been themselves, Stormont and later the British direct-rule administration, rather than the Westminster forum. Another difference marking off Ulster parties from British ones has been their need to compete for support with groups who reject constitutionalism in itself – who pursue their goals by violence or industrial action such as strikes. This division has continually demanded the attention of the political parties, especially the SDLP. More recently, after a succession of constitutional failures culminating in the Constitutional Convention's inability to design a widely acceptable form of government for the province, they have also had to face another problem – popular disillusionment with politicians themselves. Questions about their own efficacy and their future role have been sharpened by the effects of prolonged direct rule in Ulster, which deprives parties of any clearly defined function and lessens their impetus to consolidate their structures, recruit new members or seek areas of agreement with each other. On the other hand, if direct rule continues indefinitely with no sign of agreed moves towards a local administration, the importance of the Westminster forum is likely to *increase* for Ulster politicians. At the same time, the British government is having to concern itself more directly with the province's socio-economic problems and industrial policy, as well as with reform of the educational system, divorce laws, etc. Political groups in Ulster may thus pay increasing attention to the quality of the representatives they send to Westminster, and to the devices they can use to extract concessions from the mother parliament.

This raises questions about the attention Westminster must pay to Northern Ireland's political groupings. This has traditionally been slight. From the foundation of the Stormont regime in 1920 until the recent civil disorders, Westminster followed a convention of non-involvement in internal Ulster affairs, despite the efforts of concerned Catholics in the province to make Britain interested in the political injustices there and intervene as she was constitutionally entitled to do. During the recent conflict British parties have striven for a bi-partisan policy on major Ulster issues: no division has made major political impact nor been used for electoral gain by either major British party. The one significant change at Westminster in recent years has been the proclamation of an independent stance by Ulster Unionist MPs, who no longer give automatic voting support to the Conservative Party. This attempt to increase their bargaining power has won minor concessions, such as Labour's promise to review the under-representation of Ulster voters at Westminster; it is an open question whether the Northern Ireland bloc would possess the skill or the opportunity to extract more meaningful benefits in a future parliament, or threaten the survival of the governing party. One must look elsewhere than the party system to discover really significant effects which the Ulster conflict has had on British political life and values.

Violence in Northern Ireland has led the British liberal–democratic system to pass in Ulster a range of measures which depart from its declared principles. These include internment without trial, special powers legislation and non-jury courts. With the spread of the IRA bombing campaign to England, the British government has introduced such legislation as the Prevention of Terrorism Act (PTA), which suspends normal *habeas corpus* regulations and gives wide powers to the police. These measures can be used against every citizen in Britain, and are more likely to be made permanent than to be abolished or amended, as PTA renewal debates at Westminster have demonstrated. Highly developed techniques of surveillance and control have been developed in Northern Ireland: the human and technical expertise involved can readily be made operative in Britain should state agencies decide that they are necessary. Thus terrorism and counter-terrorism in Ulster have eroded the infrastructure of British political life, which all its liberal–democratic parties claim to uphold, in ways which have already changed the state of civil liberties and may alter it in more far-reaching, and as yet unknown, directions. unknown, directions.

Conclusion

Multi-Party Britain

H. M. Drucker

In a recent book Professor Giovanni Sartori has described two-party politics simply: 'We have a two-party format whenever the existence of third parties does not prevent the two major parties from governing alone, i.e. whenever coalitions are unnecessary.' He then underlines the point in other words:

> This is the same as saying that alternation in power is the distinguishing mark of the mechanics of two-partyism. One may say that 'two' differs from 'three' whenever third parties do not affect, in the long run, and at the national level, the alternation in power of the two major parties.[1]

Professor Sartori cites the United Kingdom (or 'England', as he will call it) as the perfect two-party system; but he admits that the system may be about to change.

Strange though it may seem, the notion that the party system of a Western power may change is itself rather novel. In 1967 Professors S. M. Lipset and Stein Rokkan came close to dismissing the possibility of such change in their book *Party Systems and Voter Alignments: Cross National Perspectives* – the most influential post-war book on comparative parties. Lipset and Rokkan noted:

> We have pushed our attempt at a systematization of the comparative history of partisan oppositions in European politics up to some

point in the 1920s. Why stop there? . . . The reason is deceptively
simple: the party systems of the 1960s reflect, with few but significant exceptions, the cleavage structures of the 1920s. This is a
crucial characteristic of Western competitive politics in the age of
'high mass consumption': the party alternatives, and in remarkably many cases the party organizations, are older than the
majorities of the national electorates.[2]

However, even after this statement, Lipset and Rokkan could not
dismiss from their book the notion that a new generation of dissaf-
fected youth, who had already invented new types of criminality and
styles of living, might form new parties. But they doubted it.[3]

We now know that, as far as Britain is concerned, this conservatism
was too confident. There are now more than two political parties,
some of them quite new, here. More to the point, by Professor
Sartori's test Britain no longer has a two-party system. The leaders of
the two largest parties cannot face general elections in the confident
expectation that one or other of them will form a government after it,
without help from some other party or parties.

A word or two of caution may be useful here. We are not saying that
each of the next few general elections will be followed by a coalition or
minority government. We are talking about and recording our observation of a general trend, increasingly discernible since 1955, away
from two-party politics. Our claim is that this trend has gone so far
that Sartori's criterion of two-partyness is no longer being met.

As we have seen, this is not simply a matter of the two major parties
losing support to other contenders. The two major parties have
themselves changed in important ways as they have sought to adapt
to their reduced circumstances. As Andrew Gamble has shown in this
volume, the internal changes in the Conservative Party over the past
20 years have been considerable. Where once it could confidently
govern itself and the country with few formal rules and no internal
democracy, it has now lost its nerve. It has also lost the confidence of
many of the influential institutions which once happily worked with
the party. Labour has apparently benefited from recent changes, but,
as Robert Borthwick has shown, the old working-class traditions of
loyalty and solidarity which once gave Labour so many safe seats and
ensured that Labour MPs obeyed their Whips – at least when the
party was in office – have disintegrated. The Labour Party has lost
votes and individual members. Discipline within the parliamentary
party is much looser than it used to be.

The point which the chapters of this volume demonstrate most clearly is that the various features of the party system no longer reinforce one another. The Conservative and Labour Parties are no longer able to call on the loyalty of large numbers of supporters in the constituencies – nor on the electorate. The Liberal Party is no longer able to pretend that it is the understudy if either of the two major parties should falter. The SNP and PC are impressive campaigning machines in Scotland and Wales but have weak parliamentary groups and lack solid electoral support. The politics of Northern Ireland, once so predictable, now shift and change almost monthly, and no Northern Ireland party can be counted on to support any British party in the division lobbies in the House of Commons. The major parties can no longer anathematise the parties on the left – the Marxist parties – and the right – the National Front. Indeed, the parties of the centre occasionally steal an idea or a policy from the extremist parties. The party system is beginning to break up. The old reinforcement has ceased. We may summarise this change by saying that the party system has begun to break up along two dimensions: organisational and geographical.

The organisational point is probably the more important. The electorate is moving away from the parties and yet votes for parties whose policies it dislikes. The local constituency associations and parties back some policies – the Rhodesian rebellion and wholesale nationalisation, for example – which are not attractive to the party leaders. Governments are easily cut off from feeling within their parties or within the electorate. It is no longer possible to define the party system entirely in terms of government and opposition formation – as Sartori does – nor entirely in terms of divisions in the electorate. The two respond to different rhythms. Labour governed with remarkably little difficulty between 1976 (when it lost its majority) and the general election of 1979, despite the fact that it trailed the Conservative Party in the opinion polls for most of that time. One change, however, which has happened both in Westminster and the country, is in party discipline. Both in the lobbies at Westminster and in the poll booths people are less loyal to the parties of their grandfather's choice.

The chapters in this volume by Peter Mair on the Marxist left and Martin Walker on the National Front bring out another point. The parties of the Marxist left are really cadre parties. They do contest elections from time to time, but they do not expect to win. Their existence and the vigour of their intellectual life is a standing comment on the failure of the Labour Party to convince the left – and particularly young people on the left – that Labour represents Socialism. The success of the National Front in recruiting large numbers of followers in precisely those inner-city areas where, by tradition, Labour has been strong, and where now her individual membership is negligible, is an even more poignant pointer to the failure of the Labour Party to speak for numbers of Britons. The ability of the National Front to force the Conservative leadership to bring race into the front rank of issues speaks worlds for the power of that electorally insignificant and parliamentarily non-existent party.

Roger Mullin shows that in at least one part of Britain it is possible for a quite respectable – if not positively dull – political party to organise thousands of activists. The SNP's success in Scotland is a sign of the failure in Scotland of both major parties. Its ability to win the support of 30 per cent of the Scots electorate at a general election also suggests that 'class' is not so salient a division in Scotland as it is usually thought to be. Yet Scotland is often held to be a more class-divided society than England.

But the party system is also breaking up on geographical lines. The 1955 general election was the last in which there was a uniform swing across the country. In the 1959 election the north of England, particularly the North-West, and Scotland swung to Labour, while the rest of Britain went Conservative. Since that election, differences between the various parts of the country have been increasing. Wales and Scotland now have unique electoral patterns. In each case a national party has appeared on the scene and is a strong contender for votes. Northern Irish voting was always different, of course. Its distinctiveness seems less surprising now that British voting patterns have shattered. But it must not be thought that England has remained true to class politics. On the contrary, as Michael Steed has pointed out, the country has become divided between the core and the periphery. The core – those parts of the country closest to the capital – belongs to a striking extent to the Conservative Party; the periphery belongs to the other parties, of which Labour is far the biggest. Defining South-East Britain as the core (i.e. East Anglia, the Midlands, and Southern England) and North-West Britain (i.e. Scotland, Wales, and Northern England) as the periphery, he has produced the following analysis of parliamentary seats after the February 1974 general election:[4]

Seats	Con	Lab	Others	Majority
NW Britain	81	178	19	Lab 78
SE Britain	216	123	5	Con 88

The figures in this table do suggest that the previous importance of the class division in British voting has been, to no small extent, cross-cut by a division on core/periphery lines.

The constitutional debate over devolution has been partly a response by both Conservative and Labour Parties to this increasing geographical division. As the evidence collected by the Kilbrandon Commission shows, the demand for stronger regional authorities is not confined to Wales and Scotland; it is, indeed, stronger in some parts of England than Wales, but so far the SNP and Plaid Cymru have taken the greatest advantage of the new mood. Their success in playing on the feeling of nationality amongst the Scottish and Welsh people led a Labour government to consider a measure of devolution. Distinctive Assemblies for Scotland and Wales would lead to ever more distinctive government in those two parts of the country, and thus make any future return to central domination even less likely. At the same time, for quite different reasons, the Protestant majority of Northern Ireland is no longer willing to accept the Conservative whip in Westminster. In an oblique way these changes confirm the relationship perceived by Professors Lipset and Rokkan and the whole school of comparative party theorists of the 1960s; there is a relationship between party and nation-building. What we are seeing in the UK suggests there is also a relationship between party and nation-destruction.

The reader is entitled to ask how we should classify the emerging party system. If it is no longer two-party, what is it? This is a fair question. But it can be answered only in the most general terms. The UK is now a multi-party state. Changes are still happening so fast that it would be foolhardy to go much beyond that. Nevertheless, one or two pointers can be discerned. Britain still has two parties – Conservative and Labour – which are very much larger and more powerful than the others. It is not inconceivable that either of them might form a government unaided after a future general election; and it is inconceivable that a government will be formed which excludes both of them. The other parties vary considerably. Some, the Irish parties and the Scottish and Welsh nationalist parties, contest elections only in their countries. Others, the Liberals most prominently, but also the Marxist parties and the National Front, while strongest in England, do not confine themselves to one of the British nations. Some, especially the Scottish National Party, Plaid Cymru, and the National Front are well blessed with a large number of enthusiastic supporters. None of the smaller parties are dominated by their parliamentary groups as the larger parties are. But then, most of them have small, and some have non-existent, parliamentary groups. None of the existing UK parties have much experience of coalition formation. Few are yet prepared to explain their attitude to coalitions to the electorate before elections. If coalitions become frequent – as it seems reasonable to expect – the parties will come under pressure to declare likely partners. The Liberal Party is the furthest advanced in this respect.

None of the smaller parties have a solid electoral base. Few Liberal electors yet identify their interests with the party they vote for. This lack of solid identifiers is one of the main reasons why we cannot believe that the present party system is permanent.

Perhaps the last remaining bulwark of two-party politics is the electoral system. The position of the minor parties would be handsomely improved it the country adopted proportional representation. Which of them would benefit would depend on which kind of PR was adopted. Indeed, as Andrew Gamble notes, we may use the electoral system as something of a litmus test of the party system. The continued insistence of the leaders of the Conservative and Labour Parties on the 'first-past-the-post' system is a reflection of their unwillingness to admit that they no longer live in a two-party world. If either major party were to concede the creation of a PR system for Westminster, it would also be said to have conceded the arrival of multi-party politics.

While it lasted, the two-party system was praised as a keystone in the arch of the British Constitution. It was thought to connect the machinery of government to the will of the people in a way which enabled the weight of each to support the other. That keystone is now missing. Perhaps it will be replaced. Perhaps we shall learn to live without it or any replacement. Perhaps we shall learn to reconstruct the Constitution on some new basis. Without it the government and politics of Britain cannot be quite so orderly for some time.

Notes and References

Introduction

1. Quoted from Sir I. Jennings, *The British Constitution* (fourth edn) (Cambridge, 1962) p. 62. The quotation is from *Iolanthe* by W. S. Gilbert.
2. Ibid, p. 63.
3. R. T. McKenzie, *British Political Parties* (London 1963 edn) p. 636.
4. S. H. Beer, *Modern British Politics* (London, 1965) p. 386.
5. R. T. McKenzie, *British Political Parties*, p. 636.
6. J. Blondel, *Voters, Parties and Leaders* (Harmondsworth, 1963) p. 90.
7. A. H. Birch, *Representative and Responsible Government* (London, 1964) pp. 243-5.
8. G. Moodie, *The Government of Great Britain* (London, 1964) p. 65.
9. R. M. Punnett, *British Government and Politics* (London, 1968) p. 101.
10. M. Duverger, *Political Parties* (London, 1954) p. 217; and Sir I. Gilmour, *The Body Politic* (London, 1969) p. 25. Gilmour also states that 'The party system is a far more dominating feature of the Constitution than ... any other "constitutional" feature', p. 24.
11. See the admirable summary of this theory in L. Epstein, *Political Parties in Western Democracies* (London, 1967) pp. 46-76.
12. S. E. Finer, *Adversary Politics and Electoral Reform* (London, 1975).
13. D. Butler and D. Kavanagh, *The British General Election of October 1974* (London, 1975) p. 285.
14. Lord Houghton (Chairman), *Report of the Committee on Financial Aid to Political Parties* (London, 1976).
15. I. Crewe, *et al.*, 'Partisan Dealignment in Britain, 1964-74', *British Journal of Political Science*, vol. 7 (1977) pp. 129-190. This work has been

admirably summarised in an article in *The Economist*, 17 March 1978, pp. 22–25.

16. A. King, *Why is Britain becoming harder to govern?* (London, 1976).

17. See G. Ionescu, *Centripetal Politics: Government and the New Centers of Power* (London, 1975), especially chapters II and III; R. E. Pahl and J. T. Winkler, 'Corporatism in Britain', *The Times*, 26 March 1976, p. 14.

Chapter 1

An earlier version of this paper appeared in *Parliamentary Affairs*, XXXII, no. 1 (1979).

1. See, for instance, F. J. C. Hearnshaw, *Conservatism in England* (London, 1933); J. Boyd Carpenter, *The Conservative Case* (London, 1950); Q. Hogg, *The Case for Conservatism* (Harmondsworth, 1947).

2. This has received illuminating analysis recently from Tom Nairn, 'The Twilight of the British State', *New Left Review*, 101–2 (1977) pp. 3–61.

3. An authoritative Conservative view of the Constitution is L. S. Amery, *Thoughts on the Constitution* (Oxford, 1953).

4. All figures are taken from D. Butler and A. Sloman, *British Political Facts, 1900–75* (London, 1975).

5. Cf. R. T. McKenzie and A. Silver, *Angels in Marble* (London, 1968).

6. Persuasively documented by Maurice Cowling, *The Impact of Labour, 1920–4* (Cambridge, 1971).

7. See the rigorous examination by G. Sartori, *Parties and Party Systems* (Cambridge, 1977) chapter 6.

8. Analyses and speculations on this topic include J. H. Goldthorpe *et al.*, *The Affluent Worker: Political Attitudes and Behaviour* (Cambridge, 1968); F. Zweig, *The worker in an affluent society* (London, 1961); and M. Abrams and R. Rose, *Must Labour Lose?* (Harmondsworth, 1959).

9. I. Crewe *et al.*, 'Partisan Dealignment in Britain, 1964–74', *British Journal of Political Science*, 7 (1977) pp. 129–190.

10. Ibid.

11. Labour has done better at general elections which have followed a period in government (1950, 1951, 1966, 1974 Oct.) than at those which have followed a period in opposition (1955, 1959, 1964, 1974 Feb.); 1970 is so far the only exception to this pattern.

12. Cf. McKenzie and A. Silver, *Angels in Marble*; R. D. Jessop, *Traditionalism, Conservatism, and British Political Culture* (London, 1974); F. Parkin, 'Working class Conservatives – a theory of political deviance', *British Journal of Sociology*, 18 (1967) pp. 278–90.

13. Among the more important contributions to this debate are J. Biffen, *Political Office or Political Power?* (London, 1977); Sir Keith Joseph, *Stranded on the Middle Ground?* (London, 1976); I. Gilmour, *Inside Right: a*

Study of Conservatism (London, 1977); P. Walker, *The Ascent of Britain* (London, 1977); and R. Blake and J. Patten (eds), *The Conservative Opportunity* (London, 1976).
14. Cf. P. Seyd, 'Democracy within the Conservative Party?', *Government and Opposition* (1975) pp. 219–37; and M. Pinto-Duschinsky, 'Central Office and "Power" in the Conservative Party', *Political Studies*, 20 (1972).
15. Cf. P. Seyd, 'Factionalism within the Conservative Party: the Monday Club', *Government and Opposition* (1972) pp. 464–87.
16. P. Norton, *Dissension in the House of Commons* (London, 1975).
17. See R. Blackburn, 'The Heath Government: a new course for British capitalism', *New Left Review*, 70 (1971) pp. 3–26; and P. Norton, *Dissension in the House of Commons*.
18. See Susan Strange, *Sterling and British Policy* (Oxford, 1971).

Chapter 2

1. This point is made more fully in R. Taylor, 'The Uneasy Alliance – Labour and the Unions', *Political Quarterly*, 47 (1976) pp. 398–407.
2. See, for example, D. Leonard, *Paying for Party Politics*, PEP Broadsheet No. 555 (London, 1975) p. 2; and C. Martin and D. Martin, 'Decline of Labour Party Membership', *Political Quarterly*, 48 (1977) pp. 459–71.
3. For a fuller account of the SLP, see H. M. Drucker, *Breakaway: the Scottish Labour Party* (Edinburgh, 1978).
4. On this see P. Seyd, 'Labour Party Reform', *Political Quarterly*, 49 (1978) pp. 38–43.
5. These cases are discussed more fully in A. D. R. Dickson, 'When Rejects Re-run: a Study in Independency', *Political Quarterly*, 46 (1975) pp. 271–9.
6. R. T. McKenzie, *British Political Parties*, 2nd (rev.) ed. (London, 1964) p. 635.
7. For details of the 1976 election see H. M. Drucker, 'Leadership Selection in the Labour Party', *Parliamentary Affairs*, XXIX (1976) pp. 378–95.

Chapter 3

1. The Liberal presence in the House of Lords has been important to the party. A number of hereditary peers have been Liberals, and the party possessed a number of ennobled elder statesmen (notably Viscount Samuel), which kept Liberal representation above that in the Commons. Since 1964 the party has also received life peerages and, given the Commons voting system, has put into the Lords several active leading politicians who in another party would be MPs.

2. See Michael Steed's Foreword (pp. 20–8) in Arthur Cyr, *Liberal Party Politics in Britain* (London, 1977).

3. See Cyr, *Liberal Party Politics in Britain*, p. 187 (and p. 34 for updating).

4. David Butler and Donald Stokes, *Political Change in Britain*, 2nd ed. (London, 1974) Tables 12–7 and 12–8.

5. James Alt, Ivor Crewe and Bo Särlvik, 'Angels in Plastic: the Liberal Surge in 1974', *Political Studies*, XXV (1977) p. 348. Alt *et al.* estimate that around 2¼ million February Liberal voters did not repeat their vote in October. Since the actual fall in the Liberal vote in comparable constituencies was 1.2 million (see above, p. 81), on that basis there must have been 1½ million new Liberal voters in these constituencies in October. Allowing for the probable votes in constituencies with no candidate in February, a combination of this psephological and survey evidence produces the following estimates for the 1974 Liberal vote:

Liberal vote in February and October	3.65 million
Liberal vote in February only	3.0 million
Liberal vote in October only	1.65 million
Total Liberal vote	8.3 million

Alt *et al.* further estimate (p. 349) that another 22 per cent of their sample either thought seriously about voting Liberal or would very likely have done so if the Liberal candidate had had a chance of winning locally.

6. Douglas Schoen, *Enoch Powell and the Powellites* (London, 1977) pp. 181, 184 and 185.

7. Alt *et al.*, 'Angels in Plastic'.

8. Glenn Wilson, 'The Liberal Extremists', *New Society*, 1 Nov. 1973, pp. 263–4. The data is based on a small (924) sample in January 1973, when the Liberal vote was above its core level.

9. David White, 'Nuclear power: a special *New Society* survey', 31 March 1977, p. 648.

10. Gallup Report, Political Demographics 30 November 1977–30 January 1978. Data used with permission of Social Surveys (Gallup Poll) Ltd.

11. I am indebted to John Curtice of Nuffield College, Oxford, for the secondary analysis of the Butler and Stokes data from which these figures are drawn.

12. The legacy may also be interpreted as the persistence of a cleavage; and the strong association of the core Liberal vote with religious dissent, the Welsh language minority, small farmers and the peripheral regions of Great Britain can be seen as a typical alliance in terms of the cleavage system approach. Cf. S. M. Lipset and Stein Rokkan (eds), *Party Systems and Voter Alignments* (New York, 1967) chapter 1.

13. *Sunday Times*, 22 September 1968.

14. Butler and Stokes (listed), *Political Change in Britain*, p. 322; Alt *et al.*, 'Angels in Plastic', pp. 365–6.

15. Peter H. Lemieux, 'Political Issues and Liberal Support in the February, 1974 British General Election', *Political Studies*, XXV (1977) pp. 323–42.

16. Butler and Stokes (listed), *Political Change in Britain*, p. 323; Alt *et al.*, 'Angels in Plastic', p. 359.

17. On tactical voting, see the Nuffield series of general election studies for 1966, February 1974, and, more especially, Michael Steed, 'An Analysis of the Results', in D. E. Butler and Dennis Kavanagh, *The British General Election of October 1974* (London, 1975) pp. 337–42.

18. See Michael Steed, 'Case Study: My Own By-election', *Government and Opposition*, 9 (1974) pp. 356–8, and references cited.

19. Michael Steed, 'The National Front Vote', *Parliamentary Affairs*, XXXI, no. 3 (1978).

20. See the Analysis of the Results in the Nuffield series of general election studies for these years, and also Hugh Berrington, 'The General Election of 1964', *Journal of the Royal Statistical Society*, Series A, 128 (1965) pp. 17–66.

21. The hundredth anniversary of the foundation of the National Liberal Federation in May 1877 was celebrated as the Liberal Centenary Year of 1977; but the formation of Gladstone's 1868 Cabinet had been celebrated as the first Liberal Cabinet at a centenary dinner in 1968.

22. For many years LPD operated as a part of LPO, but in 1977 it moved to a separate address in London (9 Poland Street, London W1) and has been increasingly stressing its autonomy.

23. The National League of Young Liberals and the Union of Liberal Students have co-operated closely, particularly in the 10 years from 1966, when they decided to use the umbrella title Young Liberal Movement. They are widely referred to simply as the Young Liberals. But they retain separate representation at all levels of the party.

24. Clause F1 of the constitution of the Liberal Party.

25. Cyr, *Liberal Party Politics in Britain*, pp. 166–9.

26. Gordon Lishman, 'The Inarticulate and the Deaf', *New Outlook*, 17, No. 12 (December 1977) p. 29. A letter from a former Liberal MP, Paul Tyler, in *New Outlook*, 18, No. 2 (March 1978) p. 17, expressed a typical counter opinion: 'Gordon Lishman's superficial survey of relations between the Liberal Parliamentary Party and the party hierarchy demonstrates all too well how out of touch the latter have become from the groundswell opinion of the grass roots party workers.'

27. The resolution adopted at the 1970 assembly set out the strategy as follows:

    1. a dual approach to politics, acting both inside and outside the institutions of the political establishment;

    2. a primary strategic emphasis on community politics; our role as

political activists is to help organise people in communities to take and use power, to use our political skills to redress griev-ances, and to represent people at all levels of the political structure;

3. a national strategy based on:
    (a) the recognition of the need for a comprehensive and coher-ent organisational strategy covering all aspects of our Party's work;
    (b) a national commitment to build a Liberal power base in the major cities of this country;
    (c) the provision of an aggressive political lead on issues of moral concern, injustice and oppression and the use of these campaigns to publicise Liberal attitudes and policies. We aim to identify with the under-privileged of this country and the world;
    (d) the building of a national image to capture people's imagi-nation as a credible political movement, with local roots and local successes.

The Community Politics approach was developed out of the ideas and limited successes of the late 1960s, but had earlier roots. The party decided to concentrate on building up strength in local government in 1960. See Alan Watkins, *The Liberal Dilemma* (London, 1966) pp. 108–10, who quotes Jo Grimond as saying in 1960: 'Every time a local Liberal councillor gets a bus stop moved to a better place he strikes a blow for the Liberal Party.'

Chapter 4

1. See Douglas Young, 'A Sketch History of Scottish Nationalism', in N. MacCormick (ed.), *The Scottish Debate* (Oxford, 1970) for a brief summary of early Labour party support for Scottish Home Rule.
2. For example, see C. Harvie, *Scotland and Nationalism – Scottish Society and Politics 1707–1977* (London, 1977) chapter 2. See also Michael Hechter, *Internal Colonialism – the Celtic fringe in British national development, 1536–1966*, (London, 1975) Part III; and I. Lindsay, 'Nationalism, Community and Democracy', in G. Kennedy (ed.), *The Radical Approach* (Edinburgh, 1976).
3. Tom Nairn, *The Break-up of Britain: Crisis and Neo-Nationalism* (London, 1977) chapter 1.
4. For an insider's view of party growth in this period see Billy Wolfe, *Scotland Lives* (Edinburgh, 1973). For a general appraisal of SNP growth see J. Kellas, *The Scottish Political System* (Cambridge, 1973) chapter 7.
5. *The Royal Commission on the Constitution 1969–1973*, Cmnd. 5460 (1973) 2

volumes. While the report maintained the focus on constitutional issues, this was hardly the intention when the Commission was established. In *The Diaries of a Cabinet Minister*, Vol. 3 (London, 1977) p. 235, Richard Crossman explained that 'this is a way of doing nothing'.

6. SNP Research Bulletin No. 6, May 1973, p. 3.
7. Esmond Wright, 'In Defence of the United Kingdom', in MacCormick, *The Scottish Debate*, p. 112.
8. For a consideration of the factors involved in SNP success in Conservative-held Highland seats, see M. Dyer, 'Why Tory stronghold crumbled', *The Scotsman*, 24 October 1974. More generally see D. Jaensch, 'The Scottish National Vote 1974: a Realigning Party System', *Political Studies* (September 1976).
9. V. J. Hanby, 'Current Scottish Nationalism', *The Scottish Journal of Sociology*, 1, No. 2 (April 1977) p. 98.
10. C. Harvie, *Scotland and Nationalism*, p. 176.
11. J. E. Schwartz, 'The Scottish National Party; non-violent separatism and theories of violence', *World Politics* (July 1970).
12. SNP, 'Industry policy Document' (1977) p. 1.
13. Ibid. For critical discussions of the SNP's ideological development, see H. J. Hanham, *Scottish Nationalism* (London, 1969); and more recently Keith Webb, *The Growth of Nationalism in Scotland* (Glasgow, 1977). For the views of some of the SNP's most influential leaders, see Kennedy, *The Radical Approach*.

Chapter 5

1. There is a growing literature on Plaid Cymru: see A. Butt Philip, *The Welsh Question* (Cardiff, 1975); P. M. Rawkins, *Minority Nationalism*, unpublished Ph.D. thesis (Toronto, 1976); R. D. Tanner, *Welsh Nationalism*, unpublished M.A. thesis (Bangor, North Wales, 1977).
2. Butt Philip, *The Welsh Question*, p. 15.
3. J. E. Daniel, *Welsh Nationalism – What it Stands For* (London, 1937) p. 40.
4. Butt Philip, *The Welsh Question*, p. 22.
5. See F. W. S. Craig, *British Electoral Facts, 1885–1975* (London, 1976) p. 61–2.
6. This was a period of great internal party turmoil; see Butt Philip, *The Welsh Question*, pp. 85–9.
7. Reprinted in English in *Planet*, 4 (1971).
8. In 1970 came the publication of Plaid Cymru's influential *Economic Plan*.
9. See Craig, *British Electoral Facts*, pp. 63–4.
10. For a full account of the referendum campaign in Wales, see D. Balsom and P. J. Madgwick, 'European Integration and Welsh Politics', in M. Kolinsky (ed.), *Divided Loyalties* (Manchester, 1978).

11. Plaid Cymru took control of the Merthyr Tydfil District Council and was the largest party on the Rhymney Valley District Council. For full details of local government results since reorganisation, see D. Balsom and M. Burch, *A Political and Electoral Handbook for Wales* (Farnborough, forthcoming).

12. A. H. Birch, *Political Integration and Disintegration in the British Isles* (London, 1977) p. 29.

13. Ibid., p. 28.

14. Gwynfor Evans and Joan Rhys, 'Wales', in O. D. Edwards (ed.), *Celtic Nationalism* (London, 1968) pp. 252–3.

15. Gwynfor Evans, *Non-violent Nationalism*, The Alex Wood Memorial Lecture, 1973 (New Malden, Surrey, 1973) p. 5.

16. Evans, *Non-violent Nationalism*, p. 14.

17. Saunders Lewis, *Principles of Nationalism* (Cardiff, 1975). First published in 1926 in Welsh, it was reprinted in English in 1975.

18. See N. Thomas, *The Welsh Extremist* (reprinted Talybont, 1973) p. 62.

19. Saunders Lewis, *Principles of Nationalism*, p. 13.

20. D. J. Davies, *The Economics of Welsh Self Government* (Caernarfon, 1931); D. J. Davies, *Towards Welsh Freedom*, a collection of essays etc., ed. Ceinwen Thomas (Cardiff, 1958).

21. *Planet*, 5–6, p. 9.

22. See Gwynfor Evans, *A National Future for Wales* (Cardiff, 1975); Leopold Kohr, *Is Wales Viable* (Llandybie, 1971); Leopold Kohr, *The Breakdown of Nations* (London, 1957); E. Schumacher, *Small is Beautiful* (London, 1973).

23. Details of the structure of Plaid Cymru are taken from the party *Constitution* (Cardiff, 1976) and Tanner, *Welsh Nationalism*.

24. D. Hearne, *The Rise of the Welsh Republic* (Talybont, 1975). See also *Western Mail*, 19 March 1975.

25. Plaid Cymru, *Action for Wales* (Cardiff, 1970).

26. Balsom and Burch, *A Political and Electoral Handbook for Wales*, part 4.

27. There have been several corruption cases in South Wales. See *Rebecca*, Nos 7–10.

28. P. J. Madgwick and D. Balsom, 'Changes in Party Competition at Election: the Welsh case and the British context', *Parliamentary Affairs*, 28 (1974–5).

Chapter 6

1. I would like to thank Tariq Ali, John Foster, Duncan Hallas, Pat Kane, Francis Mulhern and Dave Sherry for their help in the preparation of this chapter.

2. IMG, *Pre-Conference Bulletin No. 1* (London, 1978) p. 12, mimeo.

3. Karl Marx, 'Letter to the Labour Parliament', in Karl Marx and Frederick Engels, *Articles on Britain* (Moscow, 1971) pp. 216–17.

4. All figures derived from T. T. Mackie and Richard Rose, *The International Almanac of Electoral History* (London, 1974), and the supplements published regularly in the *European Journal of Political Research*.

5. Tom Nairn, 'The Fateful Meridian', *New Left Review* (henceforth cited as *NLR*) 60 (March–April 1970) p. 21. This brief contextual analysis is based on an argument put forward by Nairn and Perry Anderson in a series of articles in *NLR*. See also Perry Anderson, 'Origins of the Present Crisis', *NLR*, 23 (January–February 1964) and Tom Nairn, 'The English Working Class', *NLR*, 24 (March–April 1964). For an extended criticism of this thesis see Edward Thompson, 'The Peculiarities of the English', in Ralph Miliband and John Saville (eds), *Socialist Register 1965* (London, 1965), and the reply by Perry Anderson, 'Socialism and Pseudo-Empiricism', *NLR*, 35 (January–February 1966).

6. Anderson, 'Origins of the Present Crisis', p. 43.

7. Frederick Engels, 'The English Elections', in Marx and Engels, *Articles on Britain*, p. 368.

8. Ralph Miliband, *Parliamentary Socialism* (London, 1973) p. 376.

9. The large number of Marxist groups in Britain necessitates the exclusion of many from consideration in this chapter. The most important group which is excluded is the Workers Revolutionary Party, despite its intervention in the elections of 1974, when it ran nine candidates in February and ten in October. The WRP is excluded from this discussion, however, because its particularly evident isolation from other Marxist groups renders it less relevant to the future development of the British left than, say, the IMG.

10. See Fernando Claudin, *The Communist Movement: from Comintern to Cominform* (Harmondsworth, 1975) p. 16.

11. See Robert Dornhorst and Patrick Newman, 'Which Way Forward for the Communists?', *Revolutionary Communist*, 7 (November 1977) p. 4. The figures in this paragraph are drawn from Henry Pelling, *The British Communist Party* (New York, 1958); Communist Party of Great Britain, *Report of the Executive Committee to the 35th National Congress for August 1975 to July 1977* (London, 1977); and the circulation department of the *Morning Star*.

12. For the organisational and theoretical background of the SWP, see Ian H. Birchall, 'History of the International Socialists', *International Socialism*, 76 (March 1975) and 77 (April 1975); Tariq Ali, *The Coming British Revolution* (London, 1973) pp. 110–47; Alan Jones, 'The Nature of the SWP', Supplement to *Red Weekly* (May 1977); David Widgery, *The Left*

in Britain 1956–68 (Harmondsworth, 1976) and *The Origins of the International Socialists* (London, no date).

13. *The Death Agony of Capitalism and the Tasks of the Fourth International* (various editions).

14. On the IMG see Ali, *The Coming British Revolution*, and Widgery, *The Left in Britain 1956–68*. On the USFI see Pierre Frank, *A Contribution to the History of the Fourth International* (London, forthcoming) and Frank Richards, 'The Question of the International', *Revolutionary Communist*, 2 (May 1975) pp. 20–41.

15. IMG, *Pre-Conference Bulletin No. 16* (London, 1978) pp. 2–3. See also Peter Mair, 'Organisational Form and Ideological Content: the Case of the Marxist Revolutionary Party', *Rivista Italiana di Scienza Politica*, forthcoming.

16. *Aims and Constitution of the Communist Party of Great Britain*, Article 8.

17. IMG, *Pre-Conference Bulletin No. 16*, p. 11.

18. CPGB, *Inner-Party Democracy* (London, no date).

19. See *SWP Handbook* (Glasgow(?), no date). Note, however, that the SWP's use of the term 'faction' appears to differ from that of the CPGB and IMG, and appears to correspond more closely to the IMG's use of 'tendency'.

20. HC Deb, 5s, 730, c42. See also the text of Harold Wilson's broadcast during the Ulster Workers' Council strike of May 1974, when he attacked the use of the strike weapon for non-industrial purposes – text reprinted in Robert Fisk, *The Point of No Return* (London, 1975) pp. 252–4.

21. CPGB, *The Role of the Communist Party Branches in the Struggle for Socialism* (London, 1974) p. 10.

22. *Aims and Constitution of the Communist Party of Great Britain*, Article 15.

23. See Duncan Hallas, 'White Collar Workers', *International Socialism*, 72 (October 1974) p. 22.

24. IMG, *Pre-Conference Bulletin No. 4* (London, 1978) p. 9. The draft constitution of the IMG, which was agreed by the group's National Committee in March 1978, is careful to emphasise that the organisation 'has a right and obligation to insist that its militants should work to implement the revolutionary Marxist programme in all spheres – "private" as well as "public"', IMG, *Pre-Conference Bulletin No. 16*, p. 22.

25. For a succinct account of this, see Norman Geras, 'Marxism and Proletarian Self-Emancipation', *Radical Philosophy*, 6 (Winter 1973) pp. 20–2.

26. Gordon MacLennan, in *Marxism Today*, March 1977.

27. 'The Fight for a Socialist Alternative', supplement to *Socialist Challenge*, 2 February 1978.

28. 'Notes of the Month', *International Socialism*, 68 (April 1974) p. 5. 'Notes of the Month', a regular feature in the monthly *International Socialism*,

offers perhaps the best published source of information on developments in IS/SWP strategy over time.

29. CPGB, *The British Road to Socialism* (London, 1978) p. 28.
30. *The Times*, editorial, 2 February 1977.
31. Roger Kline, *Can Socialism Come Through Parliament?* (London, 1974) pp. 18–19. See also Duncan Hallas, 'How Can We Move On?', in Ralph Miliband and John Saville (eds), *Socialist Register 1977* (London, 1977).
32. 'Notes of the Month', *International Socialism*, 68 (April 1974), p. 5.
33. Steve Jeffreys, 'The Challenge of the Rank and File', and 'Notes of the Month', both in *International Socialism*, 76 (March 1975) pp. 10, 11, 3.
34. This, and the quotes earlier in the paragraph, are drawn from 'The Fight for a Socialist Alternative'.
35. Ibid., emphasis added. See also Bob Pennington, *Revolutionary Socialism: Why and How* (London, no date), and 'The Basis for Revolutionary Unity: a Draft Statement of Aims', *Socialist Challenge*, 6 October 1977.
36. 'The Next Six to Nine Months', statement adopted by the Central Committee of the SWP in November 1977, mimeo.

Chapter 7

1. See Walker, M., *The National Front* (London, 1977), chapter 2.
2. *Spearhead*, 103 (March 1977) p. 3.
3. *Spearhead*, 106 (June 1977).
4. J. Tyndall, *Six Principles of British Nationalism* (London, 1977) p. 32.
5. *Spearhead* (September 1974).
6. *Candour* (June 1967).
7. Walker, *The National Front*, p. 145.
8. Ibid.
9. Ibid., pp. 164–6.
10. A copy of this leaflet is filed with other research notes for Walker, *The National Front*, at the Institute of Race Relations, London.
11. There are several versions of this 'marching song' of the International Socialists. This one begins with the lines: 'When there's any fucking trouble, We're the first cunts in.'
12. Walker, *The National Front*, pp. 183–4.
13. Tyndall, *Six Principles of British Nationalism.*
14. *Spearhead*, 107 (July 1977).
15. *Spearhead*, 75 (May 1974).
16. Walker, *The National Front*, p. 158.
17. Ibid., p. 138.
18. *Spearhead*, 91 (February 1976).
19. *New Society*, 11 May 1976; see also M. Steed, 'The National Front Vote', *Parliamentary Affairs*, XXXI, No. 3 (1978).

20. Walker, *The National Front*, pp. 217 – 19.
21. I am grateful to Michael Steed for this analysis of the impact of various forms of PR on the NF vote.
22. As though preparing for a parliamentary presence, in October 1976 two of the NF 'intellectuals' began publishing a regular series of articles in *Spearhead* entitled 'Parliamentary Front', dealing with current events in the House of Commons, and the ways in which the NF could take advantage of them. They have suggested that a National Front MP should aim at getting a place on the Select Committee of the Commons on Race Relations, and work mainly through Question Time and amendments, since they see little chance of any major party sponsoring a Private Member's Bill introduced by a National Front MP. See *Spearhead*, 98 (October 1976) article by Ian Anderson and Ian Kingham.

Conclusion

1. G. Sartori, *Parties and Party Systems: a Framework for Analysis*, Vol. 1 (London, 1976) p. 186.
2. S. M. Lipset and Stein Rokkan, *Party Systems and Voter Alignments: Cross-National Perspectives* (London, 1967), p. 50.
3. Ibid., pp. 54 and 55.
4. M. Steed, 'Devolution – the English Dimension'. Workshop Paper, PSA Conference, University of Wales (Aberystwyth, September 1977) p. 22.

Bibliography

General

BEER, S. H., *Modern British Politics* (London, 1965).

BIRCH, A. H., *Representative and Responsible Government* (London, 1964).

BLONDEL, J., *Political Parties: a Genuine Case for Discontent* (London, 1978).

——, *Voters, Parties and Leaders* (Harmondsworth, 1963).

BULMER-THOMAS, IVOR, *The Party System in Great Britain* (London, 1973).

BUTLER, D., and STOKES, D., *Political Change in Britain* (Harmondsworth, 1974).

COOK, C., and RAMSDEN, J., *By-Elections in British Politics* (London, 1973).

CREWE, I., *et al.*, 'Partisan Dealignment in Britain, 1964–74', *British Journal of Political Science*, 7 (1977) pp. 129–90.

EPSTEIN, L., *Political Parties in Western Democracies* (London, 1967).

FINER, S. E. (ed.), *Adversary Politics and Electoral Reform* (London, 1975).

IONESCU, G., *Centripetal Politics: Government and the New Centres of Power* (London, 1975).

JENNINGS, SIR I., *The British Constitution* (London, 1941).

LEES, JOHN D., and KIMBER, R. (eds), *Political Parties in Modern Britain: an organisational and functional guide* (London, 1972).

LIPSET, S. M., and ROKKAN, S., *Party Systems and Voter Alignments: Cross National Perspectives* (London, 1967).

McKENZIE, R. T., *British Political Parties* (London, 1954).

MACRIDIS, ROY, *Political Parties: Contemporary Trends and Ideas* (London, 1967).

PULZER, P., *Political Representation and Elections in Britain* (London, 1967).

ROSE, R., *The Problem of Party Government* (Harmondsworth, 1976).

SARTORI, G., *Parties and Party Systems: a Framework for Analysis*, Vol. 1 (London, 1976).

Conservative Party

For the party literature see the publications of Conservative Central Office, particularly the Conservative Political Centre (CPC); also publications from the various groups and organisations within the party, e.g. the Centre for Policy Studies, the Bow Group, and the Monday Club.

Works by Conservatives

BUTLER, R. A., *The Art of the Possible* (London, 1971).

COLERAINE, LORD, *For Conservatives Only* (London, 1970).

GILMOUR, I., *Inside Right: A Study of Conservatism* (London, 1977).

HEARNSHAW, F. J. C., *Conservatism in England* (London, 1933).

HOGG, Q., *The Case for Conservatism* (Harmondsworth, 1947).

POWELL, J. E., *Freedom and Reality* (London, 1969).

RUSSEL, T., *The Tory Party* (London, 1978).

WALKER, P., *The Assent of Britain* (London, 1977).

Secondary works which explore further the themes raised in Chapter 1

BEER, S., *Modern British Politics* (London, 1965).

BEHRENS, R., *The Conservative Party in Opposition, 1974–7* (Coventry, 1977).

BLAKE, R., *The Conservative Party from Peel to Churchill* (London, 1970).

GAMBLE, A. M., *The Conservative Nation* (London, 1974).

GRAINGER, J. H., *Character and Style in English Politics* (Cambridge, 1969).

GREENLEAF, W. H., 'The Character of Modern British Conservatism', in R. Benewick *et al.* (eds), *Knowledge and Belief in Politics* (London, 1973).

HARRIS, N., *Competition and the Corporate Society* (London, 1972).

McKENZIE, R. T., *British Political Parties* (London, 1963).

——, and SILVER, A., *Angels in Marble* (London, 1968).

NAIRN, T., *The Breakup of Britain* (London, 1977).

PINTO-DUSCHINSKY, M., 'Central Office and "Power" in the Conservative Party', *Political Studies*, 20 (1972) pp. 1–16.

SCHOEN, D., *Enoch Powell and the Powellites* (London, 1977).

SEYD, P., 'Factionalism within the Conservative Party: the Monday Club', *Government and Opposition* (1972) pp. 464–87.

Labour Party

COATES, D., *The Labour Party and the Struggle for Socialism* (Cambridge, 1975).

DRUCKER, H. M., *Breakaway: the Scottish Labour Party* (Edinburgh, 1978).

——, 'Leadership Selection in the Labour Party', *Parliamentary Affairs*, XXIX (1976) pp. 378–95.

FORESTER, T., *The Labour Party and the Working Class* (London, 1976).

HAYTER, D., *The Labour Party: Crisis and Prospects*, Fabian Tract 451 (London, 1977).

HEFFER, E., 'Two Labour Parties, or One?', *Political Quarterly*, 46 (1975) pp. 385–94.

HOWELL, D., *British Social Democracy* (London, 1976).

JENKINS, P., 'The Future of the Labour Party', *Political Quarterly*, 46 (1975) pp. 373–84.

MARTIN, C., and MARTIN, D., 'Decline of Labour Party Membership', *Political Quarterly*, 48 (1977) pp. 459–71.

PIPER, J. R., 'Backbench Rebellion, Party Government and Consensus Politics: the Case of the Parliamentary Labour Party, 1966–70', *Parliamentary Affairs* XXVII (1974) pp. 384–96.

SEYD, P., 'Labour Party Reform', *Political Quarterly*, 49 (1978) pp. 38–43.

TAYLOR, R., 'The Uneasy Alliance – Labour and the Unions', *Political Quarterly*, 47 (1976) pp. 398–407.

Liberal Party

The Liberal Publication Department publishes all official party pamphlets and election material and also many pamphlets by groups within the party.

Historical

COOK, CHRIS, *The Age of Alignment: Electoral Politics in Britain 1922–29* (London, 1975).

DOUGLAS, ROY, *The History of the Liberal Party 1895–1970* (London, 1971).

VINCENT, J. R., *The Formation of the Liberal Party 1857–68* (London, 1966).

WILSON, TREVOR, *The Downfall of the Liberal Party 1914–35* (London, 1966).

Studies of the Liberal Party and the Liberal vote

ALT, JAMES, CREWE, IVOR and SARLVIK, BO, 'Angels in Plastic: the Liberal surge in 1974', *Political Studies*, XXV (1977) pp. 343–68.

BUTLER, DAVID, and STOKES, DONALD, 'The Liberal Presence', chapter 14 of the first edition only of *Political Change in Britain* (London, 1969).

CYR, ARTHUR, *Liberal Party Politics in Britain* (London, 1977).

LEMIEUX, PETER, 'Political Issues and Liberal Support in the February 1974 British General Election', *Political Studies*, XXV (1977) pp. 323–42.

RASMUSSEN, JORGAN, *The Liberal Party* (London, 1964).

WATKINS, ALAN, *The Liberal Dilemma* (London, 1966).

Liberal Party publications

Liberal News is published weekly by the party.

New Outlook is published monthly; it has no official association with the party but has always been close to it.

Radical Bulletin, a newsletter concentrating on internal party developments, is published by the Radical Bulletin Group.

Scottish National Party

HANHAM, H. J., *Scottish Nationalism* (London, 1969).
HARVIE, C., *Scotland and Nationalism* (London, 1977).
HECTER, M., *Internal Colonialism* (London, 1968).
KELLAS, J., *The Scottish Political System* (Cambridge, 1973).
NAIRN, TOM, *The Breakup of Britain* (London, 1977).
WEBB, K., *The Growth of Nationalism in Scotland* (Glasgow, 1977).
WOLFE, W., *Scotland Lives* (Edinburgh, 1973).

Plaid Cymru

BETTS, C., *Culture in Crisis* (Upton, 1976).
BUTT PHILIP, A., *The Welsh Question* (Cardiff, 1975).
EDWARDS, O. D. (ed.), *Celtic Nationalism* (London, 1968).
JONES, A. R. and THOMAS, G. (eds), *Presenting Saunders Lewis* (Cardiff, 1973).
MADGWICK, P. J., *et al.*, *The Politics of Rural Wales* (London, 1973).
MORGAN, K. O., *Wales in British Politics* (Cardiff, 1970).
OSMOND, J., *Creative Conflict* (London, 1978).
THOMAS, N., *The Welsh Extremist* (London, 1971).
WILLIAMS, D., *Modern Wales* (London, 1965).

The Marxist Left

There is very little easily available material concerning the Marxist left, and such books, articles and pamphlets, etc., which are relevant are included in the detailed references to Chapter 6. For information on the groups concerned, readers are recommended to look at the regular publications of the individual organisations. These are listed below.

Communist Party of Great Britain

Morning Star (daily newspaper).
Comment (fortnightly paper).
Marxism Today (theoretical quarterly).

Socialist Workers Party

Socialist Worker (weekly paper).
Socialist Review (monthly journal, replacing *International Socialism* from
   April 1978).

International Marxist Group

Socialist Challenge (weekly paper).
International (theoretical quarterly).
Also *Intercontinental Press/Inprecor* (Fourth International fortnightly
   paper, now combining the formerly separate publications *Intercontinental Press* and *Inprecor*)

Other

New Left Review (a bi-monthly theoretical journal).
Socialist Register (an annual publication).

National Front

New Society, 'The National Front and the Young: a Special Survey',
   27 April 1978, pp. 186–93, and 4 May 1978, pp. 243–4.
NUGENT, N. and KING, R. (eds), *The British Right: Conservative and
   Right Wing Politics in Britain* (London, 1977).
SKIDELSKY, R., *Oswald Mosley* (London, 1975).
STEED, M., 'Racism and the Electorate: an Examination of the
   Electoral Record of the National Front', *PSA Workshop on Contem-
   porary British Politics* (January 1977).
STUDLER, D. T., 'British Public Opinion, Colour Issues and Enoch
   Powell: a Longitudinal Analysis', *British Journal of Political Science*,
   1974.
WALKER, M., *The National Front* (London, 1977).

Northern Irish Parties

BURTON, FRANK, *The Politics of Legitimacy: Struggles in a Belfast
   Community* (London, 1978).

FARRELL, M., *The Orange State* (London, 1976).

HARBINSON, JOHN F., *The Ulster Unionist Party* (Belfast, 1973).

MCALLISTER, IAN, *The Northern Ireland Social Democratic and Labour Party* (London, 1978).

ROSE, RICHARD, *Governing without Consensus* (London, 1971).

——, *Northern Ireland: A Time of Choice* (London, 1976).

Index